I0793584

IMAGES
of America

AROUND DENVER

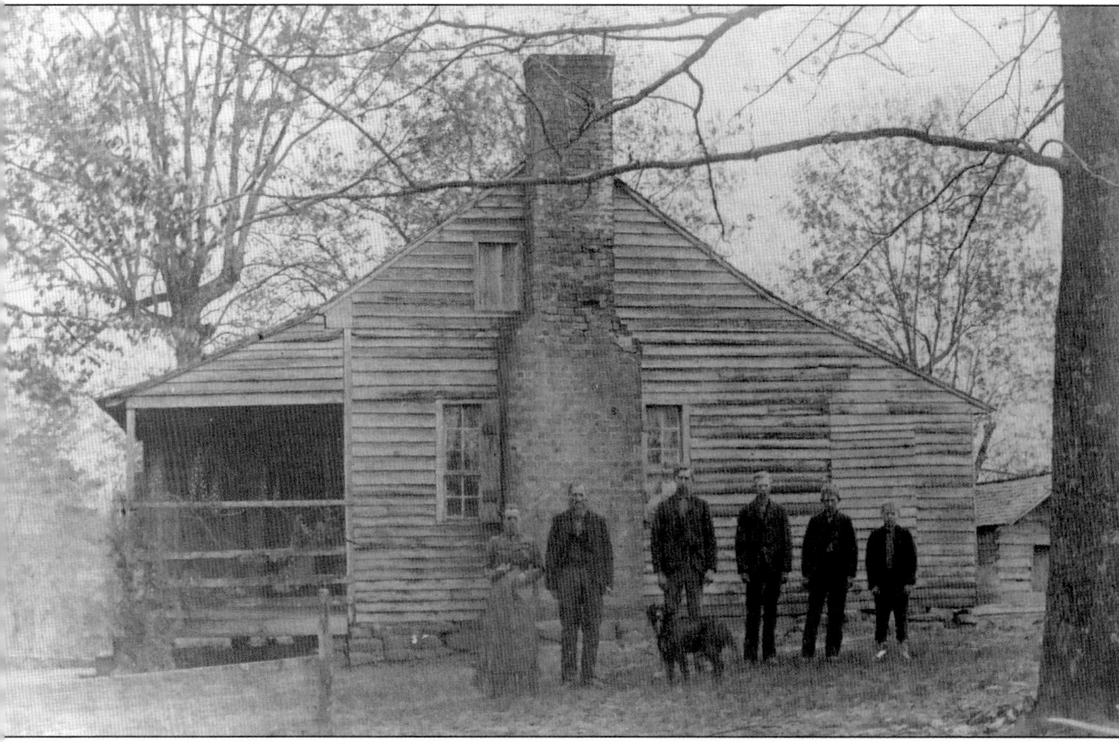

Man's best friend holds a steady pose in this photograph of the Sidney and Susan Cherry family. The Cherry house was located on the north side of Optimist Club Road near St. James Church Road in Denver. Members of the family are, from left to right, Susan Elizabeth Black Cherry (1850–1911), Sidney Durant Cherry (1846–1929), Thomas Harvey Cherry (1881–1968), Marvin Alexander Cherry (1886–1966), Horace Allison Cherry (1889–1974), and Alvin Ethridge Cherry (1892–1972). (Courtesy of Kelli Gaskill Hogue.)

On the Cover: A quiet campground and arbor set the tone for this panoramic photograph of a large group taken during the 117th session at Rock Spring on August 7, 1953. The campground was 119 years old at the time. A newspaper article that accompanied the story about the session included a note that the "Trustees announced that there will be no children's services because of the epidemic in Catawba County," but added that "there is no polio epidemic in Lincoln County." (Courtesy of Lincoln County Historical Association.)

IMAGES
of America

AROUND DENVER

Jason L. Harpe and Matt Boles

ARCADIA
PUBLISHING

ISBN 978-1-4671-1539-1

Published by Arcadia Publishing
Charleston, South Carolina

Printed in the United States of America

Library of Congress Control Number: 2015958452

For all general information, please contact Arcadia Publishing:
Telephone 843-853-2070
Fax 843-853-0044
E-mail sales@arcadiapublishing.com
For customer service and orders:
Toll-Free 1-888-313-2665

Visit us on the Internet at www.arcadiapublishing.com

Contents

Acknowledgments

It is difficult to put into words how exciting this project has been for us. Tracking down and securing photographs and learning the stories attached to them has deepened our knowledge of history in Denver and the areas around it. It was refreshing to see the nostalgic looks in the eyes of people in the eastern part of Lincoln County when we told them about our plans to put together a photographic retrospective on the places that they hold so dear. The individuals who maintain historic images in their photograph collections were more than willing to entrust us with these family treasures for a short time so that we could digitize them for this publication. We could not have assembled such a succinct, yet inclusive, group of photographs to tell the story of the areas around Denver without the help of so many supportive and encouraging people. Our hope is that they will be happy with this publication and encourage others to look through their family scrapbooks, journals, Bibles, and containers that rest at the back of closets, attics, and basements for old photographs of eastern Lincoln County that we can use in future publications. While this book is full of incredible vintage images, there are two to three times this amount that await their turn to be featured in future publications. Our hope is that the success of this publication will serve as the impetus for more books of this type on the history of eastern Lincoln County.

There are a number of people who we are indebted to for devoting an incalculable number of hours to ensure that this project was successful. They welcomed our phone calls, impromptu meetings, and incessant requests for information and contacts and got more excited as we updated them on our project. We would like to thank the following people and organizations for their contributions to this publication: Mary Abernathy, Bruce Armstrong, Kirk Bailey, Jennifer Robinson Barker, Henry Barkley, Mark Boles, Leroy Bost, Andrew Bridges, Steven Bridges, Allen Broach, Terry Brotherton, Chief Jay Flynn and the Denver Fire Department, John Cherry, Woody Cherry, the Russell and Dot Cornwell family, Denny Dellinger, Janet Duckworth, Davidson College Archives, East Lincoln Fire Department, Kellie Ellis, Anne Sherrill Eudy, Julia Fields, Celeste Lowery Frazier, Judy Gibson, Fran Goins, Ann Graham, Amy Reel Hallman, Frances Hampton, Mary Harbinson, Mike Hensdill (the *Gaston Gazette*), Amy Hilburn, John S. Hopkins, Kelli Gaskill Hogue, Shawn Howard, Janet Sigmon Jones, Doris Jean Keever, Janeen Killian, the Killian family, Frances McIntosh Kiser, Vicki Kopf, Merriel Mundy Lawing, Roddi and Nancy Long, the Library Company of Philadelphia, Lincoln County Historical Association (LCHA), Lincoln County Soil and Water Conservation District, Nancy Nixon Little, Lewis Lowery, Mary Lowery, Dorothy Beatty Maiers, Lisa Mundy Mauney, Marsha Sigmon McCall, Joyce McCumbee, Lewis McLean, Norma Morrison, Shirley Mull, Bernice Luckey Nixon, Bill and Lela Nixon, Thomas Nixon, Lincoln County Historical Association, North Carolina Office of Archives and History, Robinson-Spangler Carolina Room at the Charlotte-Mecklenburg Library, Lincoln Soil and Water Conservation District (Lincolnton), Edward and Doris Little, Jamie McCurry, Emmitt and Sharon Poole, Tina Robinette, Jimmy Robinette, Rock Springs Elementary School, Judge Theodore Royster, Sue Carolyn Sherrill, Frances Nixon Sigmon, Ann Smith, Edgar Smith, Jim Smith, Julia (Patsy) Smith, David and Janice Springs, Stonewall Jackson Foundation, Gurtha Strand, Brandi Surratt, Mary Swift, Jack Thompson, Richard and Melisa Thompson, J.J. Tindall Photography, Carolyn Pethel Washam, Betsy Watts, Webb's Chapel United Methodist Church, Doris Houk Wilkinson, J.C. Wilson, and Claire Wong.

Introduction

The history of Denver and areas around it in eastern Lincoln County is nearly impossible to write about in its entirety within the framework of this photographic retrospective. This became very clear recently when staff and volunteers of the Mundy House and History Center of Eastern Lincoln County undertook a timeline of the major historical events in this part of the county for the Mundy House Open House on October 24, 2015. After compiling a 15-page list of historical events, we realized that a historical narrative of eastern Lincoln County in the broader context of Lincoln County and North Carolina should be written at some point in the future, but it would be a major undertaking. There is no way to get all of the important dates, people, places, and events chronicled on timelines and in books with limited space.

The goal of this book is to highlight the history of areas around Denver through the medium of photographs. These priceless windows into the past afford people the opportunity to reminisce and reflect on important periods in their lives and the lives of their ancestors while helping educate younger generations and newcomers to the area about historic sites that they can visit and enjoy, how places got their names, how land and properties have been transformed through land development, and how the landscape became what they see today. To accomplish this goal, we started out this book project with some basic and abbreviated historical information that people can use as a point of reference on their journey through the pages of photographs that follow.

Denver, known locally as "Denver of the East," is an unincorporated area in the Catawba Springs Township of eastern Lincoln County, North Carolina, that was originally named Dry Pond after a small pond at the intersection of Highway 16 and Campground Road that always dried up during the hottest summer months. This intersection has served as the main crossroads and business district of Denver since the 19th century, and it is less than one mile west of Rock Spring Campground. In January 1873, D. Matt Thompson, principal at Rock Spring Seminary, spearheaded the local effort to have the area renamed after the capital of Colorado to attract railroad planners, whose lines could provide an economic boost to trading and commerce.

Rock Spring Campground, started in 1830 under the leadership of Rev. Henry Asbury, formed the social and religious center of activity in Denver during the 19th century, and by the 1870s, a small commercial district developed at the current intersection of Highway 16 Business and Campground Road. On January 21, 1871, citizens of Dry Pond assembled to consider the necessary steps for the establishment of a school at Rock Spring Campground. W.W. Munday chaired this meeting, appointing J.F. Munday as secretary, and Rev. T.P. Ricard and John Woodhouse delivered addresses on the importance of education. L.A.H. Wilkinson started Rock Spring Seminary in 1871, and by 1873, D. Matt Thompson was hired as the school's principal

In 1874, *The Charlotte Democrat* considered the area a "thrifty little village with one hundred inhabitants, but seventy of them are students." The population in Denver in 1890 was 185, and by 1910, the total had increased to 282. The population of Denver and its surrounding communities remained relatively low throughout the 20th century, and local families enjoyed an environment that changed very little from the time that their ancestors settled the area in the late 19th century. This landscape changed drastically between 1959 and 1964 with the construction of the Cowan's Ford Dam by Duke Energy and the creation of Lake Norman, the largest manmade body of fresh water in North Carolina. Lake Norman covers a surface area of more than 50 square miles and supplies water to Lincoln County, Catawba County, Iredell County, Mooresville, Charlotte, Davidson, and Huntersville. Many of Denver's old roads, historic houses, bridges, and family cemeteries fell victim to the waters of Lake Norman, and all that is left of some of these historic resources are the photographs contained within this volume.

Around Denver are other unincorporated communities such as Machpelah, Iron Station, Triangle, Catawba Springs, Lowesville, Kidville, Pumpkin Center, Ringdom, Pilot Knob, and St. James/Little Egypt.

The areas around Denver have names that are as intriguing as the history attached to them. Machpelah is named for the church and cemetery at the intersection of Old Plank Road and Brevard Place Road, and the name is derived from the Cave of Machpelah in Hebron, one of the holiest cities in Biblical lands, which is the burial place that Abraham purchased for his family after Sarah died (Genesis 23: 8–17). Iron Station was settled in the 1780s and was incorporated in 1909. The area derives its name from the iron mines, furnaces, and forges that were in operation from the 1780s to the 1880s. Triangle is just that—a triangle formed by roads at the site. The area had a post office that operated from 1878 to 1903. Catawba Springs was a very popular resort on Killian's Creek that accommodated visitors who sought a cool environment during hot summers as well as the healing qualities of its numerous springs. Its name comes from the Catawba Indians who were the first inhabitants in the area. Lowesville was named for the Lowe family, and Ringdom was tagged after all of the ringing from horseshoes hitting iron stakes during horseshoes matches. Pilot Knob was named by Pink McConnell for a pilot beacon light on a tower at the corner of what is today Pilot Knob Road and Highway 73. St. James/Little Egypt is an African American community that is named after St. James Church.

Each of these communities, regardless of size, had its own schools, churches, cemeteries, businesses, country stores, post offices, and cotton gins. Children in these communities were educated at one-room schools such as Elbow, Webb's, Joe's Old Field School, Summerow, Buffalo, McLean's, Signboard, Nantz, King's, Edward's, Poole's, Denver, Derr, Fairfield, Triangle, Lowesville, Graham's, Mariposa, Kidsville, Macedonia, Saddler, Trinity, Salem, Schrum's, Iron Station, and Asbury. Between 1920 and 1925, these one-room schools were consolidated into the larger, modern brick buildings of Rock Springs, Triangle, Machpelah, Iron Station, and Asbury. African American students attended Rosenwald schools such as Mount Vernon, Tucker's Grove, and Rocky Hill until they were bused to Newbold School in Lincolnton, or they attended Triangle School after white students were moved to Rock Springs. Although many of these treasured buildings are gone, a few have been repurposed and are still in use today.

Denver and its surrounding communities have been faced with increased development pressures over the past 40 to 50 years, but they maintain a commitment and dedication to collecting and preserving historic and cultural resources that tell the stories of its time-honored past. It is our hope that all who peruse this book will be encouraged to join the effort and preserve the history of eastern Lincoln County.

One

Keeping the Faith
Religion and Places of Worship

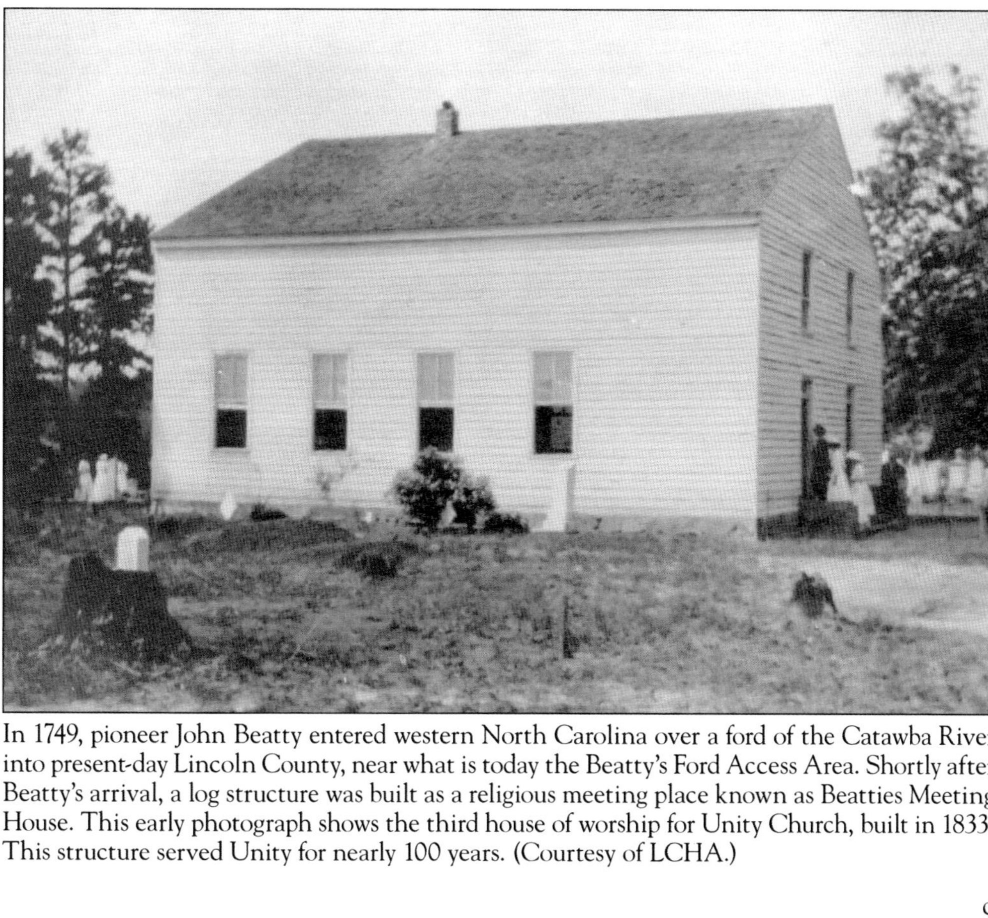

In 1749, pioneer John Beatty entered western North Carolina over a ford of the Catawba River into present-day Lincoln County, near what is today the Beatty's Ford Access Area. Shortly after Beatty's arrival, a log structure was built as a religious meeting place known as Beatties Meeting House. This early photograph shows the third house of worship for Unity Church, built in 1833. This structure served Unity for nearly 100 years. (Courtesy of LCHA.)

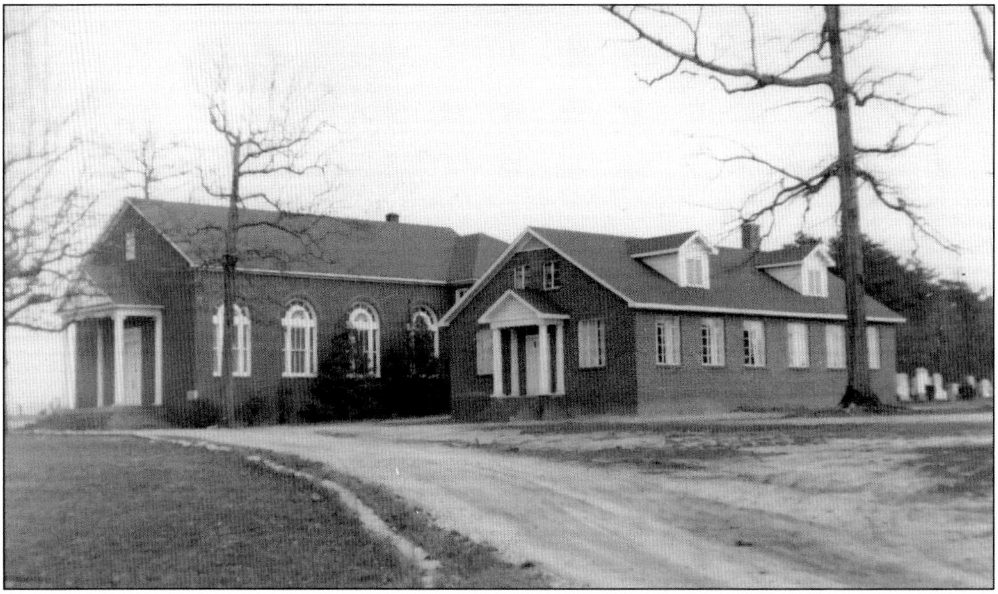

In 1931, a more modern brick structure replaced the clapboard-sided building built in 1833. The pastor, Rev. W.T. Smith, came across the river to Unity from Bethel Presbyterian in Cornelius in September 1930 and called on the services of his congregation to construct a new building. The first service was held in the church on March 15, 1931. An education and classroom building, seen to the right, was completed in 1952. (Courtesy of LCHA.)

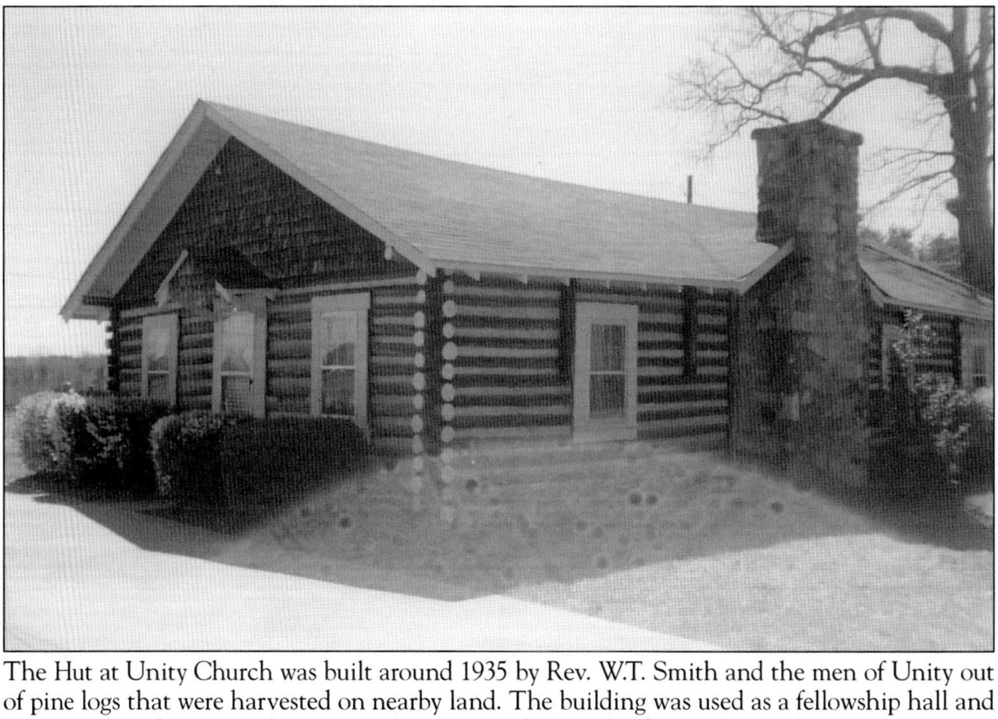

The Hut at Unity Church was built around 1935 by Rev. W.T. Smith and the men of Unity out of pine logs that were harvested on nearby land. The building was used as a fellowship hall and meeting place for years. About 2000, the Hut was disassembled to make way for a new education building. It was moved to Camp Grier in Old Fort, North Carolina, where it is still in use today. (Courtesy of Matt Boles.)

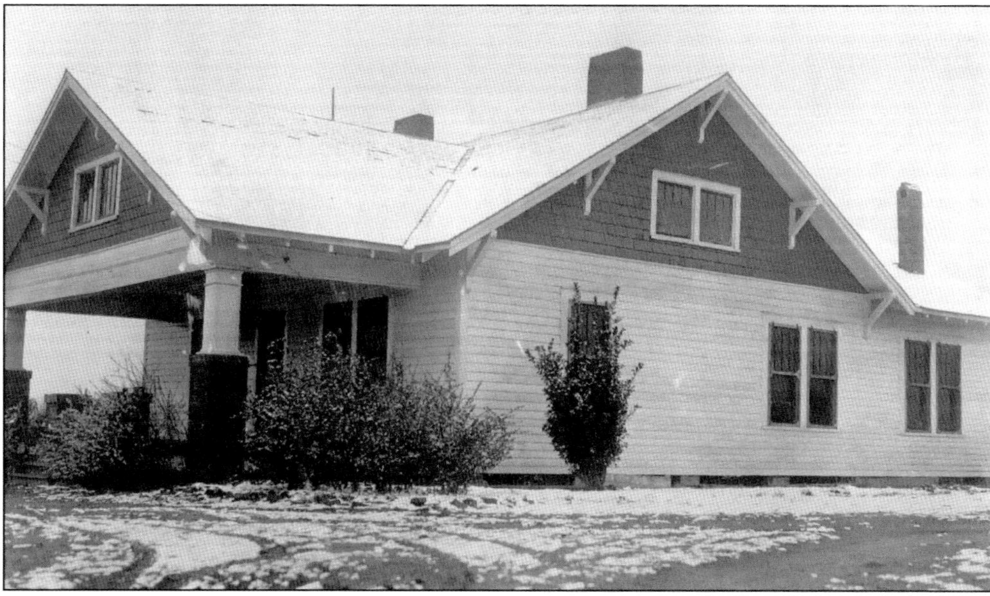

In 1924, this Craftsman-style bungalow was constructed to serve as Unity Presbyterian Church's manse. Rev. Walter Espy and Eudora Furr were the first occupants of the manse. At one time, the pastor from Unity served not only Unity, but Machpelah and Castanea Churches as well. This manse served the church for 40 years; in 1964, a new manse was constructed on property adjoining Unity. The manse was razed in the late 1990s. (Courtesy of Ann Smith.)

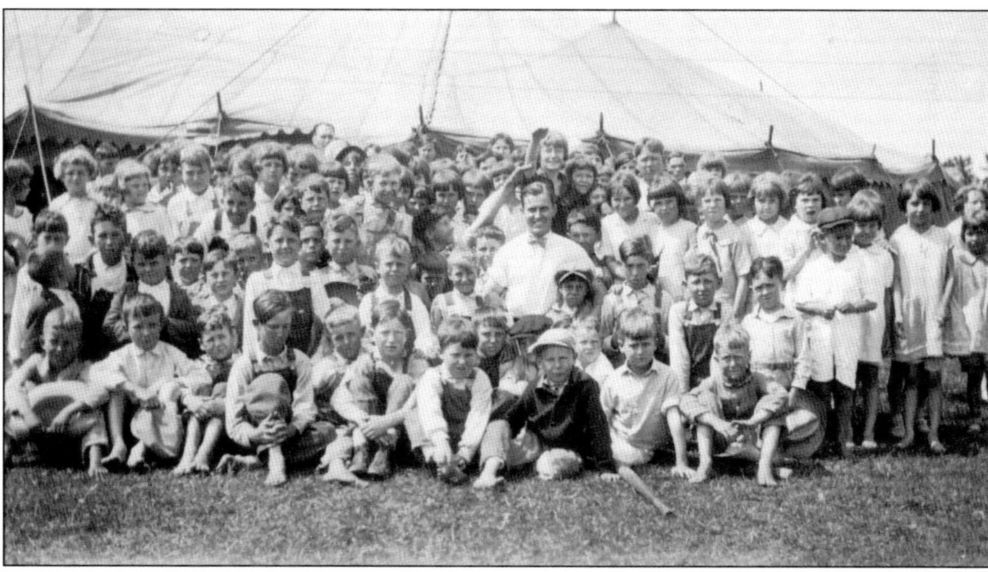

Rev. W.T. Smith, former minister at Unity Presbyterian Church, was well known for his tent revivals in the Triangle community. For this photograph from the 1930s, an unidentified man dons a large smile and a bowtie while two kids have a little fun by highlighting his place in the photograph with their hands over his head. (Courtesy of Ann Smith.)

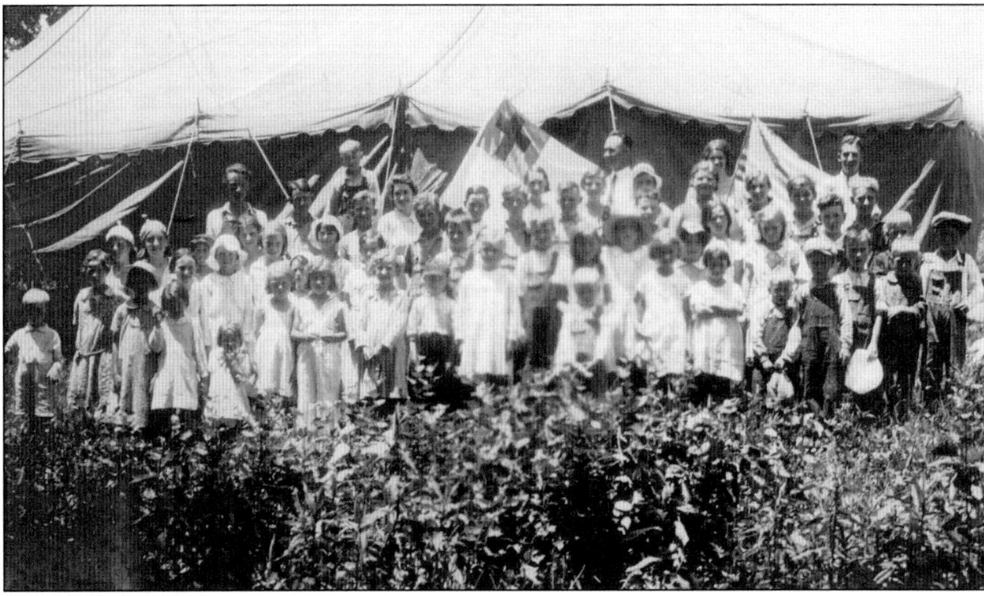

The traditional large tent of an outdoor revival stands tall behind this group of young kids in the 1930s. A group of teenagers and an adult display looks of excitement as they bear the American flag and a Christian flag. Rev. W.T. Smith held tent revivals in various counties around Lincoln County before becoming the minister at Unity Presbyterian Church in the Triangle community. (Courtesy of Ann Smith.)

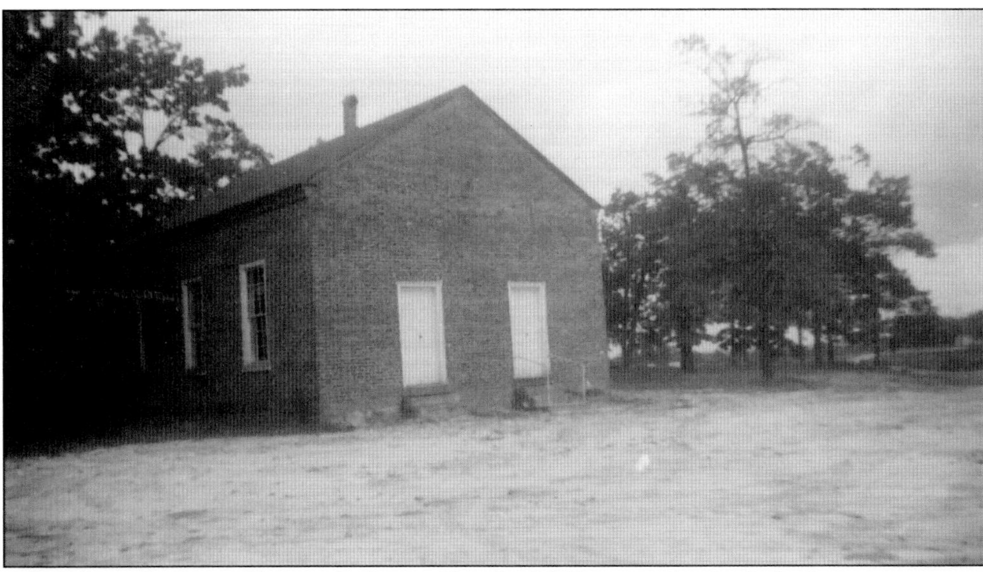

Capt. Alexander Brevard bequeathed several hundred dollars upon his death for the construction of a church building. The 30-foot-by-40-foot building was erected in 1848 as Machpelah Presbyterian Church and was recognized by the Concord Presbytery the same year. The church held services under Rev. Robert Hall Morrison from 1848 to 1889. The congregation resumed services in 1903 under Rev. W.H. Wilson, the church's second pastor. In 1976, the Presbyterian Church decided to dissolve the congregation, but the decision was reversed because of the church's historical significance. (Courtesy of LCHA.)

This 1911 photograph of the Machpelah Presbyterian Church Cemetery shows the gravestone of Rev. Robert Hall Morrison. Morrison was not only a founder but also the first president of Davidson College and served the Presbyterian Church in Lincoln County for 40 years. This cemetery was started in 1801 as a private family cemetery by Joseph Graham and Alexander Brevard on property that was midway between Graham's home, Vesuvius Furnace, and Brevard's home, Mount Tirzah. (Courtesy of LCHA.)

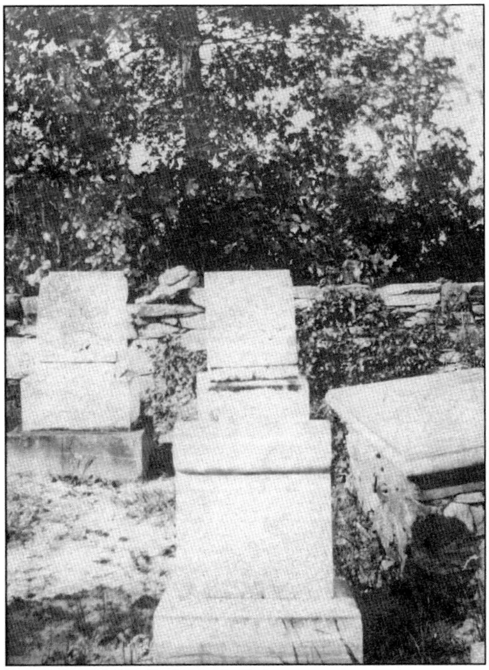

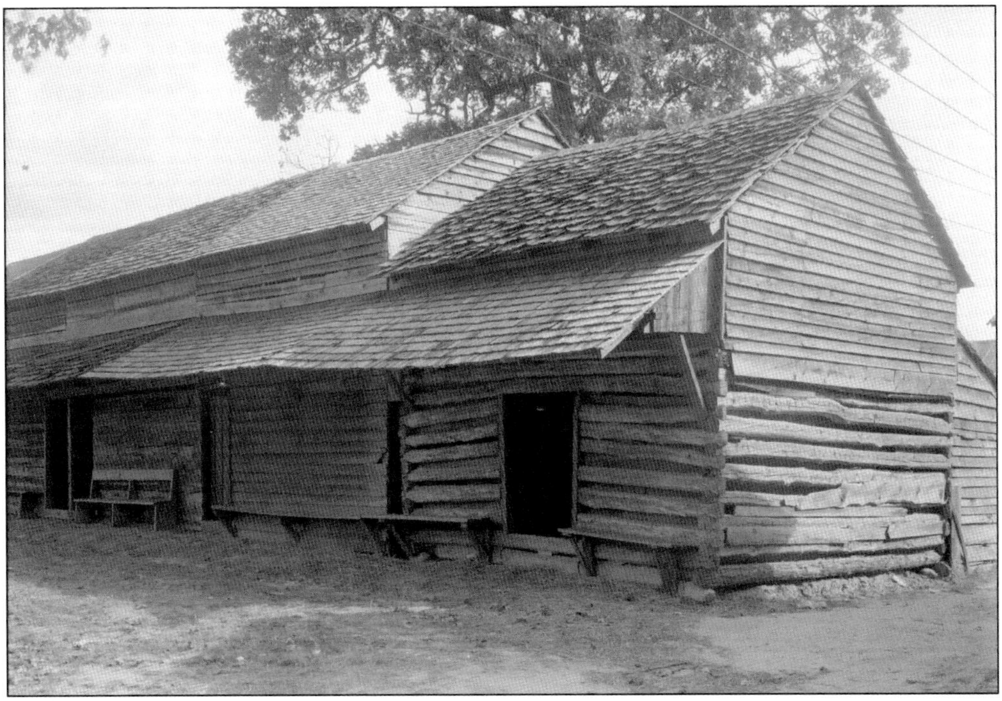

Tent No. 1 stands as a cornerstone of the Rock Spring Campground. This V-notch log structure is a reminder of many of the early wooden frame structures known as "tents." Hewn-log construction, shake shingles, and straw floors harken back to the tents of old. Fires over the years have destroyed some tents, which were replaced with more modern features: clapboard siding, concrete floors, electricity, and running water. There are some who choose to retain some of the primitive features of their tents. (Courtesy of the Library of Congress.)

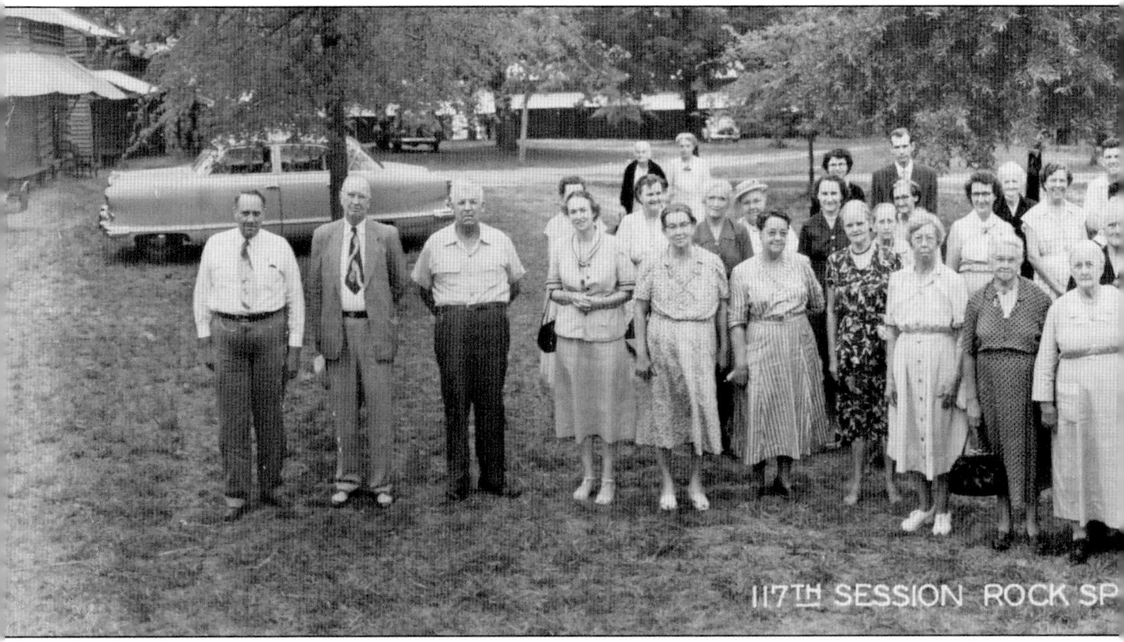

A quiet campground and arbor set the tone for this panoramic shot of a large group that lined up for a photograph during the 117th session at Rock Spring on August 7, 1953. The campground was 119 years old at the time. The newspaper article that accompanied the story about the session

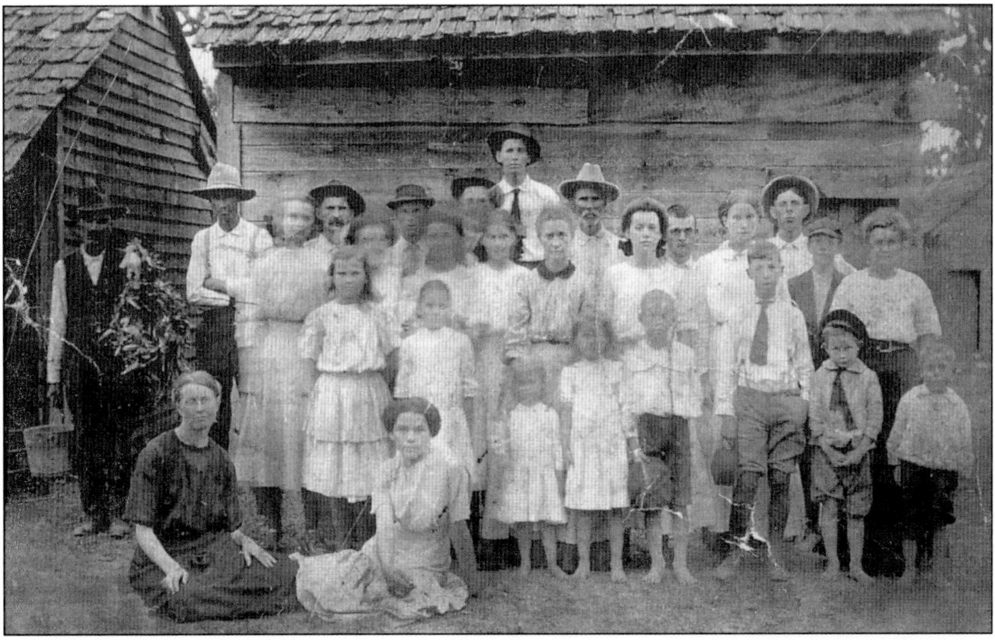

The simple majesty of tents at the Rock Spring Campground provide lodging for the members who attend the annual camp meeting in Denver. A group of attendees stand in front of a typical tent in 1910. Some of the families represented in this photograph include the Howards, Brothertons, Barkers, and Sherrills. Lewis Howard holds a bundle of fodder on his way to feed the group's horses and mules, while Mae Graham Sherrill stands to the far right with her two sons, Robert Francis (left) and Joseph Duke Sherrill (right). (Courtesy of Anne Eudy.)

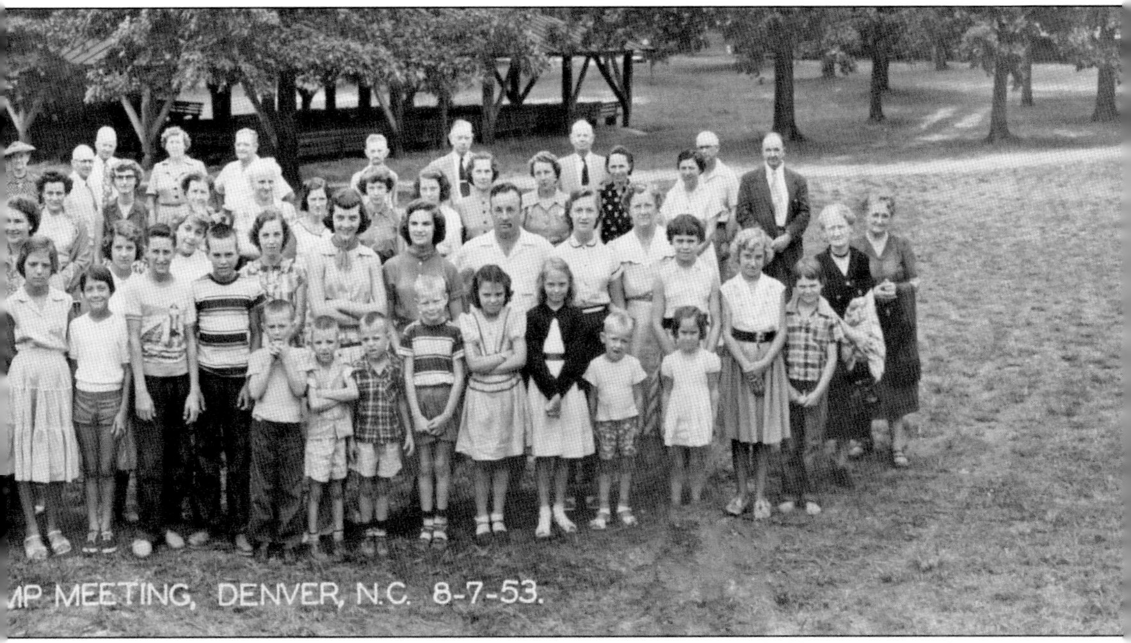

included a note that the "Trustees announced that there will be no children's services because of the polio epidemic in Catawba County," but "there is no polio epidemic in Lincoln County." (Courtesy of LCHA.)

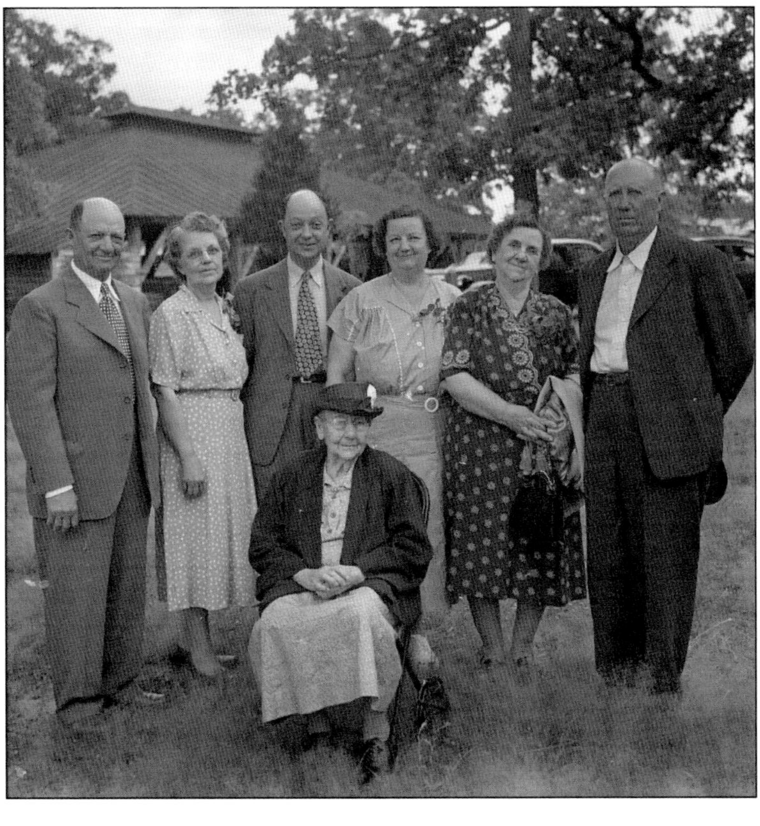

Members of the Smith and Lineberger families step away from the large group who attended an annual Smith-Lineberger family reunion at Rock Spring Campground in Denver for a photograph in 1950. Some of the reunion's activities took place under the historic log arbor that stands in the background. (Courtesy of LCHA.)

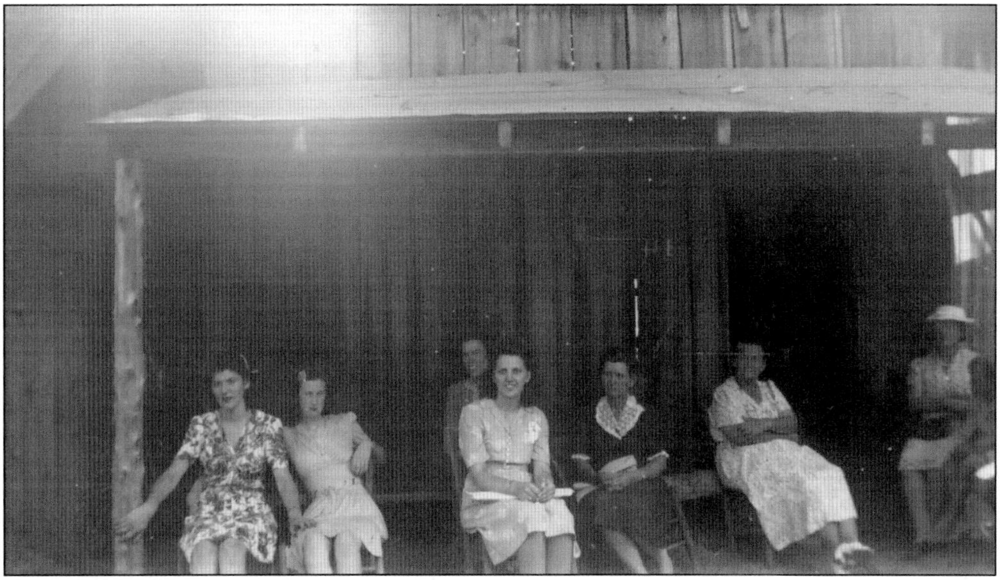

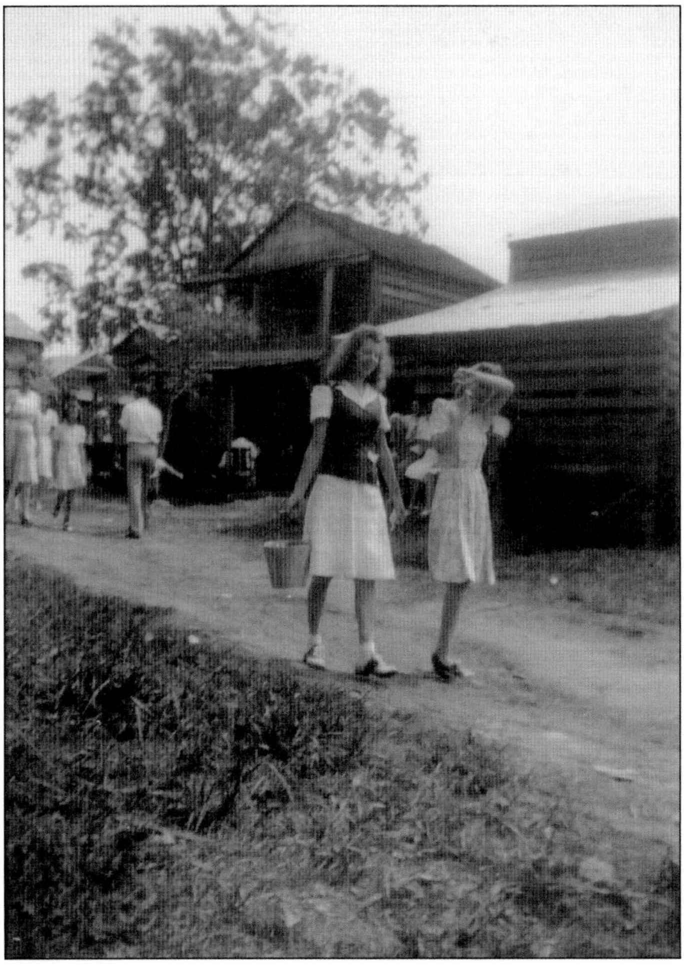

A shed roof supported by rough round logs provides shade to a group of ladies outside of Tent No. 166 at Rock Spring Campground in this 1930s photograph. The ladies are, from left to right, Geraldine Luckey, Margaret Stroupe, Bernice Luckey (in back), Muriel Luckey, Clara Beatty, and Ada Nixon. (Courtesy of Bernice Luckey Nixon.)

As tent owners rock in rocking chairs and walk around the campground to visit with friends and family, two ladies walk the well-traveled path from Rock Spring Campground to the rock spring for which the campground is named. With metal bucket in hand, the ladies retrieve water that their family will need for their weeklong stay at the campground. (Courtesy of Bernice Luckey Nixon.)

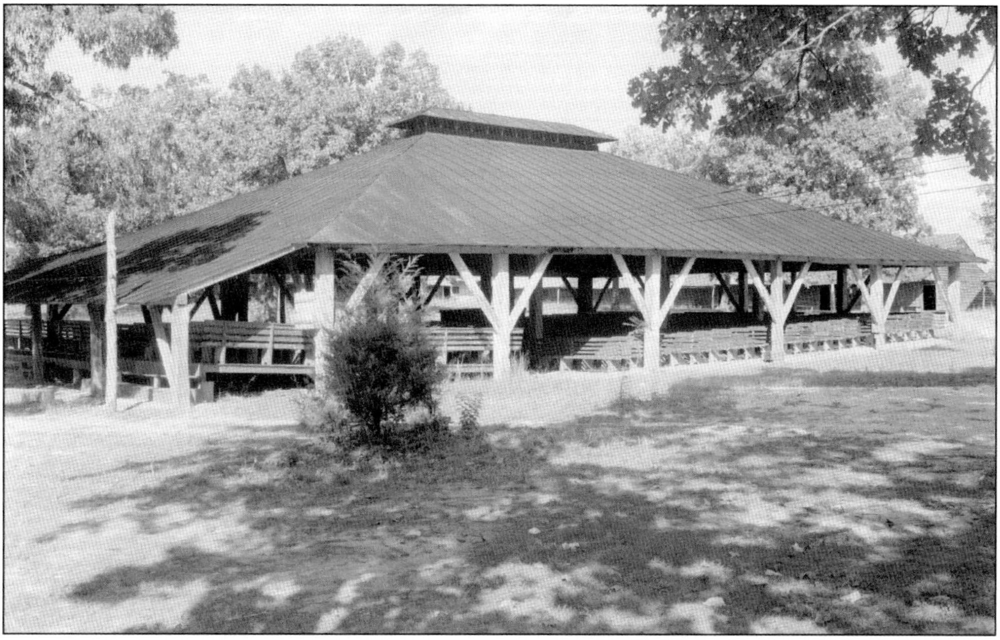

Begun in 1794 by Rev. Daniel Asbury during the Great Revival Movement in the United States, Rock Spring Campground was moved to its present site in 1830 from the Rehoboth area in eastern Lincoln County. Rock Spring Campground is listed in the National Register of Historic Places. The Trustees of Rock Spring Campground received a Historic Preservation Award from the Lincoln County Historical Association and Lincoln County Historic Properties Commission in 2014 for their restoration of the historic arbor. (Courtesy of the Library of Congress.)

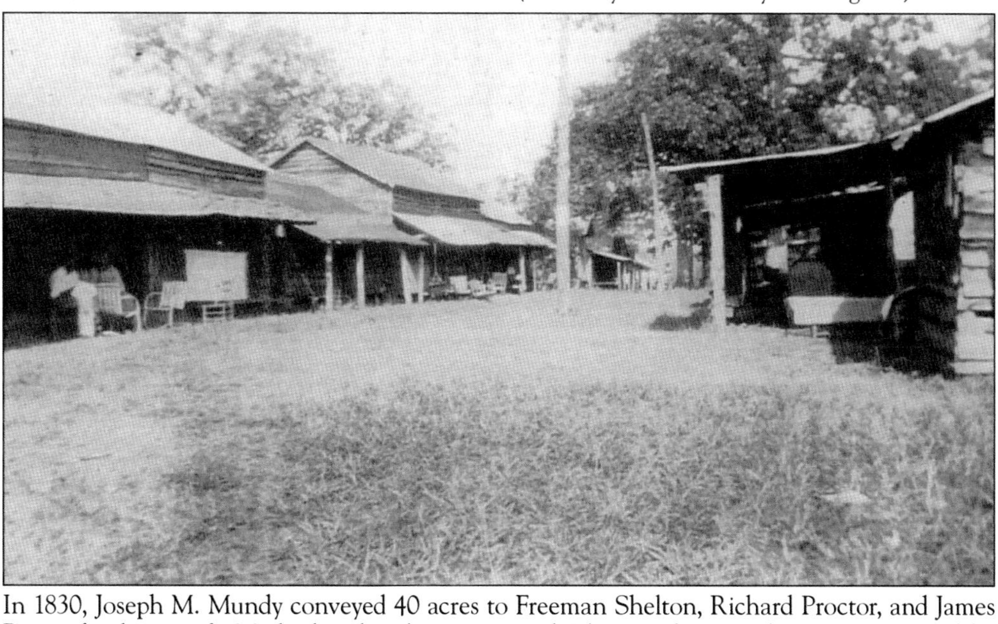

In 1830, Joseph M. Mundy conveyed 40 acres to Freeman Shelton, Richard Proctor, and James Bivens for the use of a Methodist church campground. This spot became the meeting ground for members of all denominations, and tents were built to encircle a brush arbor in the middle of the campground. The tents are privately owned, and camp meeting is held during two weeks every year. (Courtesy of Marsha Sigmon McCall.)

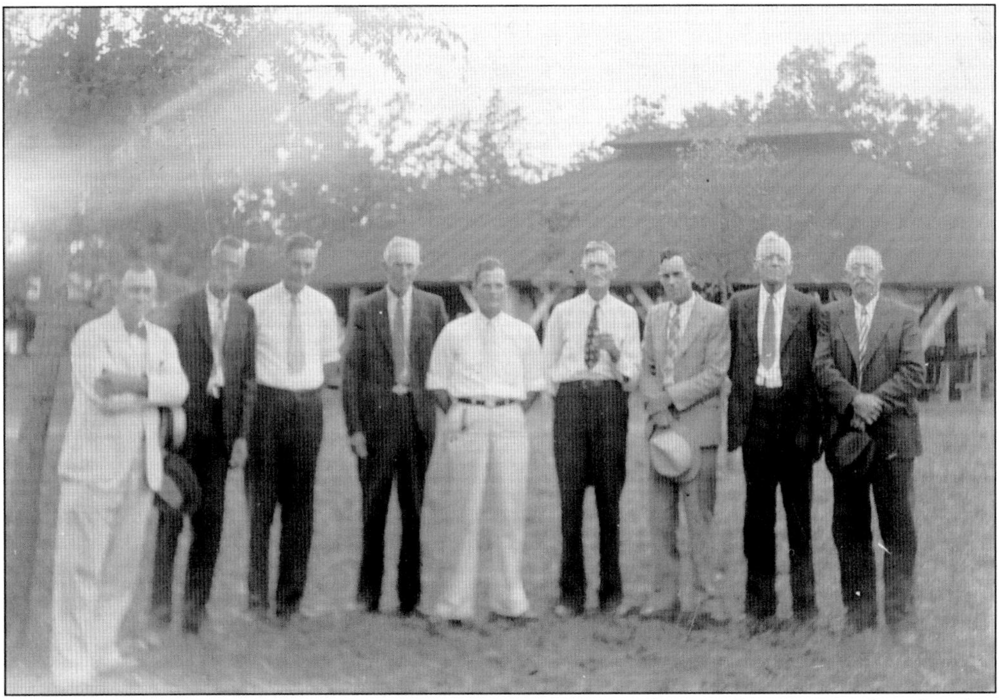

The Rock Spring Campground trustees of the 1930s stand near the iconic arbor for this commemorative photograph. Just over 100 years before this photograph was taken, the campground was started on land conveyed to trustees by Joseph M. Mundy. Pictured are, from left to right, Arnie Cashion, Will Sigmon, Louis Howard, Charles Gabriel, Dick Howard, John Sigmon, Thad Gabriel, Charlie Dellinger, and Ollie Howard. (Courtesy of Shawn Howard.)

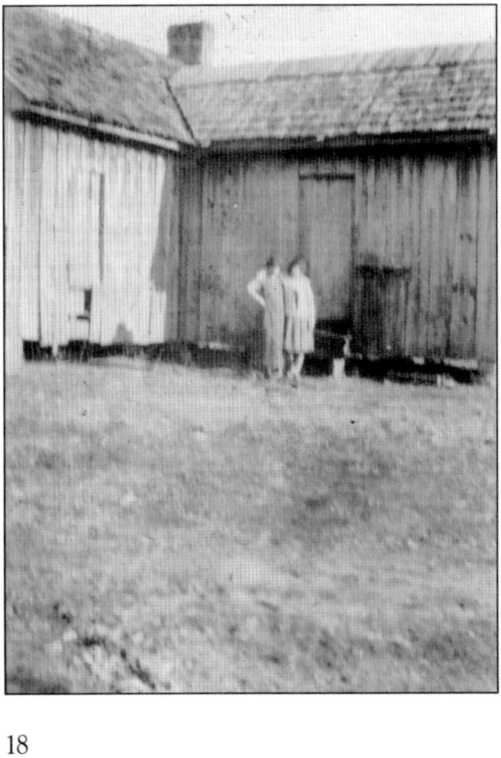

Two ladies stand outside a small frame building known as the Shack at Rock Spring Campground in 1916. No longer standing as it appears in this photograph, the Shack is now a modern concession-style building with a stone facade that occupies a prominent spot at the campground near the entrance. People patronize the Shack for food, homemade milkshakes, and children's novelty toys. (Courtesy of Richard and Melisa Thompson.)

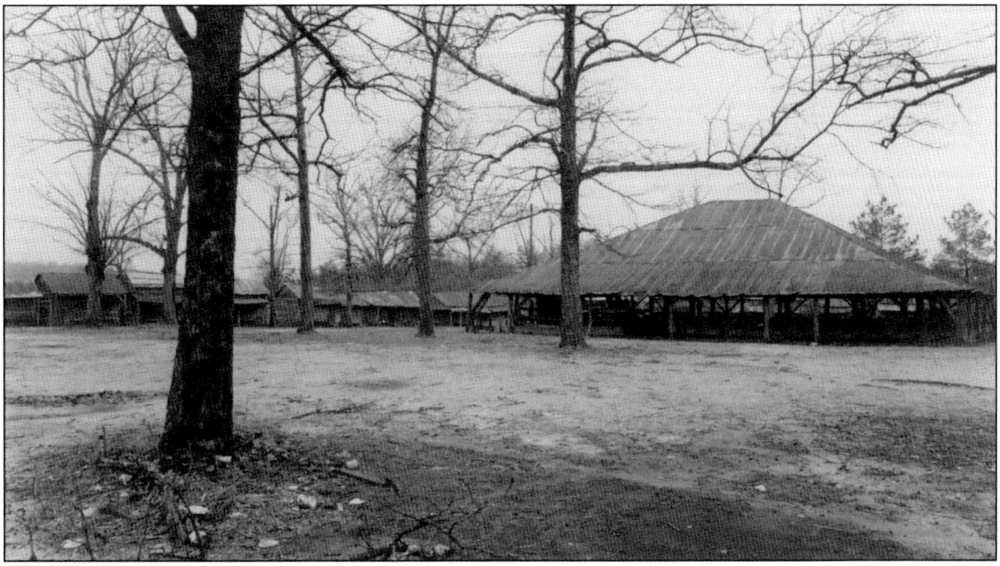

Tucker's Grove is an African American Methodist campground on Highway 73 in Iron Station that has tents encircling an arbor. Founded in the first half of the 19th century by the Methodist Episcopal Church, camp meeting at Tucker's Grove has been continually functioning since 1876 as an A.M.E. Zion camp meeting site. In 1879, Mary E. Tucker donated the oak grove where the campground is located to the trustees of Tucker's Grove Campground. (Courtesy of North Carolina Office of Archives and History.)

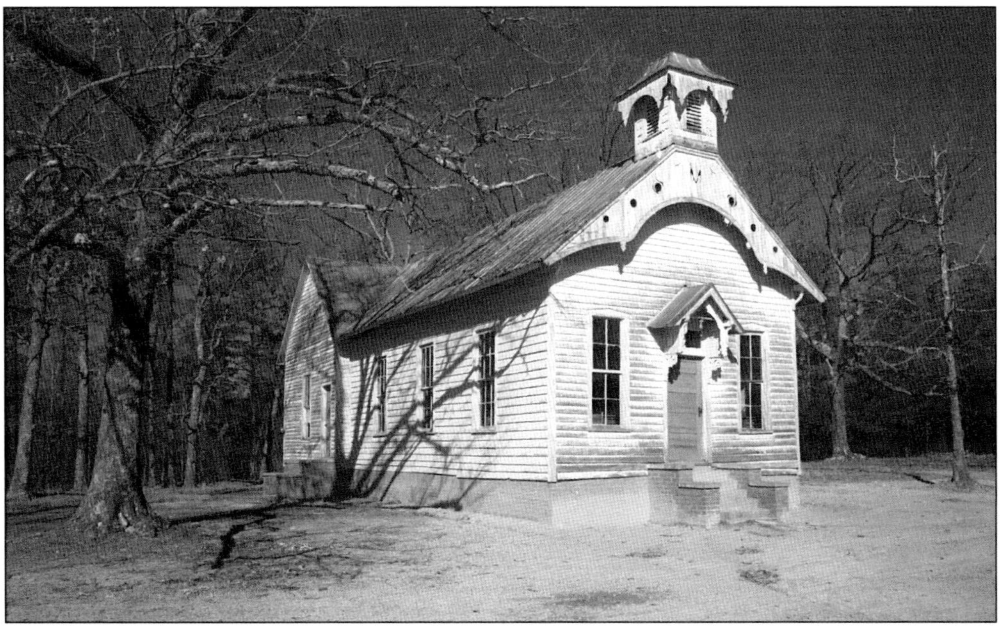

A mansard-roofed bell tower surmounts intricately cut, incised, and pierced boards of Brevard Chapel's front gable and single central entryway. According to architectural historian Marvin Brown, the church building is the "most fanciful expression of the Carpenter Gothic style in the county," and it has served an A.M.E. Zion congregation for more than 120 years. The church was most likely started in the 1870s for African Americans who had worshipped at Rock Spring Campground, which is less than 100 yards west of the church. (Courtesy of Mike Reavis.)

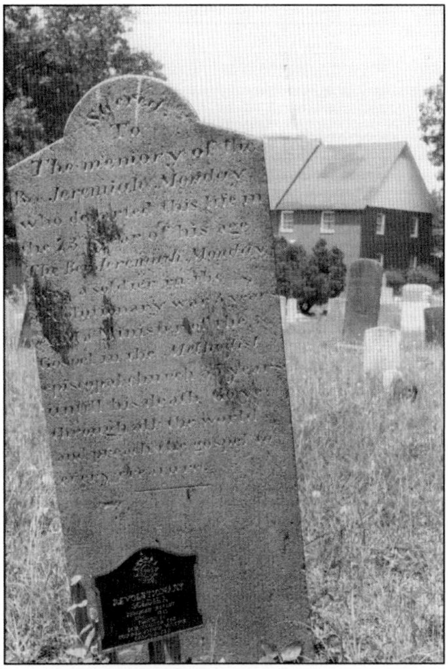

Bethel United Methodist Church was organized in 1791 by Rev. Daniel Asbury (1762–1825) and is one of the oldest congregations in Lincoln County. Rev. Jeremiah Monday (1760–1835) was one of the church's earliest ministers, and his soapstone gravestone stands in the church's cemetery. Monday, born in Pittsylvania County, Virginia, was a soldier during the American Revolution and was one of the founders of the Rock Spring Camp Meeting. His son Joseph Matthias Mundy deeded more than 45 acres to Rock Spring Camp Meeting for the Rock Spring Campground on August 7, 1830. (Courtesy of the North Carolina Office of Archives and History.)

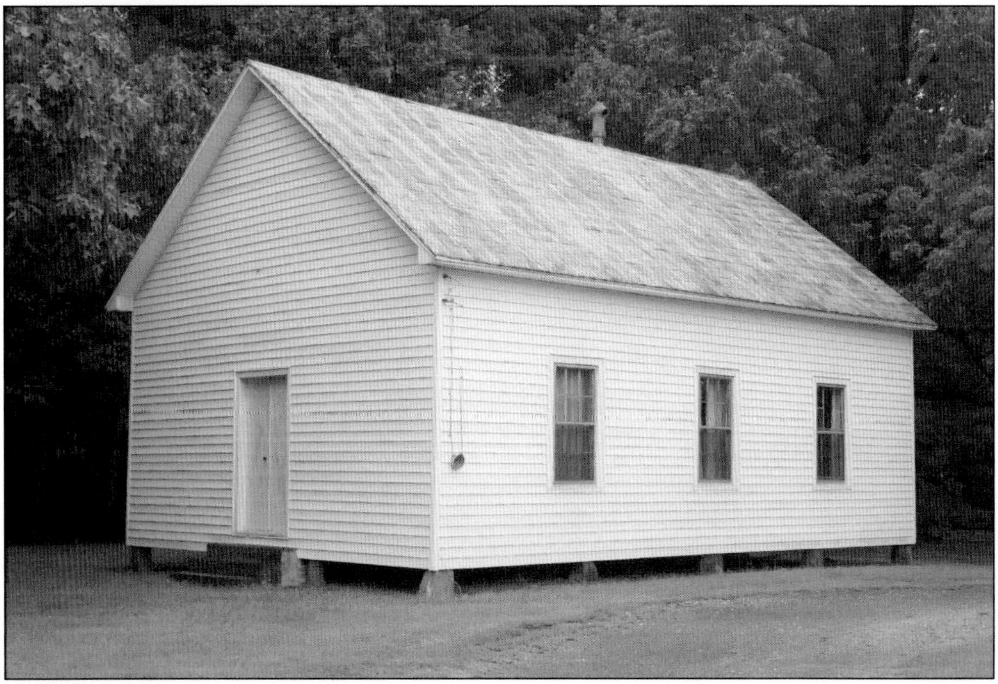

Located on Killian Farm Road in Denver, this small, one-story, frame church building stands near a cemetery originally known as the old Salem Graveyard. Sterling Womac sold one and a quarter acres to Simon Barker, Frank Womac, and Enos Hager, trustees of the old Salem Graveyard, on January 8, 1908, and the men built this church building "designated as Martha's Chapel, to be used as a place of union worship, burial service, and Sunday School by any religious group in the neighborhood," according to the Frances Hampton Papers at LCHA. The church building was named for Martha Womac Sifford (1855–1907). (Courtesy of Jason L. Harpe.)

Born on October 25, 1855, Martha Womac Sifford was the daughter of Sterling Womac and his first wife, Mary Ann Elizabeth Lawing. Martha married Albert Franklin Sifford, and they had three children. When Martha died, her body was taken to the old Salem Graveyard, and a terrible storm ensued. They were unable to bury her for several days. Her husband, distraught at her passing, would sit by her grave and weep. One day, she appeared to him in a vision and told him to build a church by the cemetery, and in 1908, a group of men built the small white structure now known as Martha's Chapel. (Courtesy of Frances Hampton.)

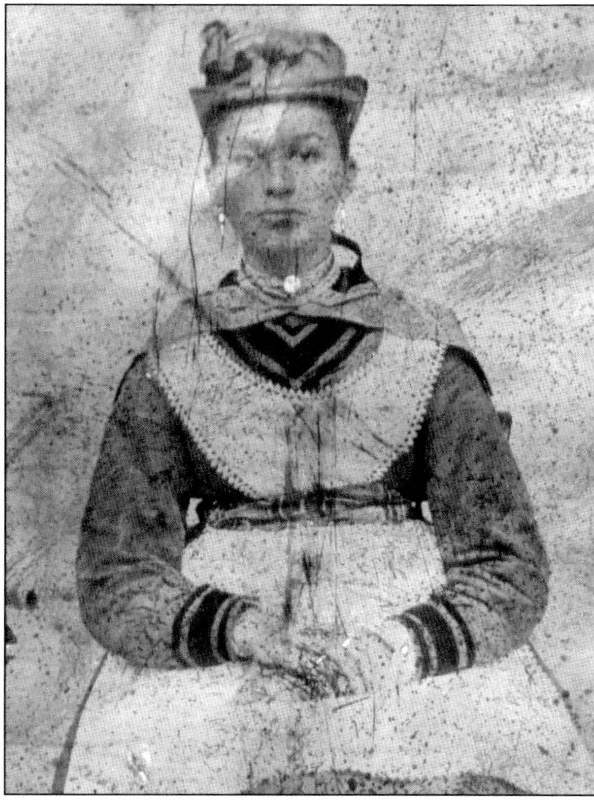

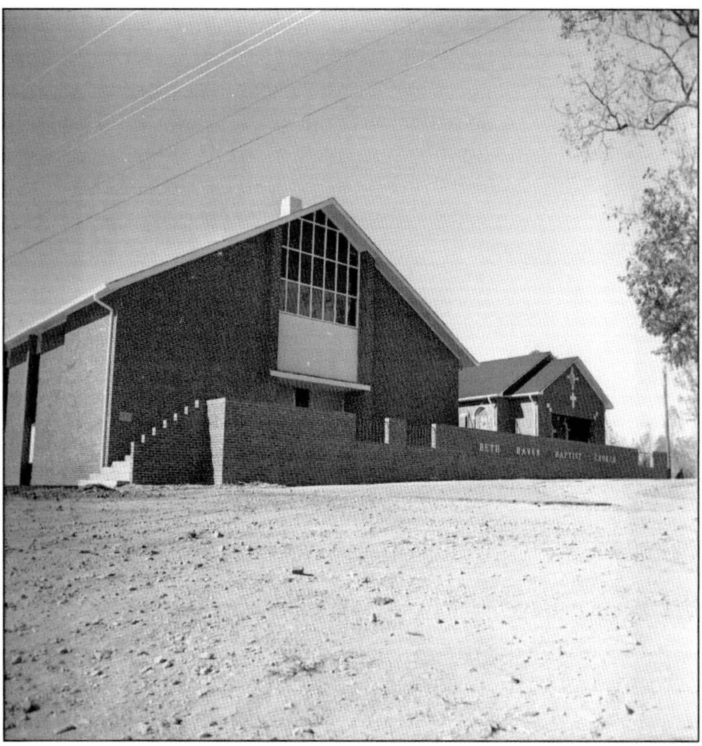

By 1890, services were being held in a one-room white church known as Marvin Methodist, located in the Kidville area. Marvin was one of the seven churches on the Rock Spring Charge. The church thrived until 1952, when membership fell to the point that the remaining members were transferred to Denver United Methodist. After Marvin disbanded, there was a need in the community for a Baptist church. Some local families constructed Poole's Chapel, and in 1973, they built Beth Haven Baptist Church, seen here. (Courtesy of LCHA.)

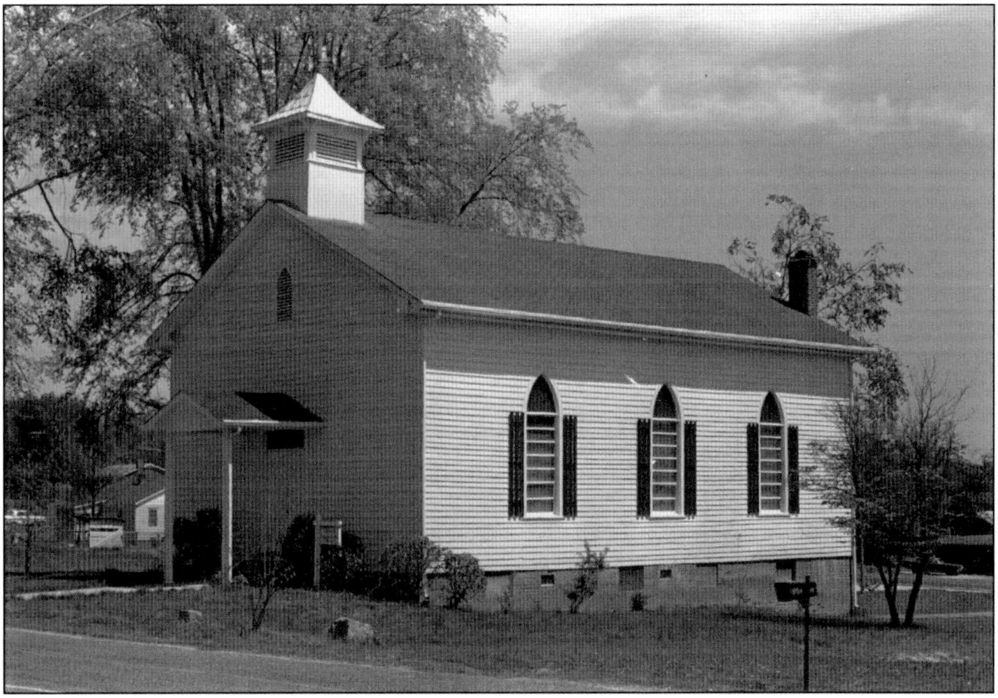

The congregation of Ironton Presbyterian Church in Iron Station began meeting under the pastorate of Rev. Robert Z. Johnston (1834–1908), who was the pastor at First Presbyterian Church in Lincolnton, in 1873. The church was officially organized in 1882 under the direction of Reverend Johnston, with 16 women and four men, and they built their church in 1889 on land donated by Joseph E. Reinhardt. (Courtesy of the North Carolina Office of Archives and History.)

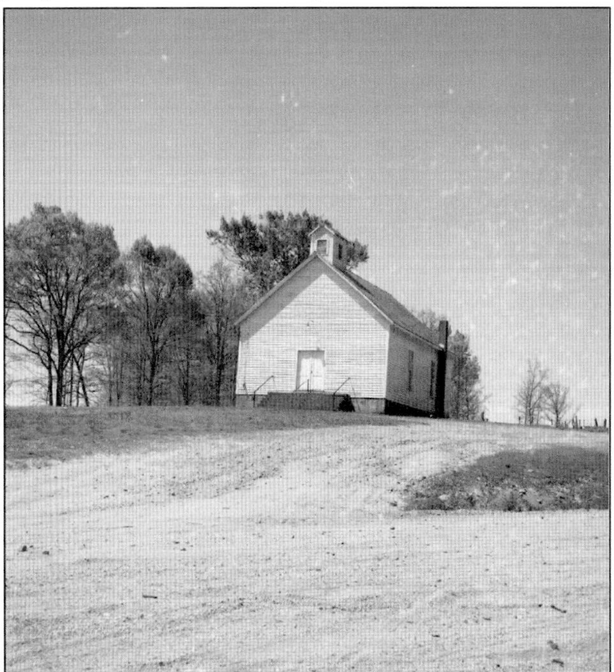

Built in 1857, the frame church building of St. Luke's Lutheran Church in Pumpkin Center is a treasured relic of the congregation, which holds fond memories of its eldest members. The congregation had numerous names since being organized by Rev. Johann Gottfried Arends in 1766, including Lebanon, Liberty, and Ore Bank, before becoming St. Luke's in 1858. The church was called Ore Bank because of the rich ore deposits that supplied the local iron furnaces for over 100 years. The frame church building pictured here was razed in 1974, and the church constructed a brick building. Wood from the old church was used to make a wooden cross that now hangs over the altar. (Courtesy of LCHA.)

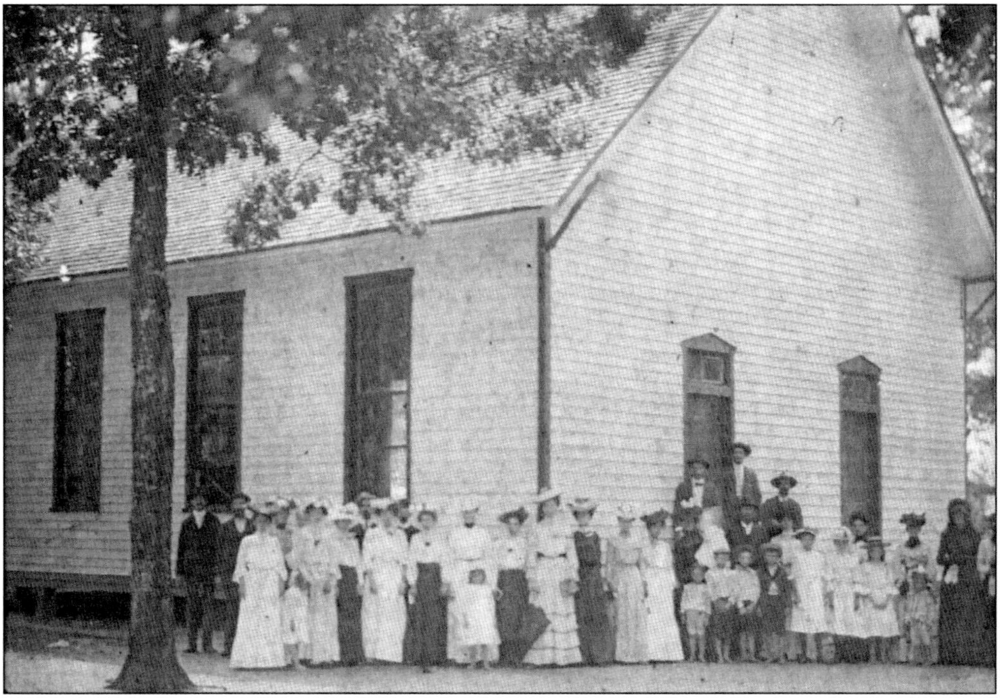

Hats are the accessory of the day for this undated photograph of Webb's Chapel United Methodist Church. The church was started because the Methodist Conference saw a need for a meeting place near the bend in the Catawba River. In 1888, Rev. Richard Stanford (R.S.) Webb (1837–1901) came to Denver and was appointed to the Rock Spring Circuit by the Conference of the Methodist Episcopal Church, South. He served the Confederacy in the 44th Regiment of the North Carolina Infantry as chaplain. The building in this photograph was constructed in the 1890s and still stands on the property. The exterior was veneered with brick, and the church added a vestibule. (Courtesy of Terry Brotherton.)

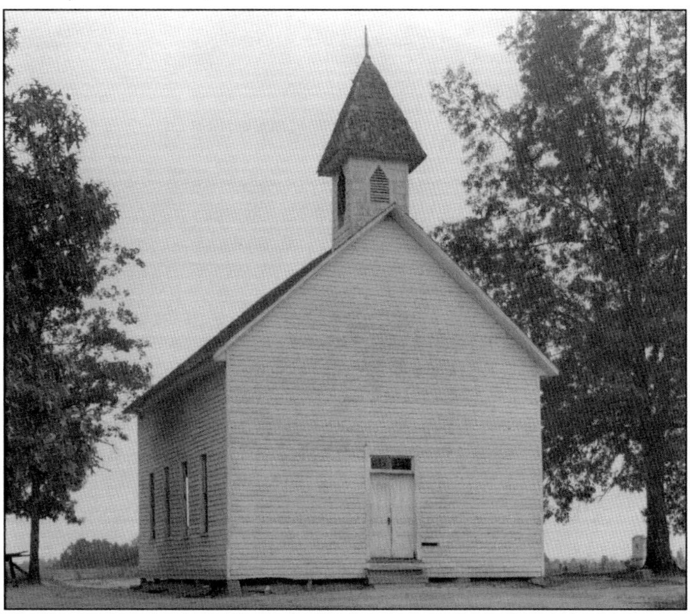

Amity Baptist Church was founded in 1905 in Iron Station. With the number of local revivals going on in the area, members of the community saw a need for a place of worship. James Patrick and Emily Lowe Mullen, along with H.F. Killian, donated the land necessary to build a church and cemetery. Other members in the community donated the timber and labor to build the first Amity Baptist Church building. (Courtesy of Joyce McCumbee.)

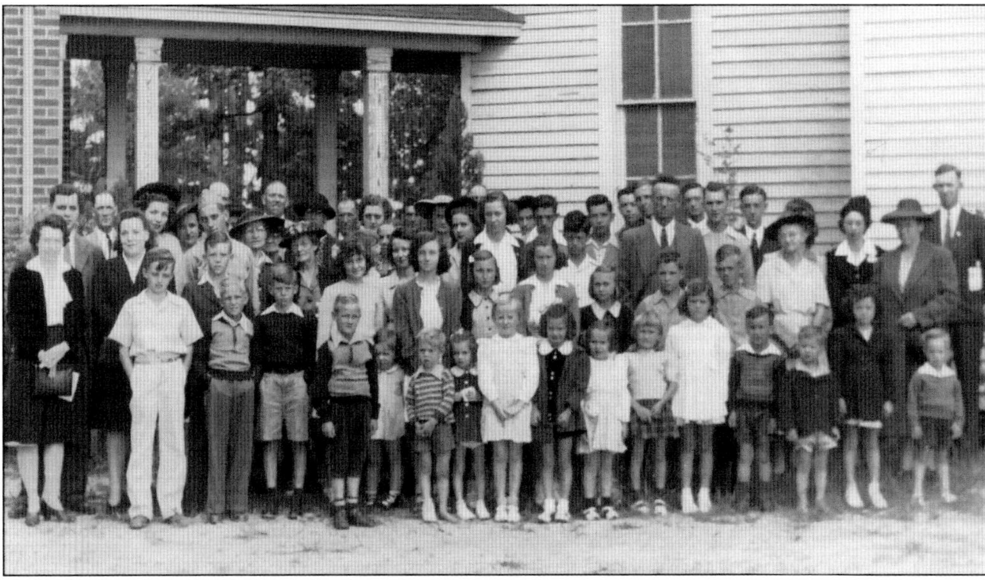

People of all ages wore their Sunday best for this photograph at Hills Chapel United Methodist Church in Lowesville. The original church building was constructed around 1862, after William P. Connell donated two and a quarter acres to D.A. Lowe, Thomas Rozelle, and Alfred Childress, trustees of Hills Chapel Church, on August 27, 1857. The church was named for Rev. Jacob Hill, a noted pioneer Methodist minister and father-in-law of Thomas Rozelle. Col. John Nixon of Lowesville was contracted to build the first church building. (Courtesy of Doris Jean Keever.)

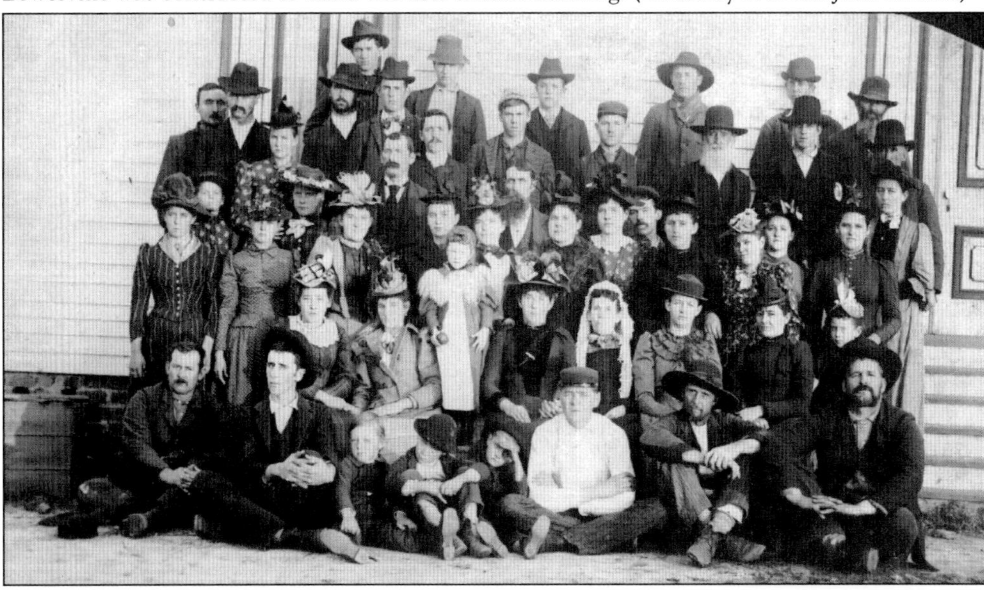

According to church history, Salem Church appeared on official records of the Lincoln Circuit in 1828, the date used as the official beginning of the church. By 1854, the community had grown considerably, and a new building was built across from what is today Martha's Chapel. In 1885, the church relocated to its present site, and a one-room building was constructed. In this 1890s photograph, Monroe Augustus Nixon stands at center with the long, dark beard, surrounded by the congregation. Families pictured include the Duckworths, Hagers, Littles, Luckeys, Kings, Nixons, McIntoshes, and Proctors. (Courtesy of Kellie Ellis.)

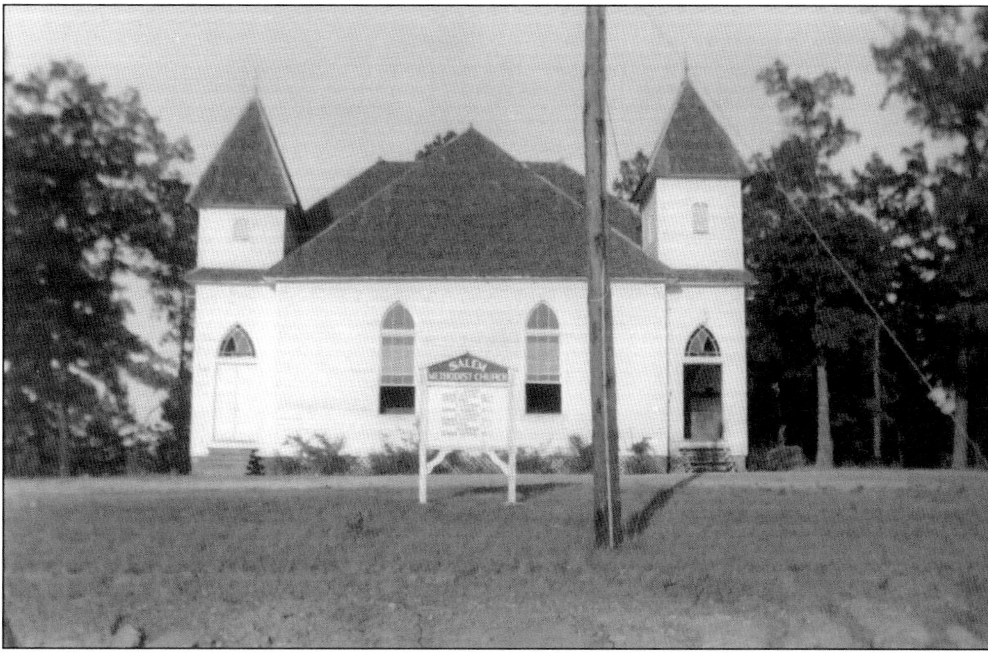

The congregation of Salem United Methodist Church dates back nearly 200 years, and the church moved to its current location at North Pilot Knob Road in Triangle in 1885. A small, one-room building was constructed at the site, but by 1919, the church added two Sunday school rooms on each side of the main building. During renovations, the church built two towers at the front corners with two front doors and a vestibule leading into the sanctuary. (Courtesy of Bernice Luckey Nixon.)

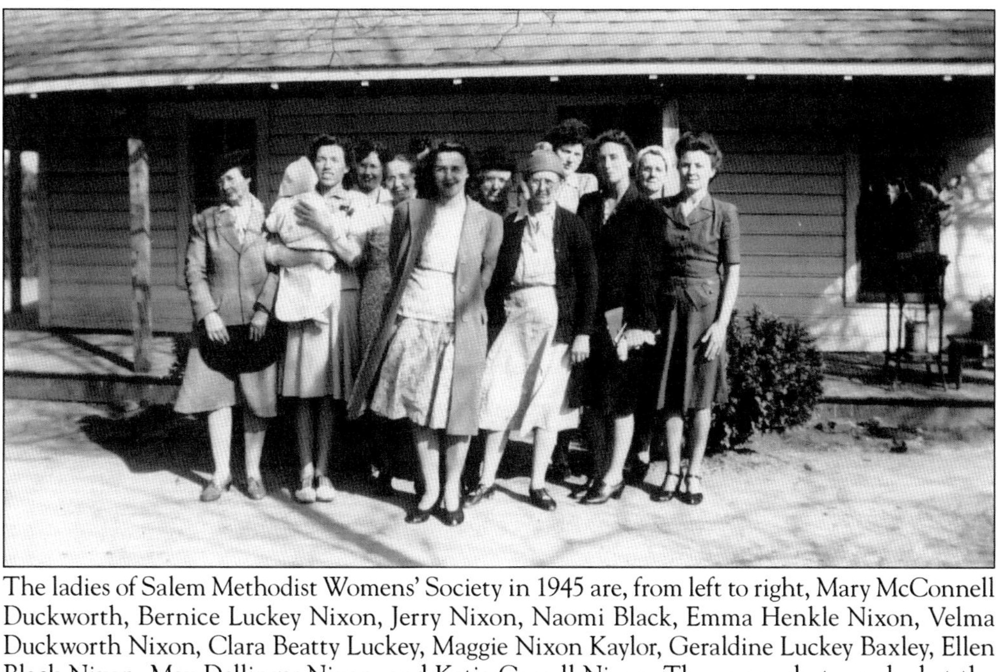

The ladies of Salem Methodist Womens' Society in 1945 are, from left to right, Mary McConnell Duckworth, Bernice Luckey Nixon, Jerry Nixon, Naomi Black, Emma Henkle Nixon, Velma Duckworth Nixon, Clara Beatty Luckey, Maggie Nixon Kaylor, Geraldine Luckey Baxley, Ellen Black Nixon, May Dellinger Nixon, and Katie Carroll Nixon. They were photographed at the home of Walter and Emma Nixon. (Courtesy of Bernice Luckey Nixon.)

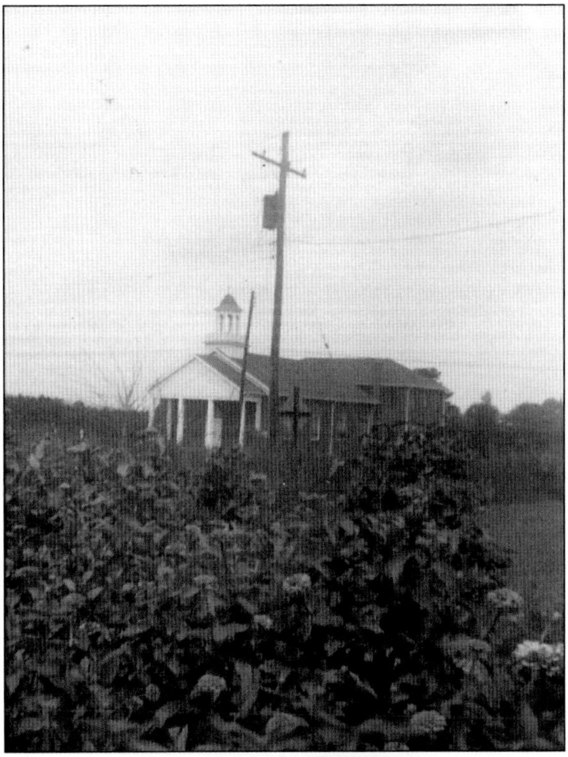

Denver United Methodist Church, pictured here, was dedicated on Mother's Day, May 12, 1957. The cornerstone of this building was laid in 1950, and construction began the following year. The building was completed in February 1952, and the church held its first service on February 10, 1952. The congregation was organized in the 1880s but did not have its own house of worship until it built a frame church in 1907. (Courtesy of Sue Carolyn Sherrill.)

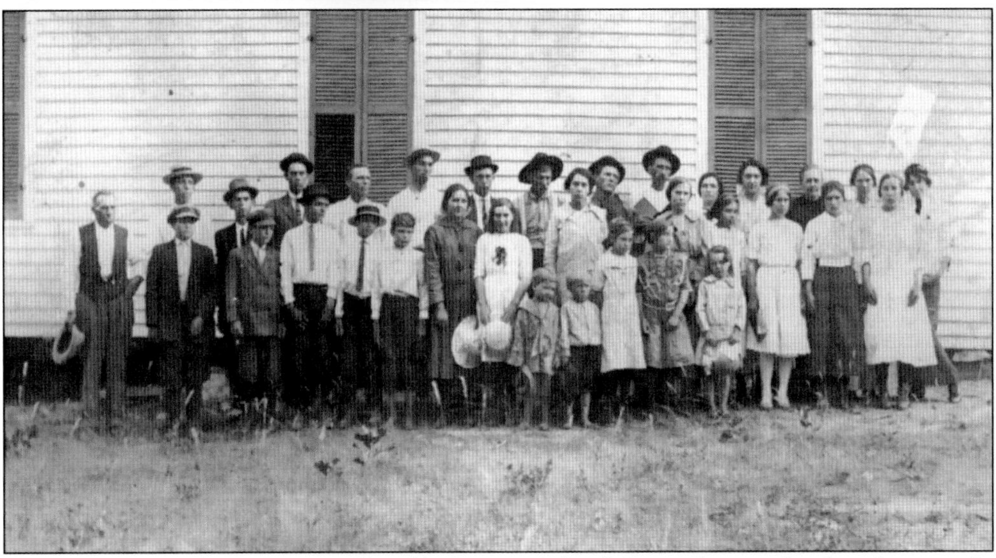

Members of Macedonia Baptist Church's Singing School Group line up for this photograph. From left to right are (first row) Robert E. Lee, Delbert Norwood, Ha Shook, Rhoda Bell Link, and Hazeline Norwood; (second row) D.A. Chapman, Robert D. Lee, Cobb Link, Joe Goodson, Osborne Lawing, Rosco Goodson, Grace Lee, Rosa Chapman, Mercedes Lee, Geguetta Chapman, Eva Shook, Belin Armstrong, Ella Goodson, and Margaret Chapman; (third row) Lee Chapman, Dorie Lawing, Gaither Lee, W.W. Moore, Klutz Clippard, Walter A. Potts, John McAlister, James Norwood, W.F. Lee, Addie Lee, Carrie Lee, Minnie Lee, Ira Goodson, and Eva Lee. (Courtesy of LCHA.)

Two

BAND OF CHARACTERS
EASTERN LINCOLN COUNTY PEOPLE AND FAMILIES

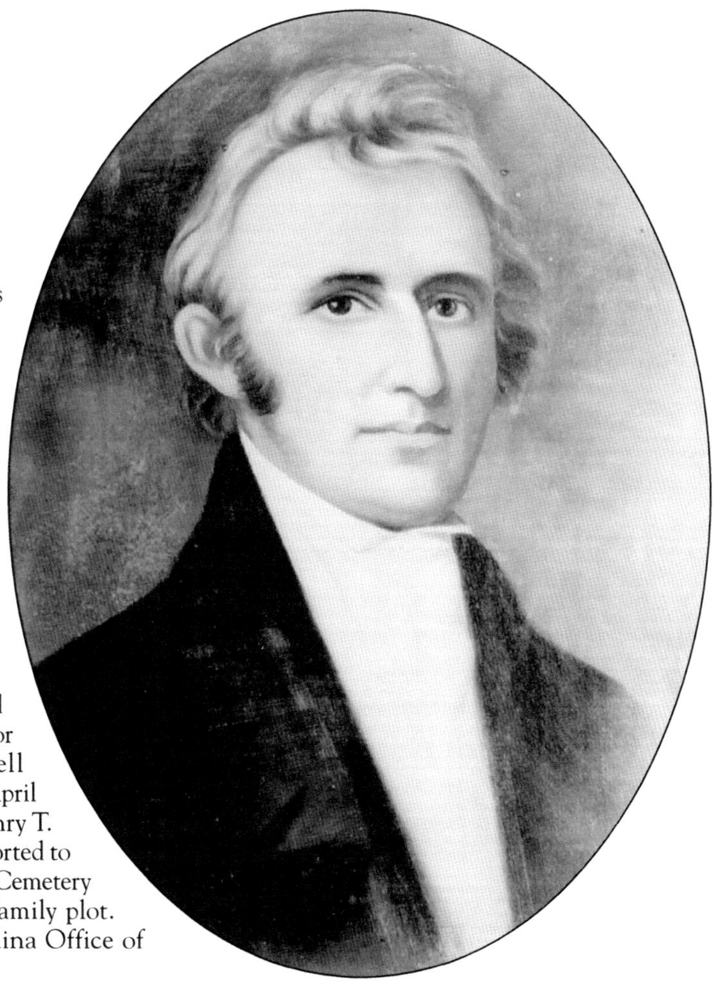

Hutchins Gordon Burton was raised in Granville County, North Carolina, and served in the state legislature as a representative of Mecklenburg County in 1809 and 1810. In 1810, the legislature elected him attorney general. Burton was elected governor of North Carolina, serving from 1824 to 1827. While on a trip from Halifax to Beatties Ford to visit his cousins, Robert H. and Alfred M. Burton, Governor Burton fell ill in Iredell County, where he died on April 21, 1836, at the home of Henry T. Sloan. His body was transported to Unity Presbyterian Church Cemetery for burial in the Burton family plot. (Courtesy of North Carolina Office of Archives and History.)

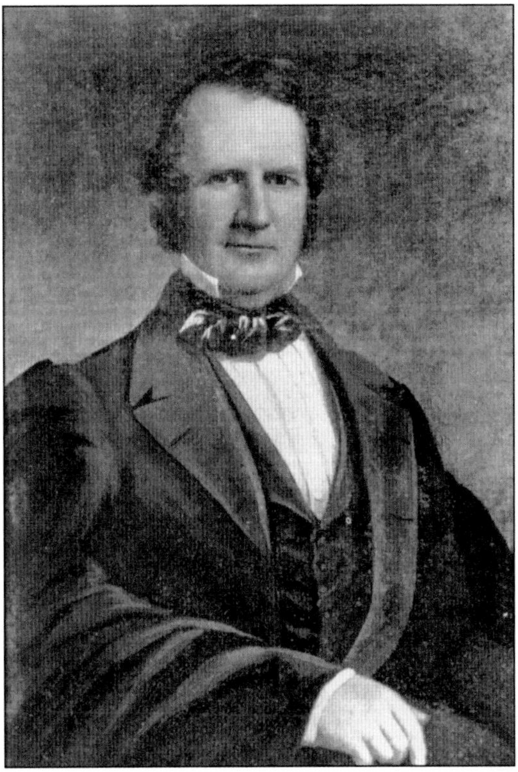

William A. Graham, son of Gen. Joseph and Isabella Graham, was born at Vesuvius on September 4, 1804. He graduated from the University of North Carolina in 1824 and married Susan Washington on June 8, 1836. He moved to Hillsborough and, as a young lawyer, served in the US Senate (1840–1843), as governor of North Carolina (1845–1849), and secretary of the Navy (1850–1853). Graham ran as a vice presidential candidate on the Whig ticket in 1852 with Gen. Winfield Scott. Graham died unexpectedly on August 11, 1875, and is buried in the cemetery adjacent to the Hillsborough Presbyterian Church. (Courtesy of North Carolina Office of Archives and History.)

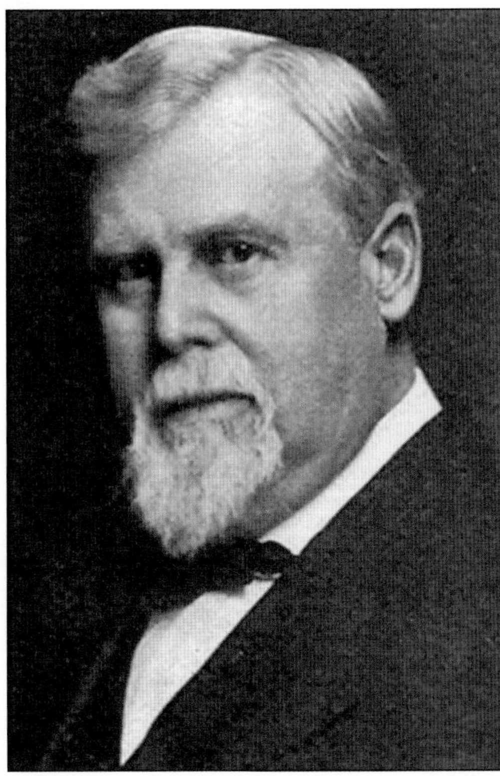

William Alexander Graham Jr. was born on December 26, 1839, in Hillsborough, North Carolina, the son of Gov. William Alexander and Susannah Sarah Washington Graham. He received an artium baccalaureus degree from Princeton University in 1860 and earned the rank of major during the Civil War. He was a leader in the Farmers' Alliance and served as the commissioner of agriculture for North Carolina from 1908 until his death in 1923. He is buried at Machpelah Cemetery. (Courtesy of North Carolina Office of Archives and History.)

Joseph Graham, born in Chester County, Pennsylvania, on October 13, 1759, married Isabella Davidson, daughter of Maj. John Davidson and Violet Winslow Wilson Davidson, on August 2, 1787. During the American Revolution, he served under Generals Griffith Rutherford and Jethro Sumner in a campaign near Charleston, South Carolina, and participated in the Battle of Charlotte. After the war, he was commissioner in Mecklenburg County (1783–1784) and sheriff of Mecklenburg County (1784–1785). He engaged in the iron industry in Lincoln County in 1789 and built the Vesuvius furnace and his house in the 1790s. He died in 1836 and is buried at Machpelah Presbyterian Church Cemetery. (Courtesy of Ann Graham.)

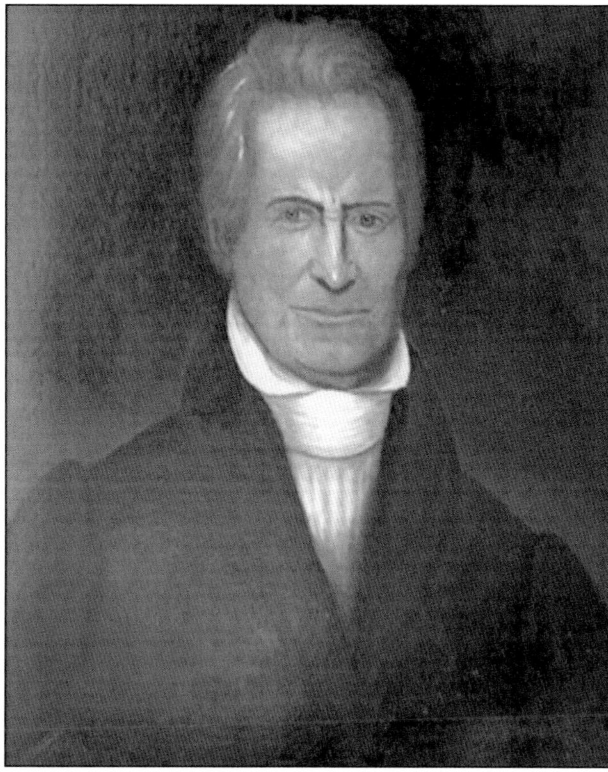

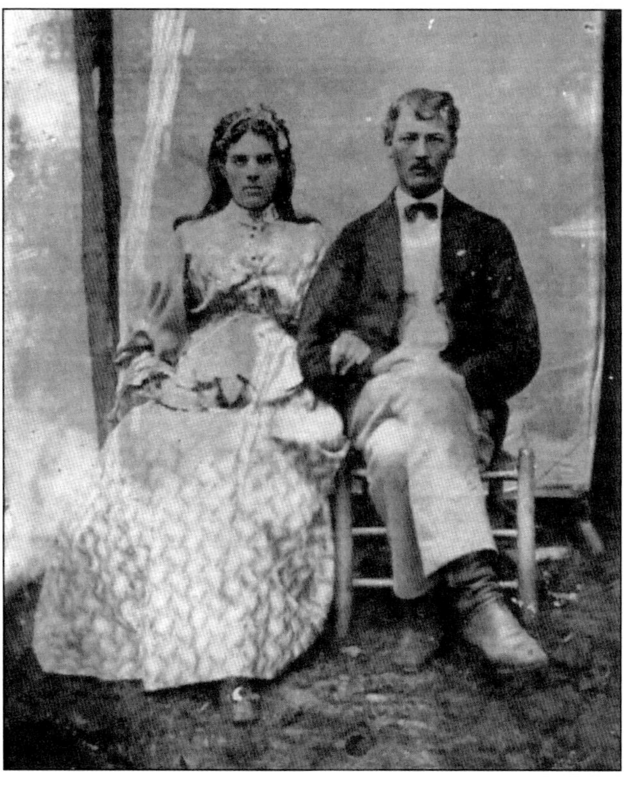

A simple sheet in a wooden frame shades Adolphus Haywood and Mary Shelton King while they sit for this photograph. Adolphus was born on March 30, 1852, the son of William Alexander King (1810–1892) and Frances "Fannie" M. Proctor (1812–1892), and married Mary Ellen Shelton (1852–1902) in Catawba County on January 24, 1872. Adolphus was a farmer in the Catawba Springs Township and was appointed postmaster of Harvey Post Office on June 8, 1895. Both Adolphus and Mary are buried at Unity Presbyterian Church. (Courtesy of Mary Swift.)

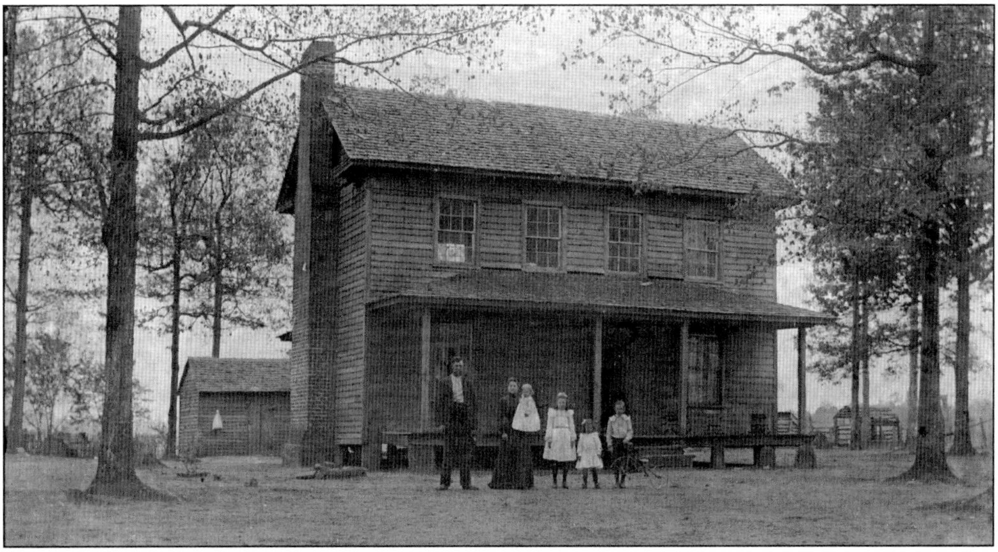

A swept lawn marks this timeless photograph of Robert "Big Bob" Nixon and his family in front of a two-story, frame I-house in Triangle. Big Bob Nixon was born on December 21, 1868, the son of Robert (1814–1884) and Millie Elmira Womack Nixon (1834–1929), and married Nannie Elizabeth Kayler (1866–1918). Big Bob and Nannie were the parents of Robert Lee (1894–1972), Lottie Louise (1901–1962), Annie Fay Nixon Cherry (1905–1966), and Houston Brown Nixon (1906–1962). Big Bob and Nannie are buried at Unity Presbyterian Church in Triangle. (Courtesy of LCHA.)

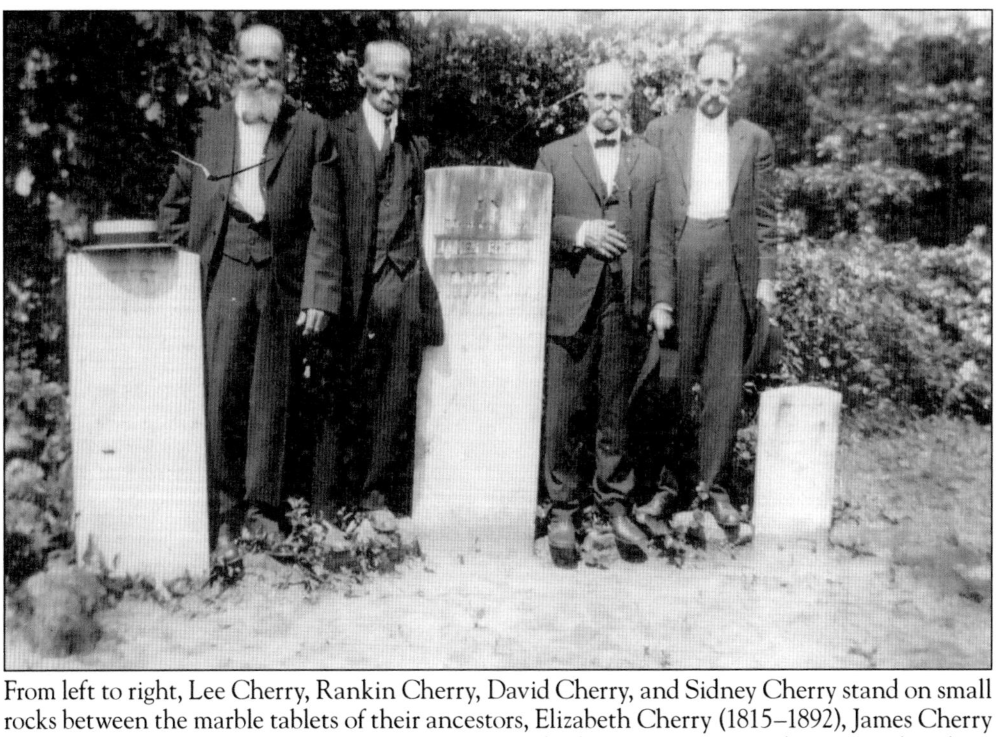

From left to right, Lee Cherry, Rankin Cherry, David Cherry, and Sidney Cherry stand on small rocks between the marble tablets of their ancestors, Elizabeth Cherry (1815–1892), James Cherry (1806–1862), and Harvey Cherry (1860–1862), at the historic Unity Presbyterian Church in Triangle. (Courtesy of Kelli Gaskill Hogue.)

Members of the Enos and Mary Lou Sifford Hager family pose for a turn-of-the-20th-century photograph at their home in eastern Lincoln County. The house was built after the Civil War on the farm that Aaron Sifford (1817–1897) bought in 1850. Originally, the farmstead included a log house and log kitchen. Members of the Hager family are, from left to right, Bly, Mary Lou Sifford, Albert Franklin, Louise, Paul, James, Elmer Lee, Dewey, and Enos. (Courtesy of LCHA.)

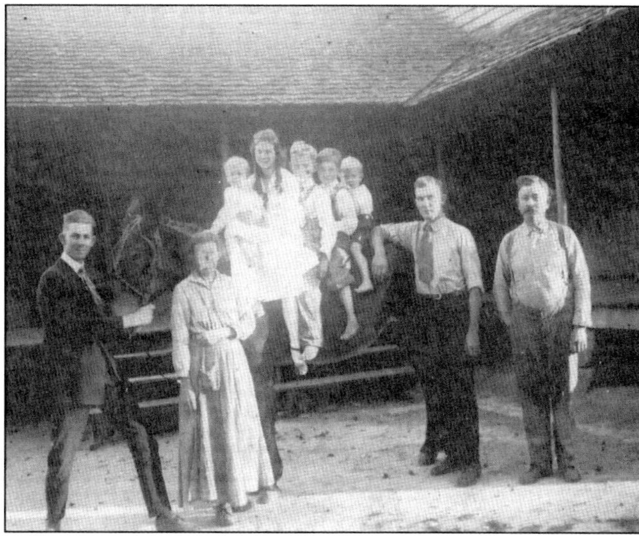

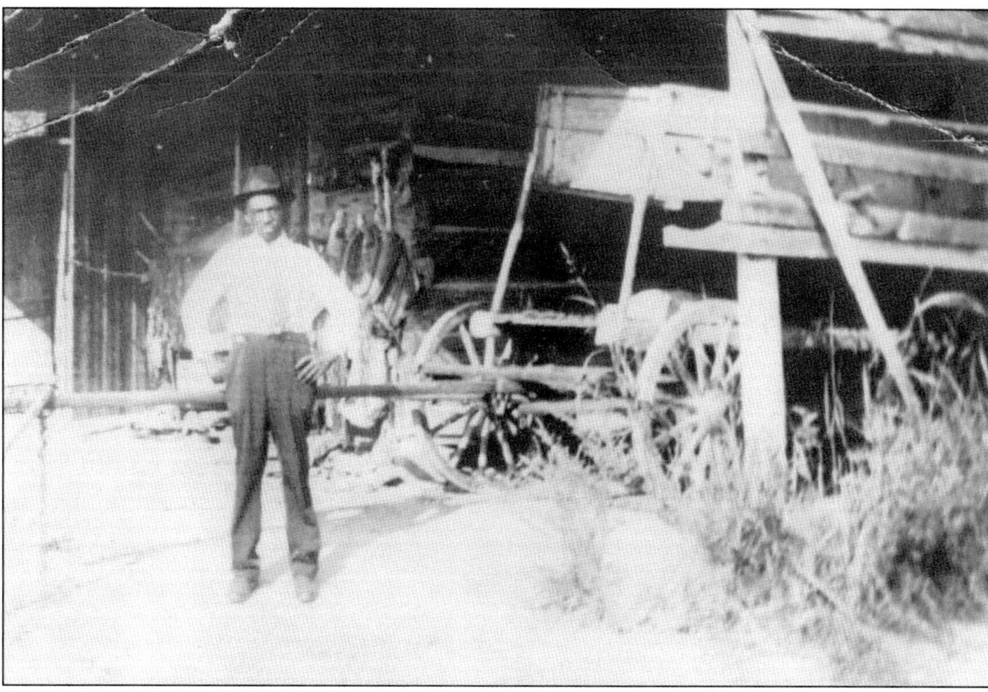

Forney Lowe Nance (1877–1945) poses in the 1920s beside an outbuilding on the property where he lived and worked in Lowesville. Nance was the husband of Victoria McCorkle Nance (1875–1961), whom he married in February 1900. The couple attended Rock Hill United Methodist Church on Old Plank Road in Lowesville. Forney was a blacksmith and ran a shop at the corner of present-day Old Plank and June Dellinger Roads. He had 17 children, including Beulah Nance Costner, Bertha Nance Wilson, Rosco Nance, Archie Nance, Novella Nance Hall, and Letha Nance Shipp. (Courtesy of Mary Lowery.)

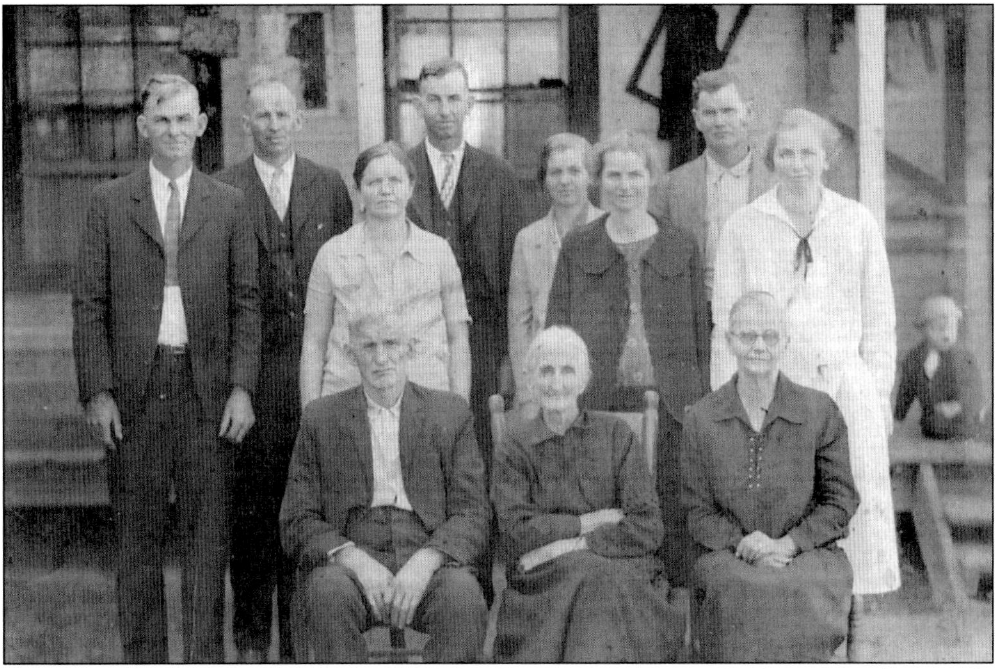

Members of the Houk family pose outside of their house in Iron Station for this c. 1926 photograph. From left to right are (first row) James Jackson Houk, Crinner Elizabeth Burgess Houk, and Harriett Houk; (second row) Monroe Harrison Houk, Maude Rebecca Houk Noles, Jennie Lila Elizabeth Houk Ballard, and Johnsie Ada Houk Ballard; (third row) James Alonzo Houk, John Gordon Houk, Laura Gertrude Houk Campbell, and William Grover Houk. James Lester Ballard, son of Johnsie Houk Ballard, sits on the porch in the background. (Courtesy of Doris Houk Wilkinson.)

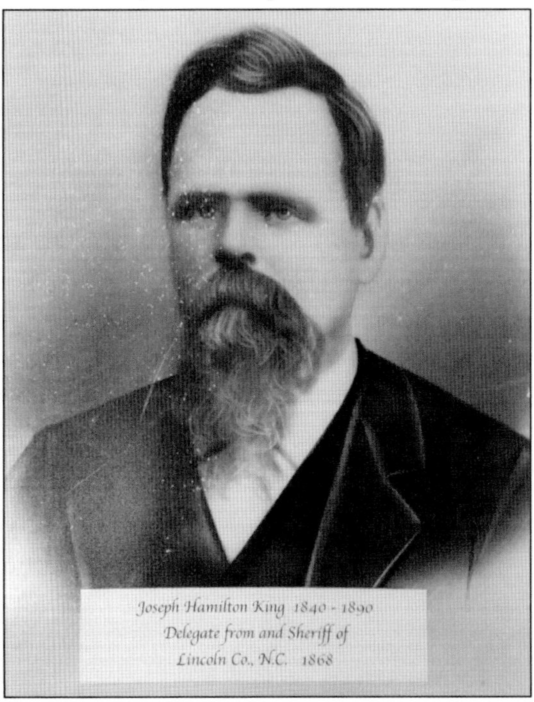

Joseph King served as a delegate from Lincoln County to the Constitutional Convention of 1868. He was elected sheriff of Lincoln County in 1868 to fill the vacancy left by Sheriff Logan H. Lowrance. He served in this capacity until 1871, when he was defeated by John Alfred Robinson. He died of typhoid fever in July 1890. (Courtesy of LCHA.)

Henry D. Nixon was born on January 4, 1858, the son of Rufus (1826–1902) and Hettie Luckey Nixon (1835–1904), and married Eliza Mundy (1862–1953), the daughter of Isaac and Charlot Mundy, on January 11, 1883. He was a blacksmith in Triangle. He and Eliza are buried at Ebenezer United Methodist Church Cemetery in Triangle. (Courtesy of LCHA.)

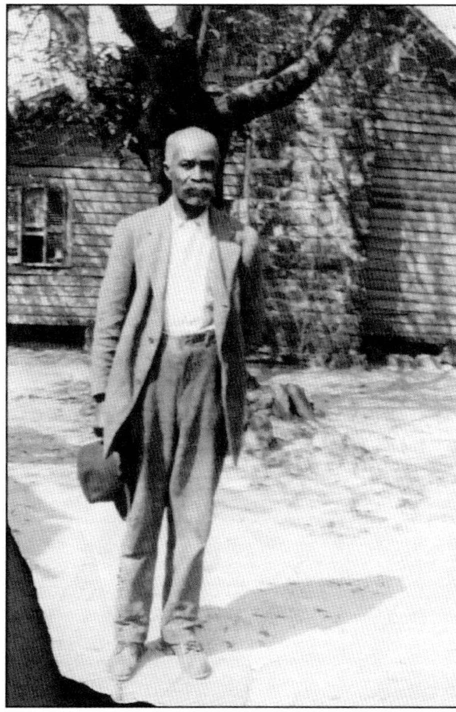

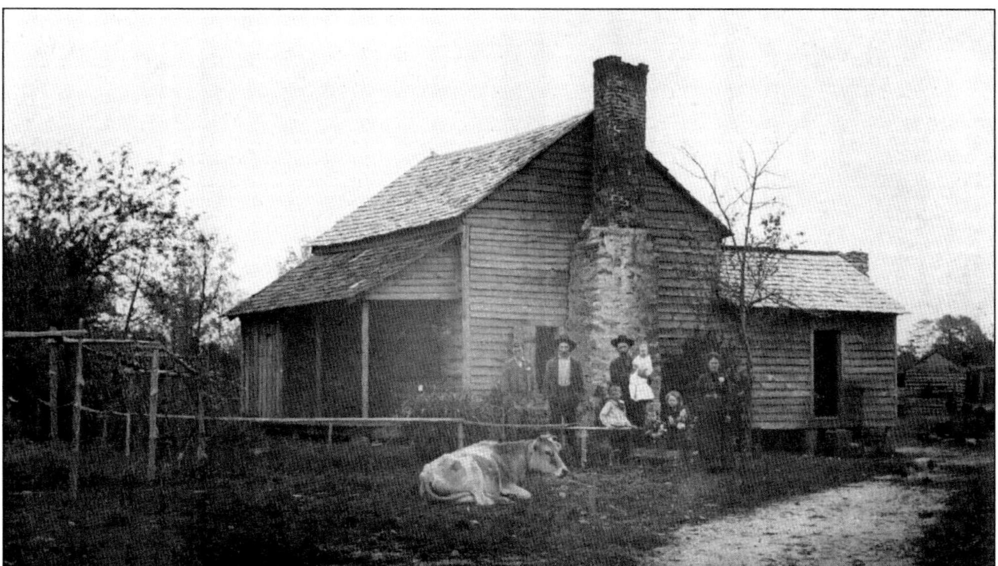

The family cow takes front stage in this c. 1900 Monroe Augustus Nixon family portrait in the Pilot Knob area near Salem United Methodist Church. Nixon (1851–1924) holds the newest addition to the family, Ella Mae (1902–1963), while his youngest son, Richard Vance (1896–1958), wears his hat and tie at center. Younger sisters (from left to right) Aletha (1898–1984) and Madge (1900–1993) made sure to bring their dolls and wagon, while Monroe's third wife, Julia Elizabeth McIntosh (1872–1966), stands beside the family dog. The two men at left are likely Monroe's sons from previous marriages, Clarence Eulie (left, 1886–1946) and Stamey Van Buren (1878–1939). (Courtesy of Kellie Ellis.)

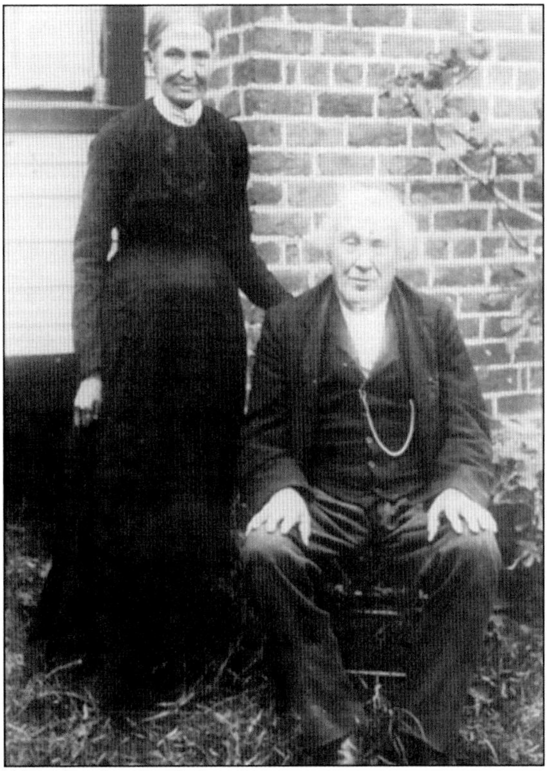

James Patrick Mullen was born to Irish immigrant Patrick Mullen in 1831 in the Iron Station area of eastern Lincoln County. James farmed his land, ran a mercantile business, and was the postmaster of the Derr Post Office. He and his wife, Emily, were one of the founding families of Amity Baptist Church, donating the land where the first church was built. (Courtesy of Mary Harbison.)

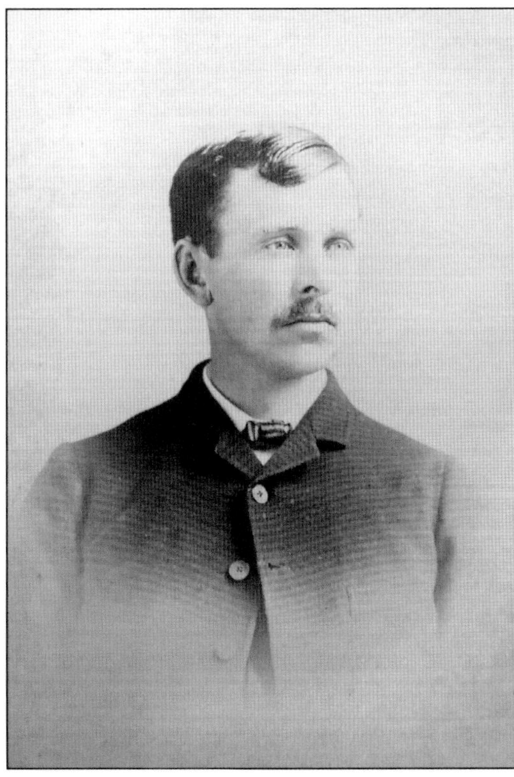

Alfred Nixon (1856–1924) is one of the most notable members of the Nixon family. The second son of Robert Nixon and Millie Womack Nixon, he was born at the Nixon family homestead in Triangle. He received his early education at area public schools and received further instruction from Prof. D. Matt Thompson at Rock Spring Seminary in Denver. He graduated from the University of North Carolina in 1881 and moved to Lincolnton to assume the position of sheriff in 1884. On April 3, 1882, he was appointed county surveyor, and over the next 40 years, Nixon was superintendent of public instruction and clerk of court for Lincoln County. Alfred Nixon married Iola Jane Robinson on October 19, 1882. He was a public historian who wrote *The History of Lincoln County* and published booklets on numerous Lincoln County families. He is buried at Hollybrook Cemetery in Lincolnton. (Courtesy of Mary Harbison.)

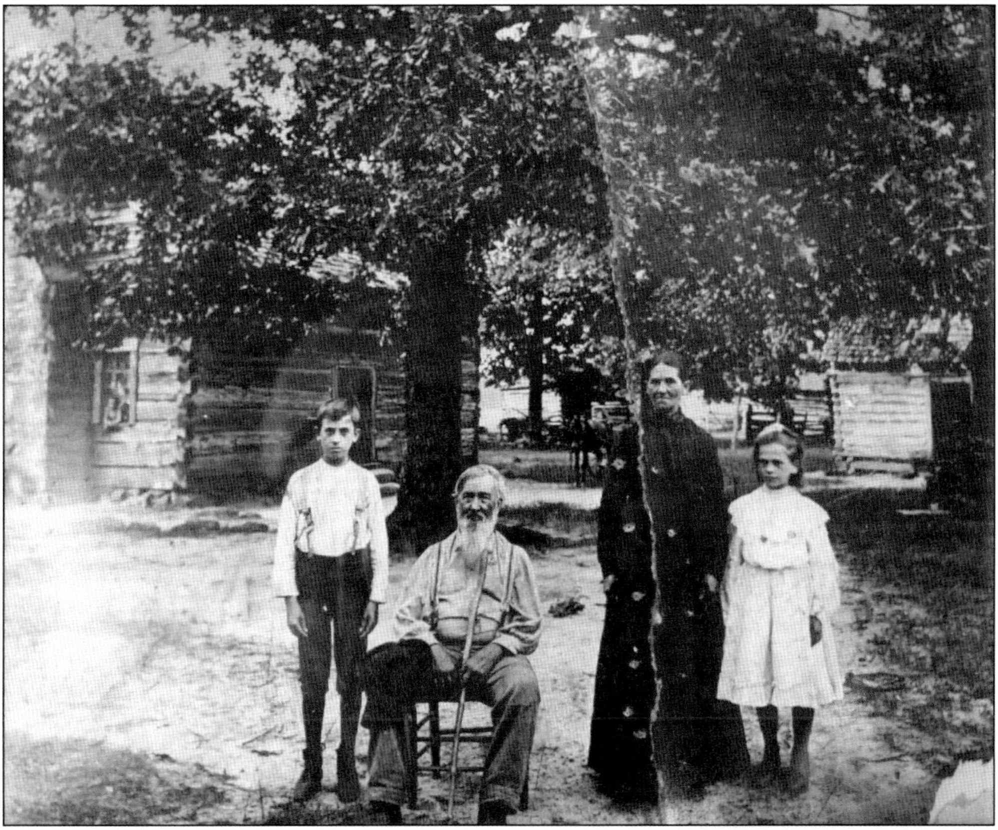

A young man props himself in the side window of the log building in the left background, while members of the Killian family pause on their property in eastern Lincoln County for a photograph during the 1890s. Also visible are horses and other log buildings. (Courtesy of the Killian family.)

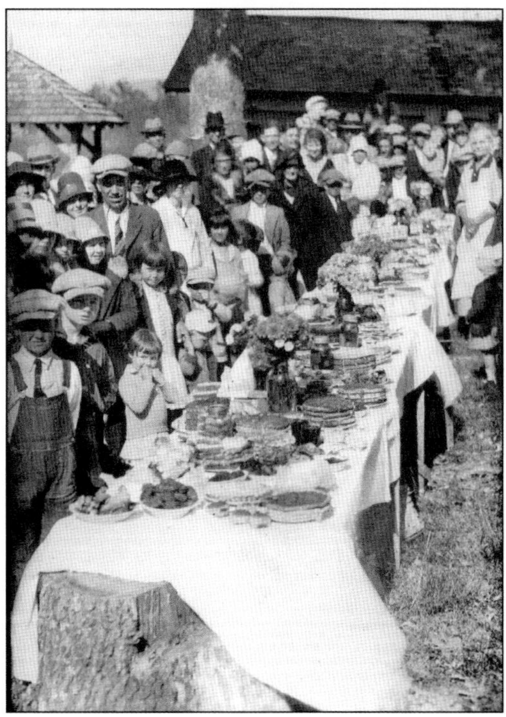

Attendees at a dinner at the Houk family homeplace wait for the photographer to capture this image around 1927. James Jackson Houk (1860–1941) and Crinner Elizabeth Burgess Houk (1861–1935) bought their home, previously known as the Smith place, in eastern Lincoln County in 1915 and moved in during the flood of 1916. They came from Burke County and lived in the Daniels community in western Lincoln County before moving to the Smith place. James and Crinner Houk are buried at Macedonia Baptist Church Cemetery in Denver. (Courtesy of Doris Houk Wilkinson.)

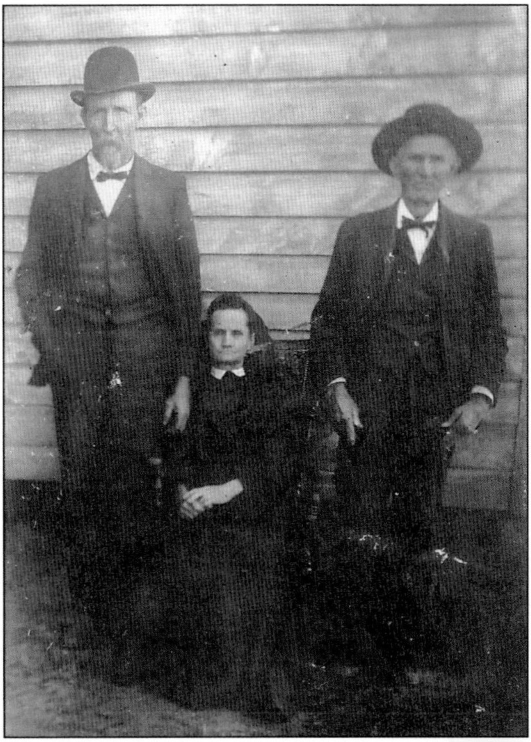

James Nixon (1843–1927) stands to the left of his wife, Mary Arabella Proctor Nixon (1844–1926), while her father, Richard S. Proctor, stands to the right. Richard S. Proctor was born near Hager's Ferry on February 17, 1817, the son of Benjamin J. and Annie Shelton Proctor, and married Elizabeth King (1819–1907). Proctor was appointed postmaster of the Catawba Springs Post Office on March 7, 1856, before enlisting at the age of 47 with the North Carolina 4th Senior Reserves in 1864. He died on October 12, 1909, and is buried at Bethel United Methodist Church in Denver. James and Mary Nixon share a marble headstone in the Unity Presbyterian Church Cemetery in Triangle. (Courtesy of LCHA.)

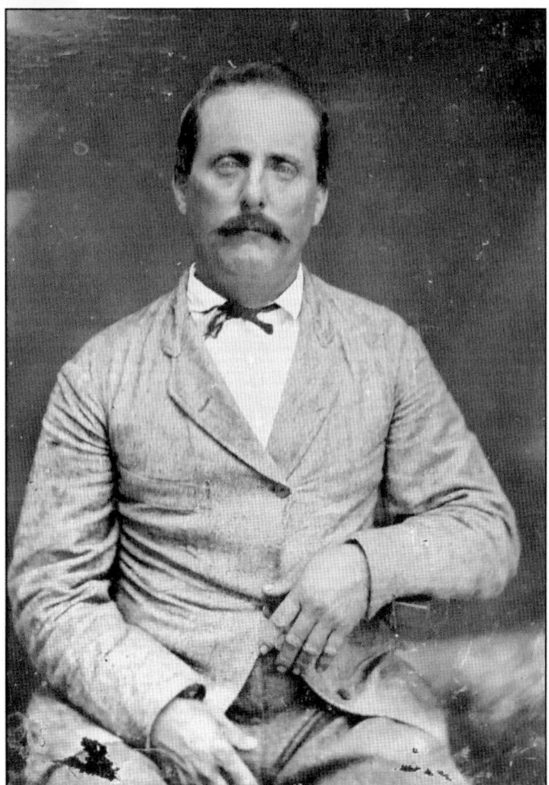

A young Abner Goodson Jr. sits for a tintype that has remained in impeccable condition. Goodson (1834–1899), the son of Abner Goodson Sr. (1791–1837) and Lucretia Seitz (Sides) Goodson (1796–1877), served the South during the Civil War as a member of Company H, 52nd Regiment, North Carolina Troops, and was wounded in the Battle of Gettysburg in July 1863. He married Emily Virginia Asbury (1847–1939), the daughter of Henry (1799–1874) and Emily Middleton Bradshaw Asbury (1813–1889). (Courtesy of LCHA.)

William Julius Peter Hager and Annie Priscilla McIntosh Hager rest in small wooden chairs as wheat straw covers the ground for this photograph. J.P. Hager was born in November 1849, the son of Simon S. and Nancy L. Hager, and married Annie McIntosh (1853–1932) on July 17, 1873. Hager is believed to have built his house in Lowesville in 1888. In addition to farming, he also operated the Hager Post Office out of his home. He died on January 5, 1929, and is buried at Hills Chapel United Methodist Church. (Courtesy of Jamie McCurry.)

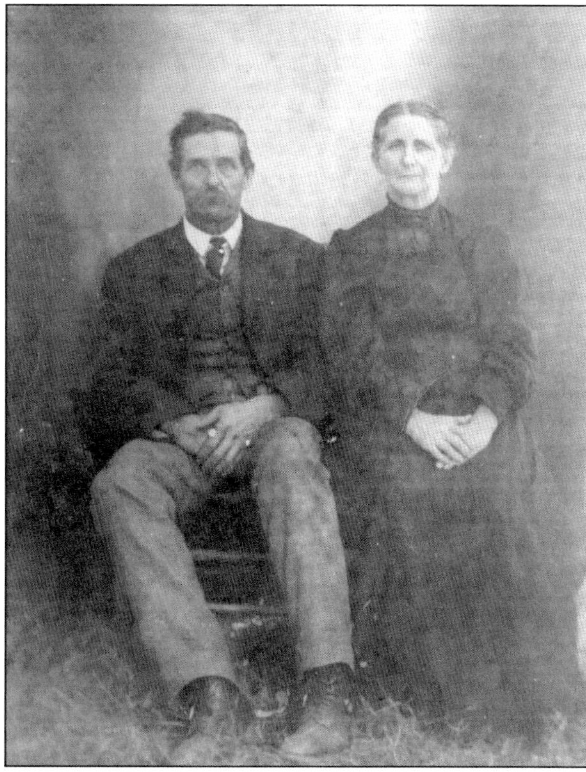

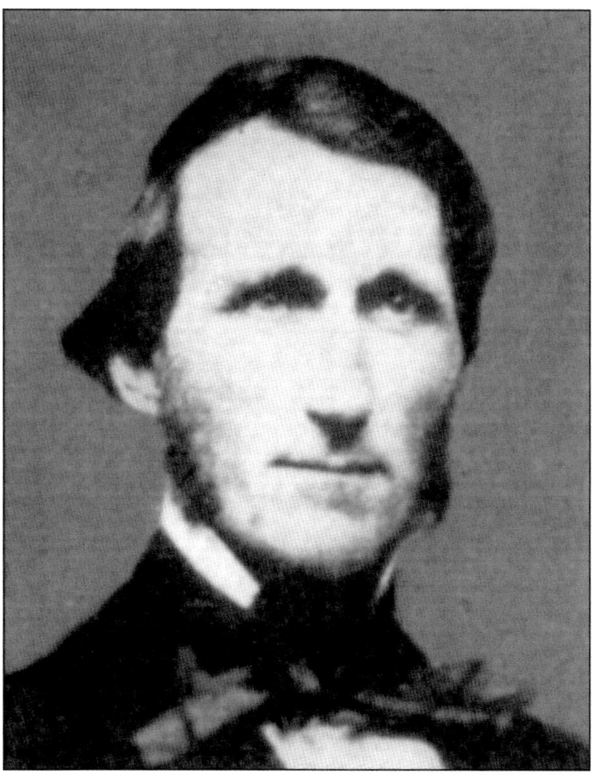

Dr. Cyrus L. Hunter was born in Mount Holly, Gaston County, North Carolina, on December 13, 1807, the son of Rev. Humphrey Hunter, who helped draft the Mecklenburg Declaration of Independence and was one of the earliest pastors at Unity Presbyterian Church. He married Sophia Graham Forney, daughter of Gen. Peter Forney, on January 16, 1834. After the death of Sophia, Hunter married Catherine L. Lyman (1813–1865). He was a doctor, botanist, mineralogist, geologist, mathematician, civil engineer, and historian, and wrote *Sketches of Western North Carolina* in 1877. He died on December 15, 1881, and is buried at Machpelah Presbyterian Church cemetery. (Courtesy of LCHA.)

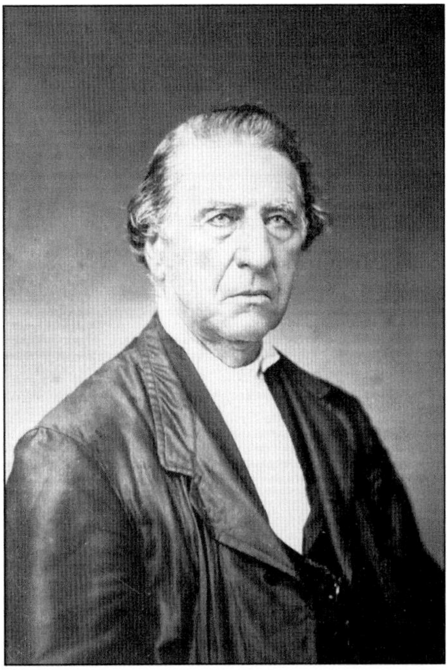

Rev. Henry Asbury, the son of Rev. Daniel and Nancy Lister Morris Asbury, was born on May 29, 1799, and married Susannah Elizabeth Robinson in Lincoln County on August 10, 1821. His second marriage was to Emily Bradshaw on July 17, 1838. Reverend Asbury is credited with beginning the camp meeting tradition in eastern Lincoln County at Rock Spring. The campground was officially incorporated in 1851, and Reverend Asbury was one of the trustees. He died on October 1, 1874, and is buried in the Rehoboth United Methodist Church Cemetery in Terrell. (Courtesy of John Hopkins.)

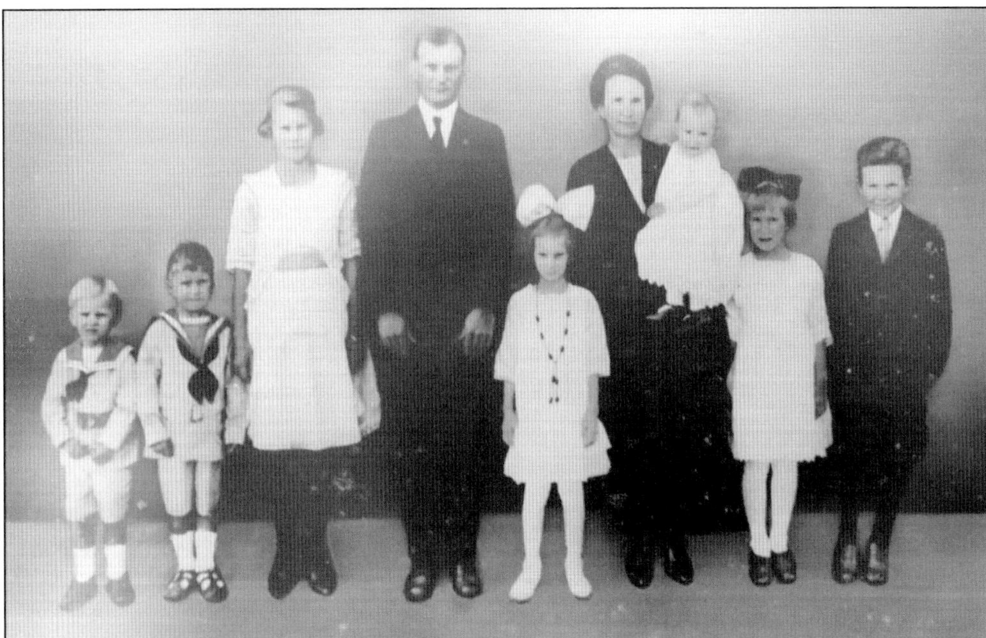

Large bows, sailor suits, and black suits are the dress of the day for this photograph of the Robert F. Graham family of Triangle. From left to right are Robert Gilbert Graham (1916–2002), Bennie Taylor Graham (1913–1980), Roberta Graham Wilson (1905–1987), Robert F. Wilson (1884–1954), Mary Anderson Graham (1910–1986), Cordia Gilbert Graham (1882–1969), Margaret Wilson Graham (1918–2012), Virginia Graham McKee (1917–2001), and Rev. James Franklin Graham (1908–1984). William A. Graham (1923–2009) was born after this photograph was taken. (Courtesy of J.C. Wilson.)

Ira Henderson Howard (1874–1960) and Nancy Jane Nance Howard (1873–1907) pose with what is most likely their first two children, Hazelean Howard Cherry (1895–1962) and Blannie Howard Proctor (1896–1978), for this turn-of-the-20th-century photograph taken in the Mountain Creek area. After Nancy died, Ira built a new home and moved the family to Triangle. In 1909, Ira opened a meat market in Charlotte with James Stowe, and in 1914, he married Linnie Bell Barker Howard (1892–1932). They had Edwin Yates "E.Y." Howard (1915–1992), Excell Howard Long (1913–1993), and Margaret (1918–1919), who died in infancy. In 1919, Ira was part of the Lincoln Guard, which went to Charlotte to manage a riot. In 1921, he is listed as a deputy sheriff who busted up a still in the Marvin area of eastern Lincoln County. (Courtesy of Nancy Long.)

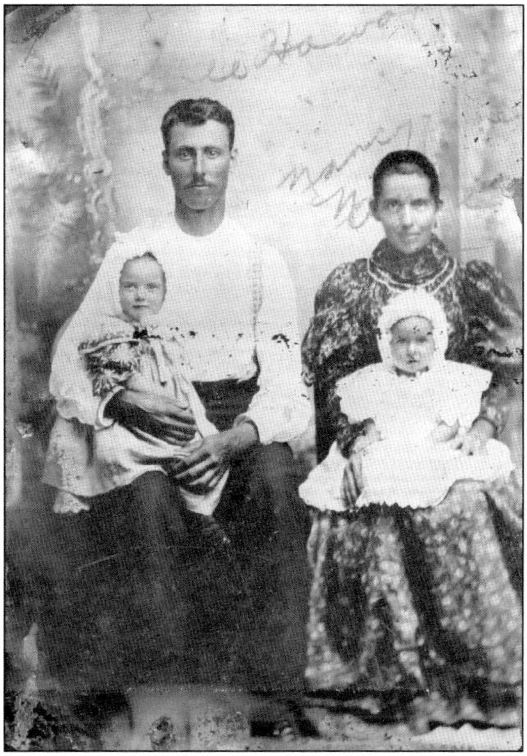

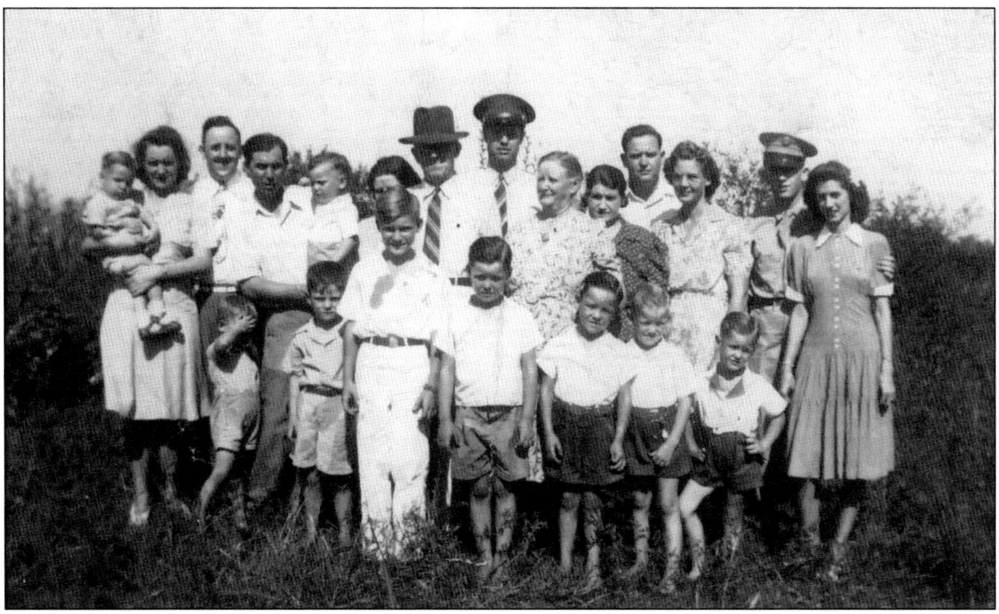

A large gathering of the Robert McIntosh family stands near their home on Hager's Ferry Road. From left to right are Connie May McIntosh, John McIntosh, Gaither Sigmon, Katie McIntosh Sigmon, Robert McIntosh, Edgar McIntosh, Julia Edith Jenkins McIntosh, Lucy Hyder McIntosh, Oliver McIntosh, Mabel Hager McIntosh, Robert McIntosh, and Ola Russell McIntosh. The children are, from left to right, John David, Bob, Ken, Dean (held by Gaither), Howard, Robert, Raymond, Richard, and Reuben. (Courtesy of Judy Gibson.)

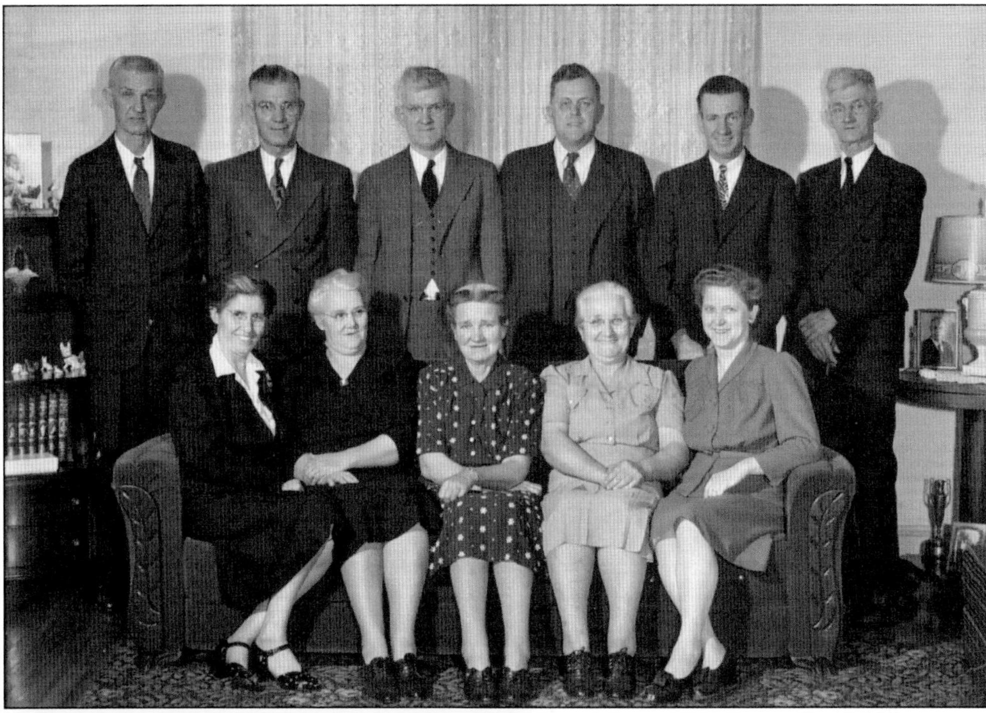

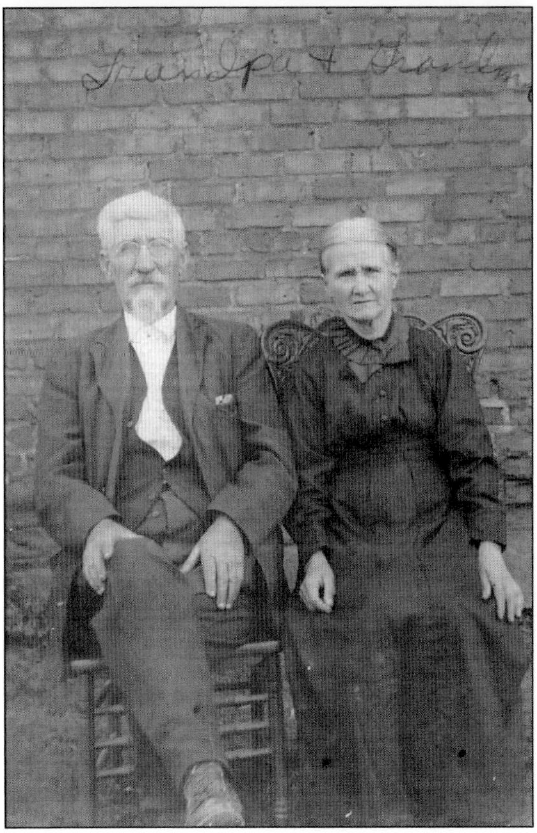

Hartwell O. Proctor (1852–1925) and Zora Aveline Howard Proctor (1858–1920), pictured at left, lived in a two-story brick house that he and his family built a quarter-mile south of Webb's Road on the east side of Highway 16. The Proctor family was instrumental in the early formation of Fairfield United Methodist Church in Westport, and Hartwell's father, Hartwell Spain Proctor (1818–1893), was an early preacher at Fairfield. Some of the offspring of Hartwell and Zora and their spouses are pictured above. From left to right are (seated) Blannnie Howard Proctor, Buena Howard Proctor, Cordia Aveline Proctor Hager, Sarah Lucy Proctor Williamson, and Ruth Arney Proctor; (standing) James Preston Proctor, Rozzelle Roscoe Proctor, Marion Oliver Proctor, John Preston Williamson, Pat Lowe Proctor, and Marvin Alexander Proctor. (Both, courtesy of Carolyn Washam.)

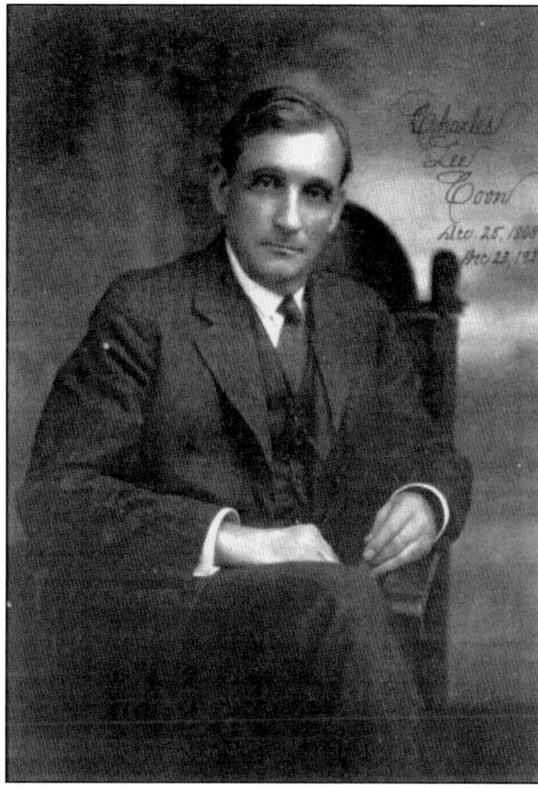

Charles Lee Coon (1869–1927) became a teacher after graduating from Conover College in 1887. Some of his positions include principal of Denver Academy (1889–1891), teacher at Conover College (1891–1896), principal of Lincolnton Schools (1896–1897), teacher in Charlotte Schools (1897–1899), superintendent of Salisbury Schools (1899–1903), secretary of the Bureau of the Southern Educational Board in Knoxville (1903–1904), chief clerk of North Carolina Superintendent of Public Instruction under J.Y. Joyner (1907), and superintendent of Wilson County Schools (1913–1927). He published *The Beginning of Public Education in North Carolina* in 1908 and *North Carolina Schools and Academies, 1790–1840* in 1915. (Courtesy of LCHA.)

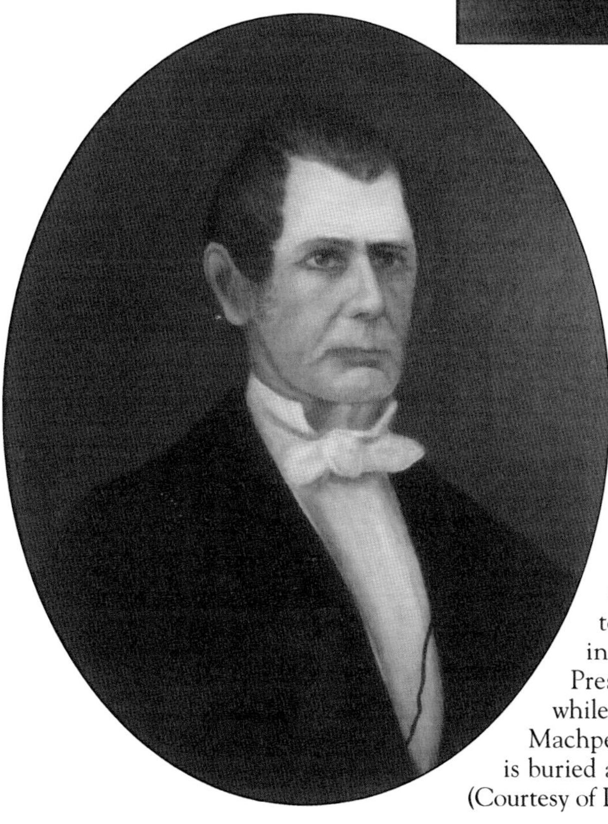

The Reverend Dr. Robert Hall Morrison was born on September 8, 1798, in Rocky River, Cabarrus County, North Carolina, and graduated from the University of North Carolina. He attended Princeton Theological Seminary, and the Concord Presbytery ordained him in 1820. Dr. Morrison was the first president of Davidson College, served for three years, and then retired to his farm and house, Cottage Home, in Lincoln County. He served Unity Presbyterian Church for 40 years and, while there, organized Castanea Grove and Machpelah. He died on May 13, 1889, and is buried at Machpelah Presbyterian Church. (Courtesy of Davidson College Archives.)

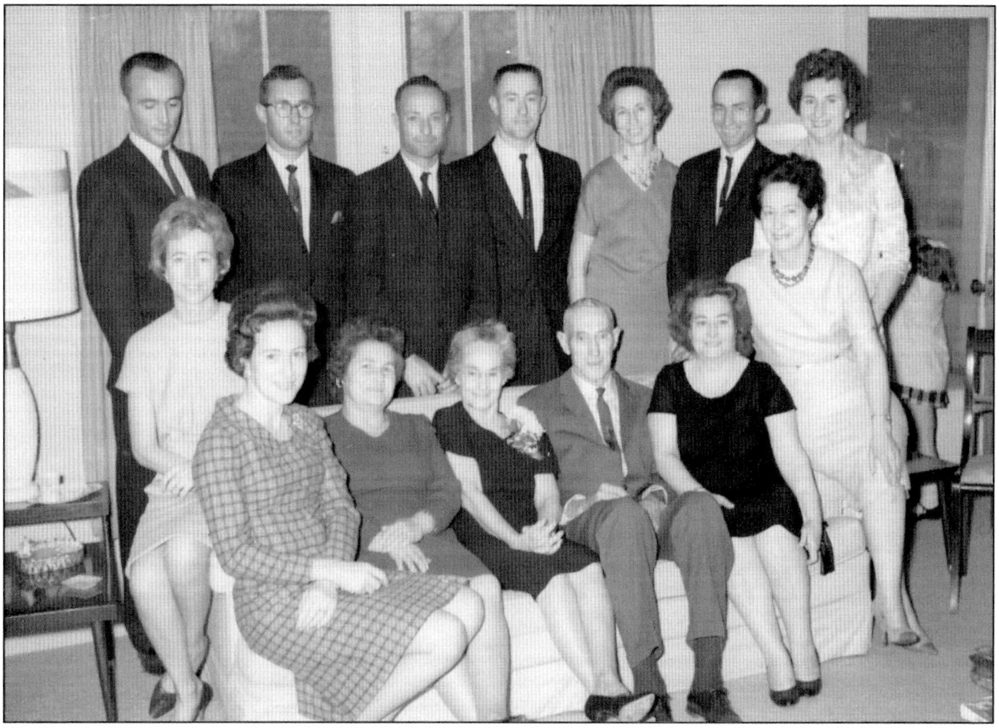

Finley and Effie Burgin (seated at center) celebrate their 50th wedding anniversary at their home in Alexis, just inside the Lincoln-Gaston County line. Their children are, from left to right, (first row, seated) Penta, Lela, Lorena, Effie, Finley, Mabel, and Beatrice; (second row, standing) Austin, Mervin, Luther, Coy, Della Mae, Thurmon, and Betty. (Courtesy of Lela Burgin Nixon.)

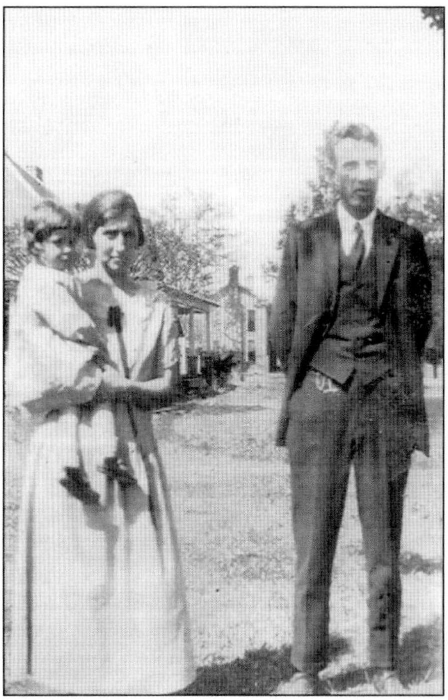

Hettie Smith was born on August 22, 1895, the daughter of Theodore Franklin Smith and Luzetta Mundy Smith. Upon the death of her husband, Frank King, who worked for the railroad, she lived on Campground Road in Denver with her brother Robert "Bob" Smith, a World War I veteran who was disabled during service. According to her nephew Jim Smith, "Aunt Het was always a joy to be with, and she had forty years perfect attendance at Denver United Methodist Church, where she is buried at the Denver Community Cemetery." Smith explained that Hettie King was very active. She had an outhouse and well when everyone else in the community had indoor plumbing. She mowed an acre of property with a push lawn mower until she died in 1976. (Courtesy of LCHA.)

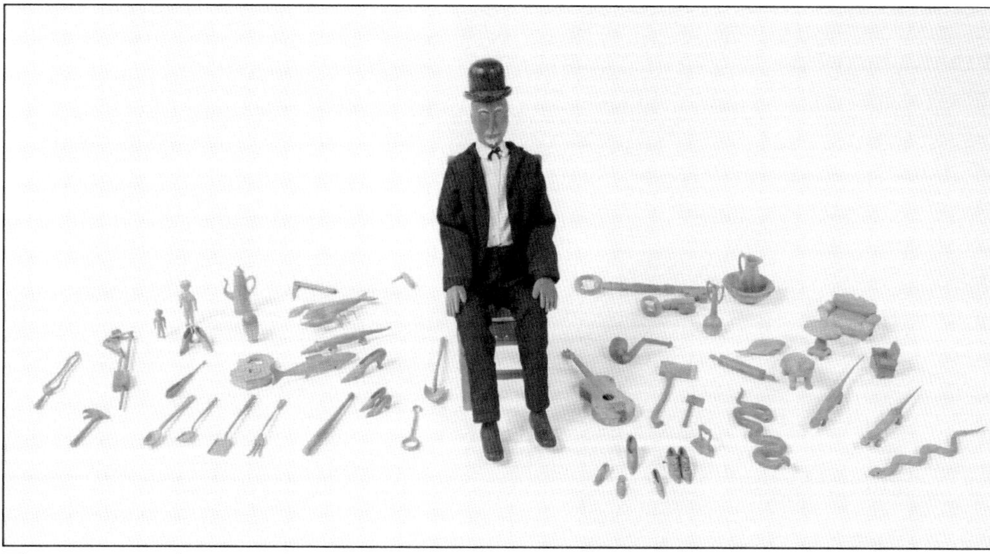

The Hettie Smith King Collection at the Lincoln County Museum of History includes carvings of snakes, frogs, lizards, and an alligator, knives, locks, spoons, shovels, forks, baby dolls, pairs of shoes, axes, a guitar, bowls, rolling pins, and other utilitarian household items. This collection exemplifies King's connection to the rural environment of eastern Lincoln County during the early 20th century and her interest one summer in taking up woodcarving. Upon completing the collection, she stored it away in an old sideboard with little knowledge that it would someday be preserved, documented, and valued for its artistic and decorative qualities. The detailed figure that measures 15 inches in height with painted facial features and hand-stitched clothing of linen is Robert Nixon. Nixon lived on Campground Road in Denver, and King remembered him as a crotchety older man who was sedentary in an old straight chair. (Courtesy of J.J. Tindall Photography.)

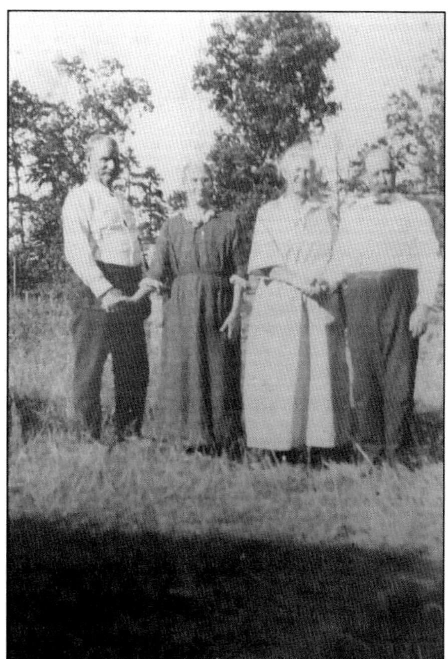

Sisters stand with their husbands with hands clasped in this c. 1910 photograph from the Lowesville area. From left to right are John Wiley Sifford; his wife, Sallie "Sarah" Nixon Sifford; Mathilda "Tilda" Nixon Hager; and her husband, Samuel Adolphus "Dolph" Hager. Dolph and Tilda lived in a large house on what is today Highway 73 in Lowesville. (Courtesy of Frances Hampton.)

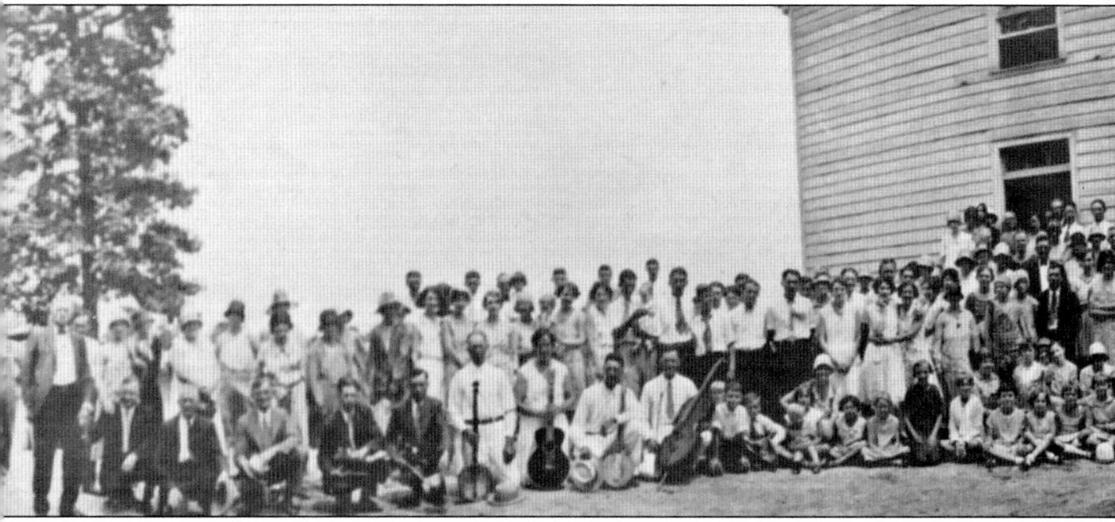

On Wednesday, July 31, 1929, several hundred descendants of Revolutionary War soldier Robert Barkley and wife Eleanor Cathey Barkley held their fourth annual reunion on the grounds of the old Unity Presbyterian Church. Robert Barkley, a patriot, fought at the Battle of Ramsour's Mill

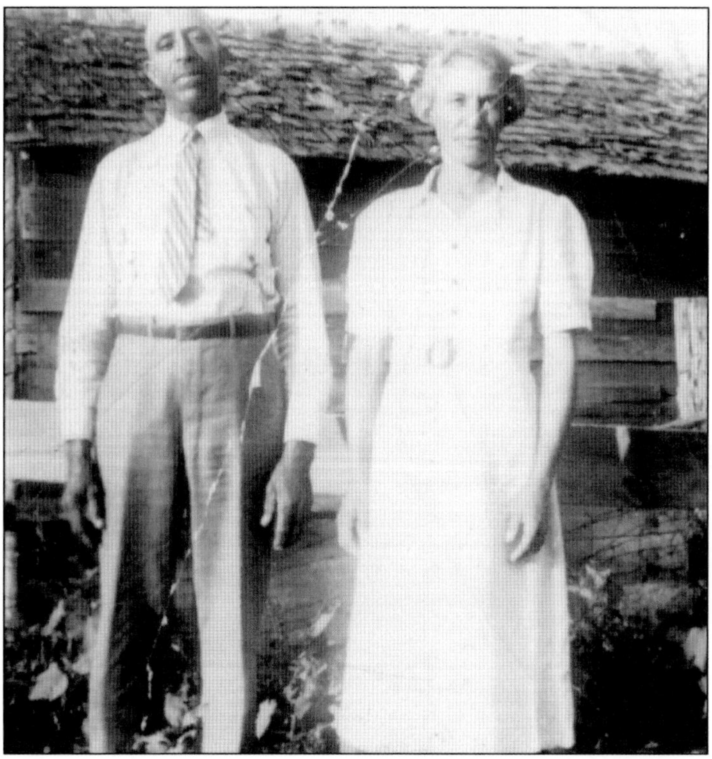

Haywood Simpson Nixon (1883–1971) and his wife, Sadie Hoyle Nixon (1891–1971), stand for this picture at their home on Beth Haven Church Road near Beth Haven Baptist Church. Haywood was the grandson of Rufus Nixon, one of the earliest known African American Nixons in eastern Lincoln County. He spent the majority of his life farming the land near his home. Haywood and Sadie left a long legacy, as many of the Nixons of eastern Lincoln County today are their descendants. (Courtesy of Thomas Nixon.)

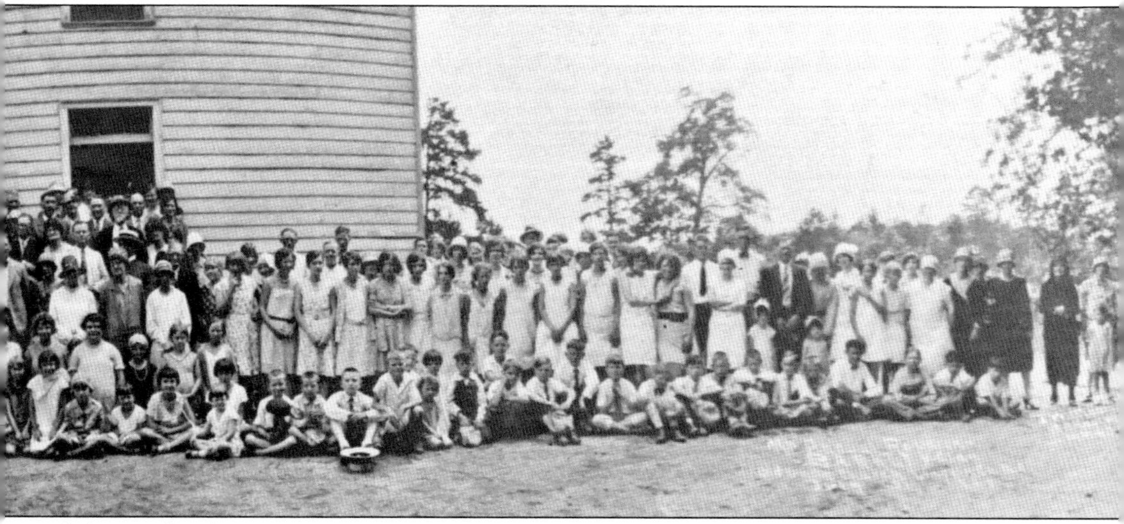

and the Battle of King's Mountain. Kentucky senator Alben W. Barkley, a Barkley descendant and future US vice president under Harry Truman, spoke at the event. A monument was placed in the cemetery to honor their pioneer ancestors of Lincoln County. (Courtesy of J.C. Wilson.)

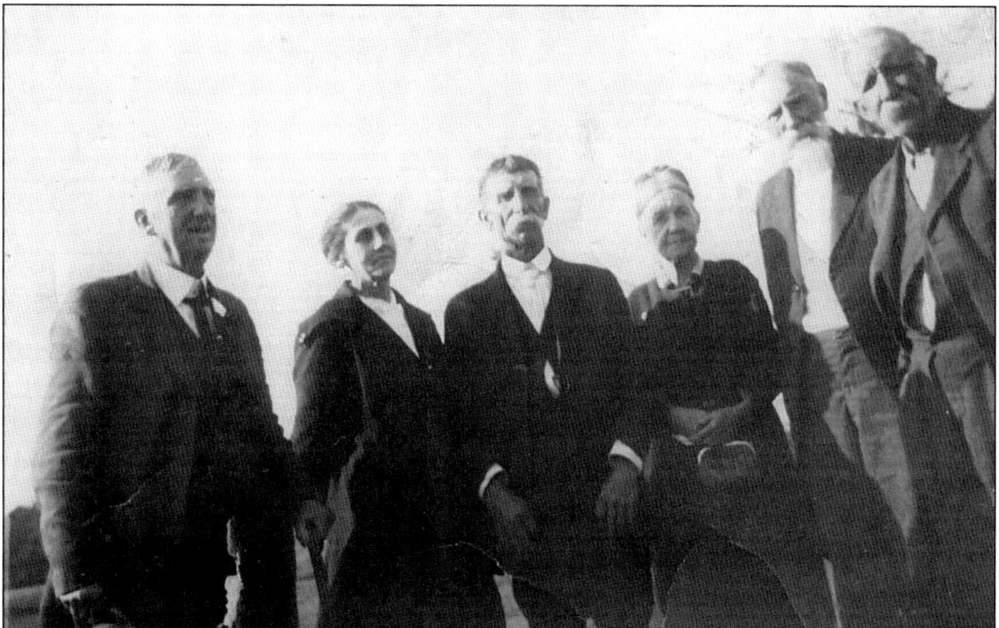

Elder members of the Mundy family stand for a group photograph at what is believed to be a funeral for Frances Rebecca "Fannie" Killian Mundy (1844–1914) or Mary Roxanna Lowe Mundy (1848–1917). Pictured are, from left to right, Freeman Pinkney Mundy (1851–1923), Frances Emma "Fannie" King (1860–1942), Osburn Wells "O.W." Mundy (1856–1940), Eliza Jane "Jennie" Mundy (1853–1933), James Coleman Thompson (1849–1924), and Rufus Milton "Doc" Mundy (1846–1922). (Courtesy of Lisa Mundy Mauney.)

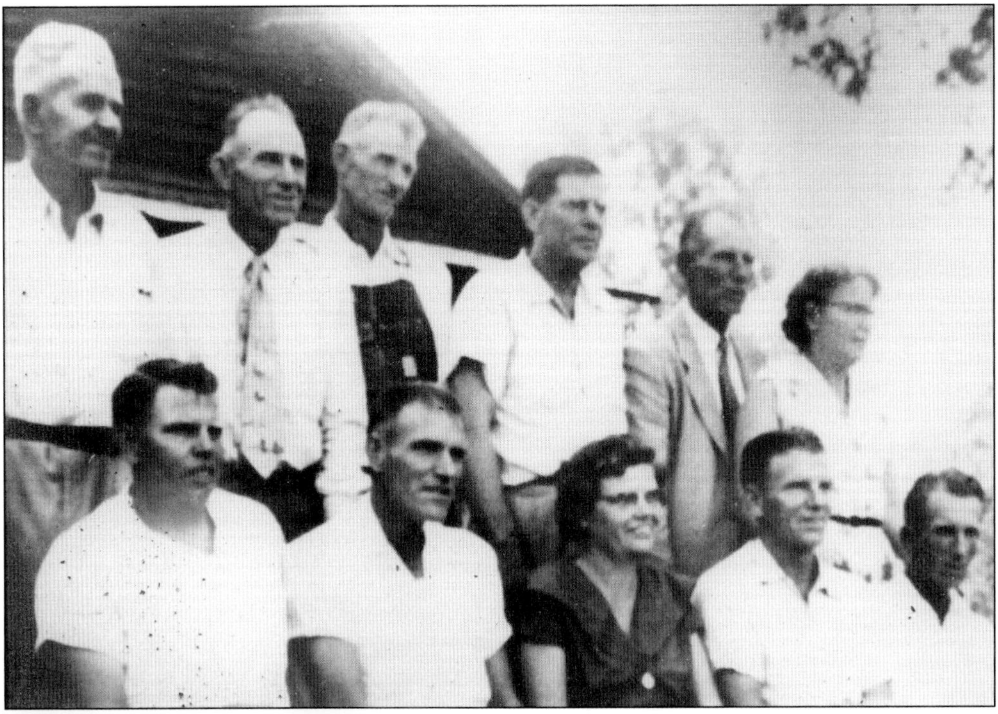

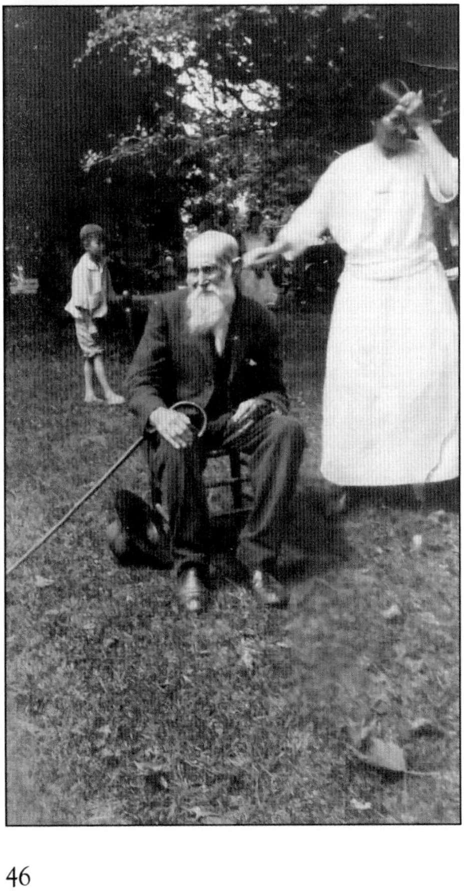

The children of William David and Cora Wingate Luckey smile for a 1960s family photograph. The Luckey family lived off what is today Graham Road in Triangle, and descendants own and live on property that has been owned by the Luckey family for many years. From left to right are (first row) Graham Luckey, James Luckey, Margie Luckey Sherrill, Harry Luckey, and Ray Luckey; (second row) Lloyd Luckey, Sid Luckey, Clarence Luckey, Fred Luckey, Charlie Luckey, and Georgia Luckey. (Courtesy of David and Janice Luckey Springs.)

Born in Iredell County on August 27, 1827, William Freeman Kelly moved to the Denver area with his family at the age of three. He spent most of his life working the fields, and was a magistrate for 30 years on the side. He was one of the original trustees when Rock Spring Campground was incorporated in 1871, and it is rumored that he only missed one meeting in over 80 years. He was held in high regard by all who knew him, and was admired for his sharp mind and ability to recall history. At the time of his death at 96, he was considered the oldest living citizen of Lincoln County. (Courtesy of LCHA.)

Zettie Kelly Cherry (1880–1964) stands in the middle of family and friends in the front yard of her son and daughter-in-law Harold Harvey Cherry (1920–1993) and Lockie Jane Howard Cherry (1917–2001), ready to celebrate another family gathering. From left to right are Leckie Kelly, Sally Black, Conrad Black, Zettie Cherry, Mary Cherry, and Connie Cherry. Sliced bread, cold cuts, deviled eggs, pickles, cookies, pies, and cakes are the fare. (Courtesy of Kelli Gaskill Hogue.)

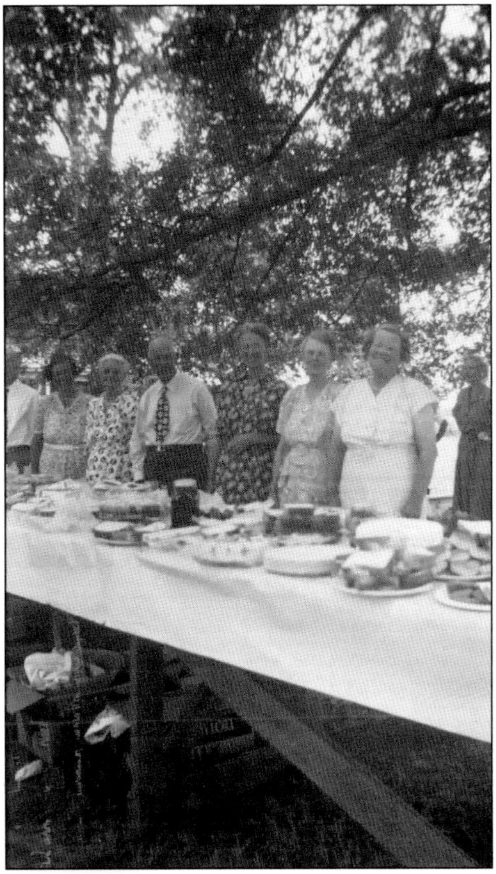

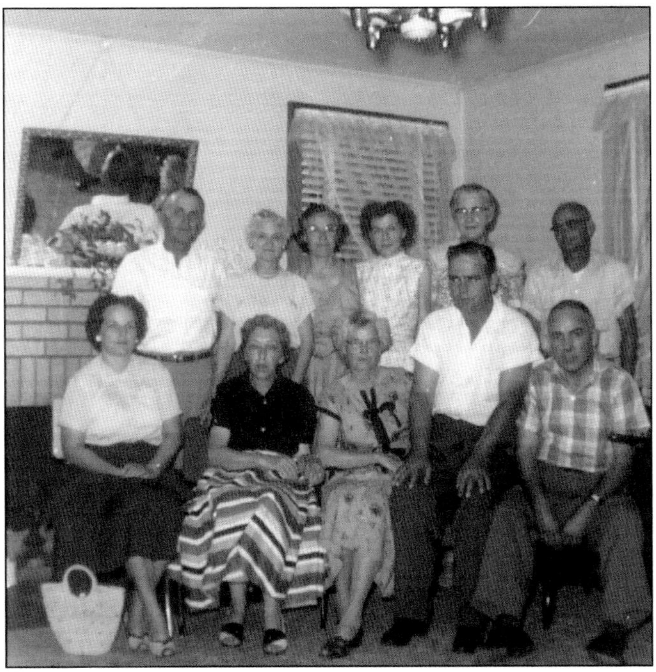

Members of the Kelly and Cherry families gather in the living room after a day of socializing for this family photograph. From left to right are (first row) Ethel Cherry Patterson, Eleanor Spratt, Bernice Cherry Cashion, Leslie Kelly, and Howard Cherry; (second row) Charles Black, Lolabell Kelly Black, Mary Iva Kelly Blue, Mary Agnes Kelly, Grace Kelly Armstrong, and Clyde Black. (Courtesy of Kelli Gaskill Hogue.)

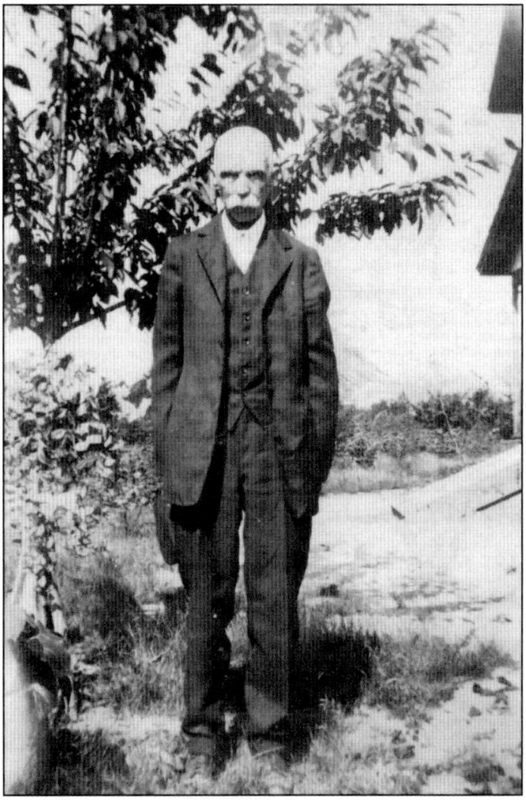

Charles Rucker "Rooker" Kelly was born in either Iredell County or Lincoln County, North Carolina, the son of Andrew Jackson Kelly (1815–1896) and Ann Rebecca Mendenhall Kelly (1813–1887), on September 19, 1847, and married Nancy Matilda Nixon (1851–1904). He served as a private in Companies B and H, 2nd Regiment, North Carolina Artillery, 36th North Carolina State Troops during the Civil War. According to the *Lincoln County News*, he was one of the 17 boys who went to war at age 17. He died on January 27, 1933, and is buried at Unity Presbyterian Church in Triangle. (Courtesy of Kelli Gaskill Hogue.)

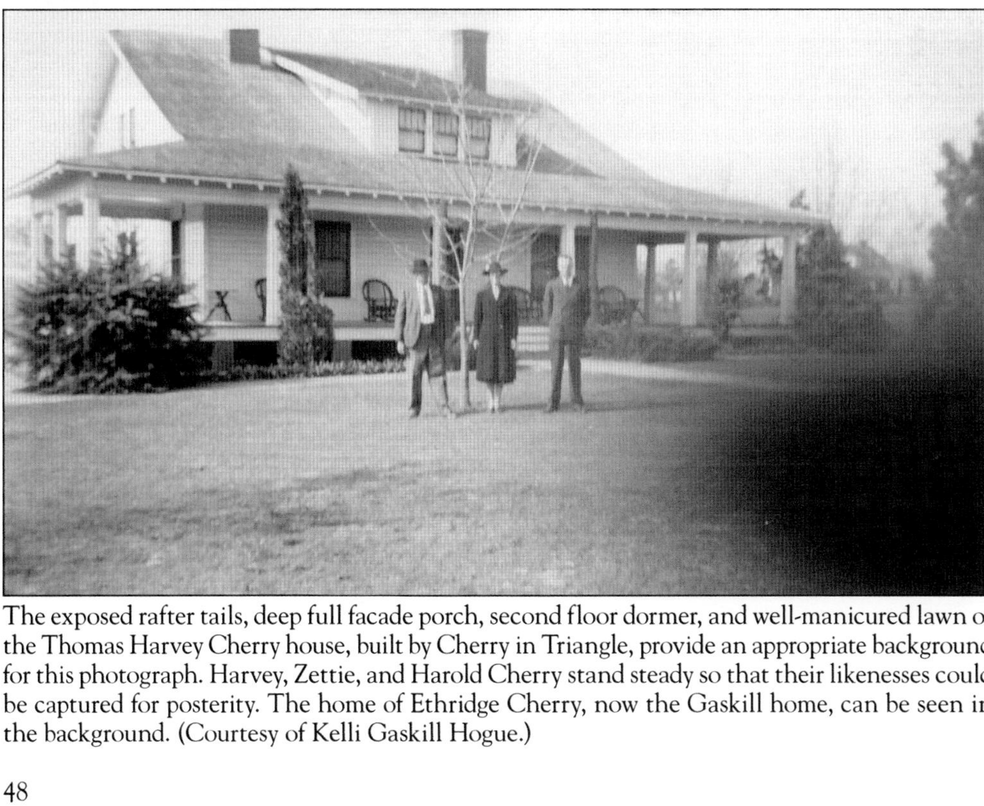

The exposed rafter tails, deep full facade porch, second floor dormer, and well-manicured lawn of the Thomas Harvey Cherry house, built by Cherry in Triangle, provide an appropriate background for this photograph. Harvey, Zettie, and Harold Cherry stand steady so that their likenesses could be captured for posterity. The home of Ethridge Cherry, now the Gaskill home, can be seen in the background. (Courtesy of Kelli Gaskill Hogue.)

The simple soapstone tab-in-socket headstone of Hugh A. "Hua" Little stands in the cemetery of Fairfield United Methodist Church in Westport with a less-than-simple story about how he died on February 25, 1863. Little was murdered by two of his slaves, Bill and Frank, the *Charlotte Democrat* reported on April 7, 1863; they admitted to the murder and "were merely instigated by the devil to commit the horrid crime." They were tried for the crime in April and were hung on May 22, 1863. The site of the hanging was about 1,500 feet southwest of what is today the Little Creek Access Area and boat ramp on Lake Norman. The area is now known as Gallows Woods. (Courtesy of Matt Boles.)

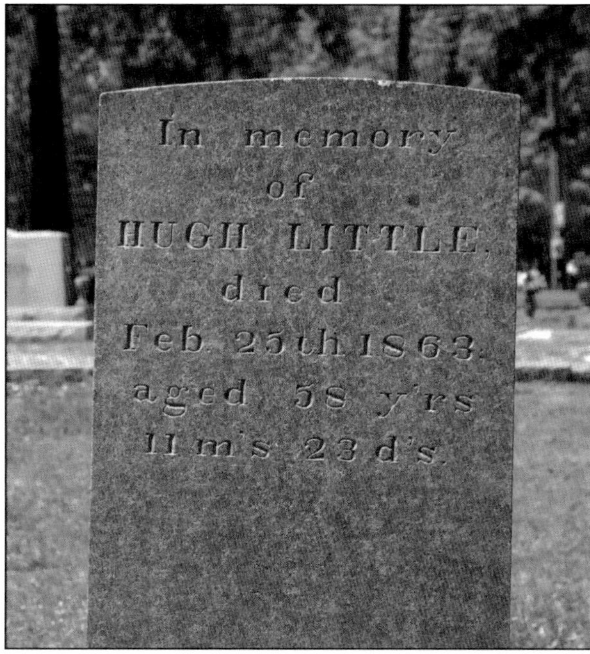

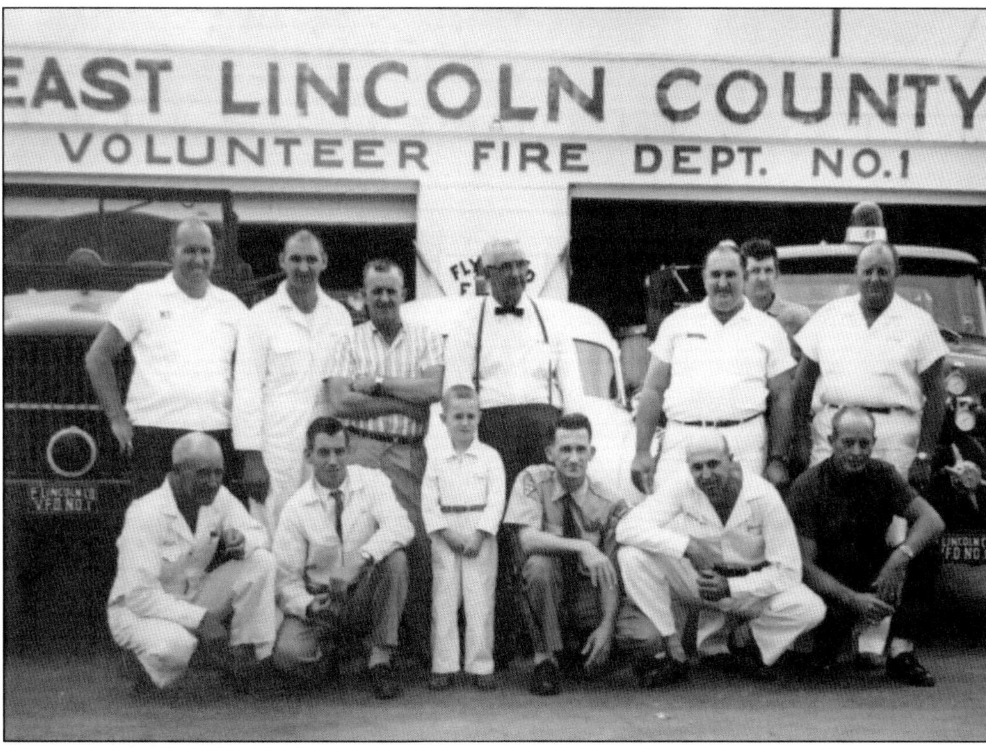

Bearing prideful smiles for their enjoyment serving the community during the 1960s, members of the East Lincoln Volunteer Fire Dept. No 1. are, from left to right, (first row) Bill Grice, Carl Grice, Roddi Long, Deputy Roy Lee Abernathy, James Hinkle, and Anderson Primm; (second row) Bob Nixon, Bob Duckworth, Graham Long, Ed Hager, A.O. Duckworth, Erstin Hager, and Grady Long. (Courtesy of East Lincoln Fire Department.)

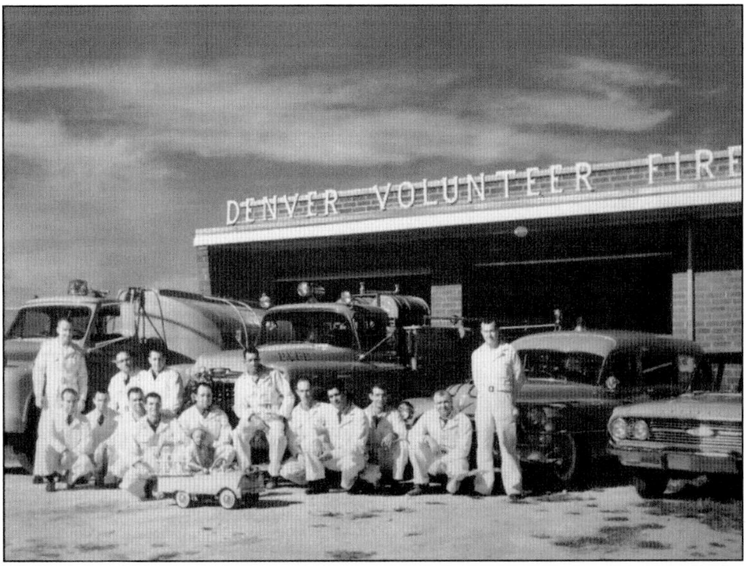

The sleekness of mascot Tim Killian's car in front of the Denver Volunteer Fire Department group in 1957 matches the modernist feel of the cars and trucks and the building that houses the department. (Courtesy of Denver Fire Department.)

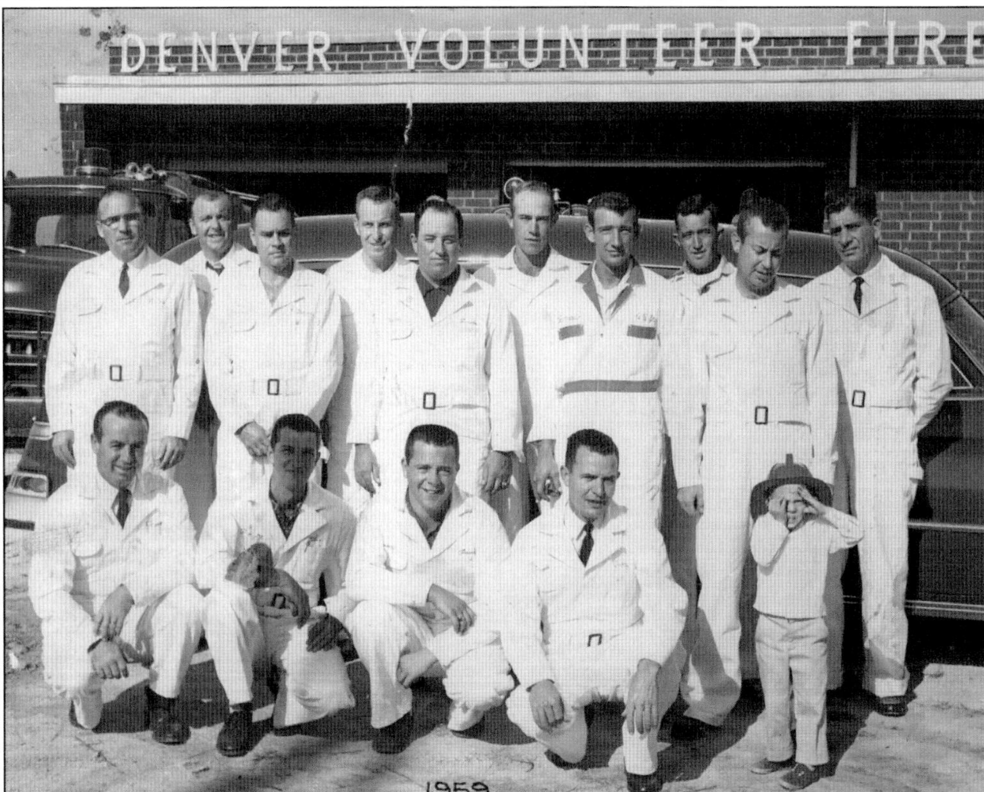

The men of the Denver Volunteer Fire Department pose in their pearly white uniforms in 1959. From left to right are (first row) Jesse Carpenter, Q.L. Moore, Jimmy Poole, Troy Dellinger, and Tim Killian (mascot); (second row) Walter Abernathy, Thomas Christie, D.L. Turbyfill, and Richard Armstrong; (third row) Raymond Ballard, Joe F. King, Monroe Sherrill, Richard Sigmon, and Ken McCall. Not pictured are Lee Beatty Killian and Wade Fox. (Courtesy of Denver Fire Department.)

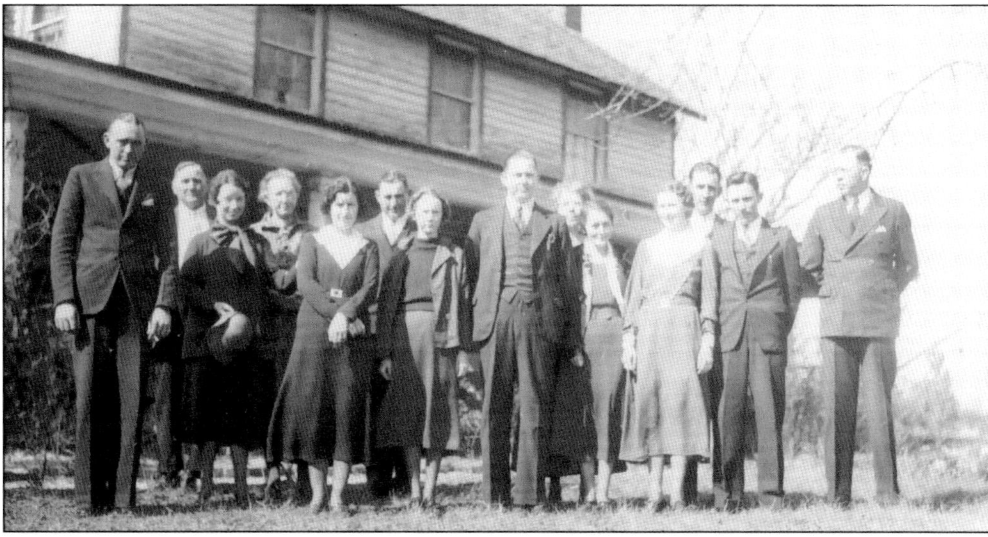

The James Ivey Cherry family stands in front of their two-story frame house with a full-facade porch for this mid-1940s photograph. James, the son of Alfred Lee Cherry (1851–1918) and Rosa Virginia Howard Cherry (1853–1941), was born on June 28, 1878, and married Daisy Udora Nixon (1878–1947). From left to right are Thomas Lee, James Ivey, Mary Esther Wright Cherry, Daisy Udora, Millie Cherry White, Gene, Myra Cherry Sherrill, Don, Laura Nixon, unidentified, Pearl Cherry Beam, George, John Beam, and unidentified. James died on October 12, 1947, and is buried at Unity Presbyterian Church in Triangle. The Cherry house still stands at the southern intersection of Triangle Circle, Optimist Club Road, and Rufus Road in Triangle. Millie and her husband, Neil White, lived in the house and ran a jewelry store in the back for many years. (Courtesy of Ann Smith.)

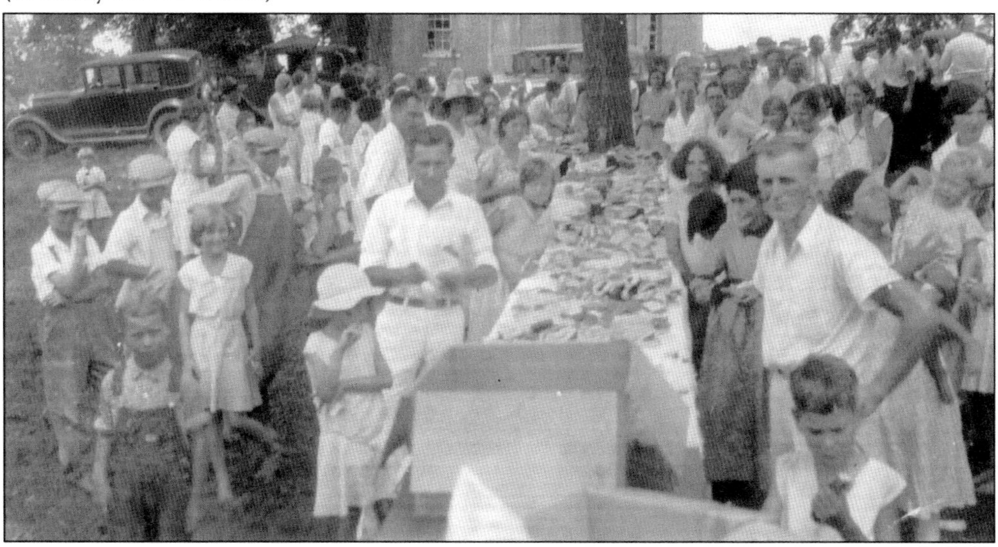

With the Elmwood office in the background, a large group of people have unpacked boxes of food on long tables for what was likely a gathering of the Unity Presbyterian Church Sunday School during the 1930s. Elmwood stood near what is today Graham Road near Unity Presbyterian Church, and many Lincoln County families whose ancestors helped settle this part of the county have fond memories of this great old aristocratic estate, specifically their time enjoying leisure activities on the Catawba River. (Courtesy of Ann Smith.)

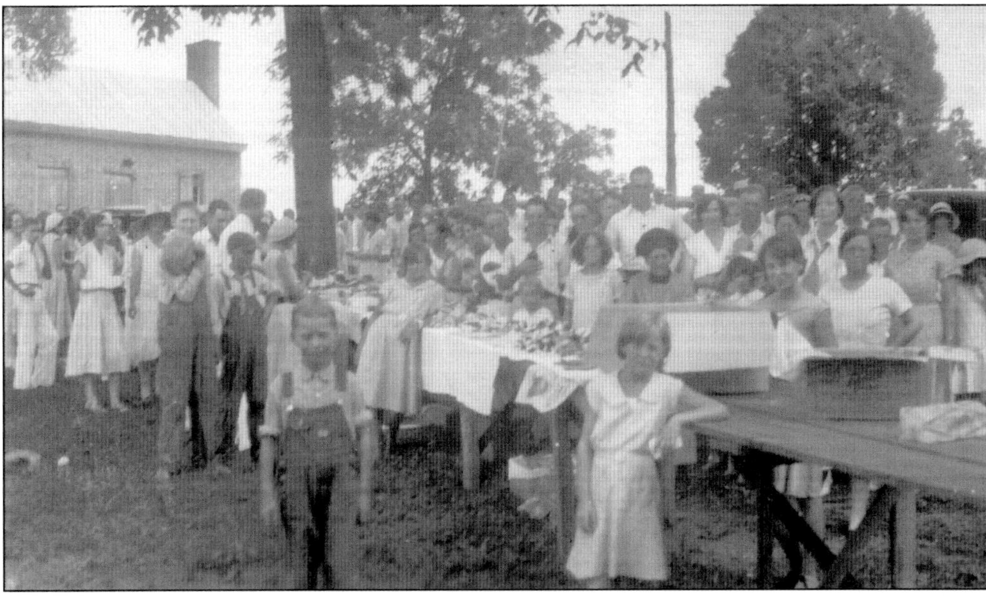

With food waiting to be consumed and the crowd growing, this group waits anxiously for the photographer to capture the image for posterity. Elmwood was one of a few early-19th-century homes that were lost when the Catawba River was flooded for Lake Norman. Many of the home's architectural features were removed and stored by Charles and Mary Babcock of Winston-Salem, only to be lost later in a fire. (Courtesy of Ann Smith.)

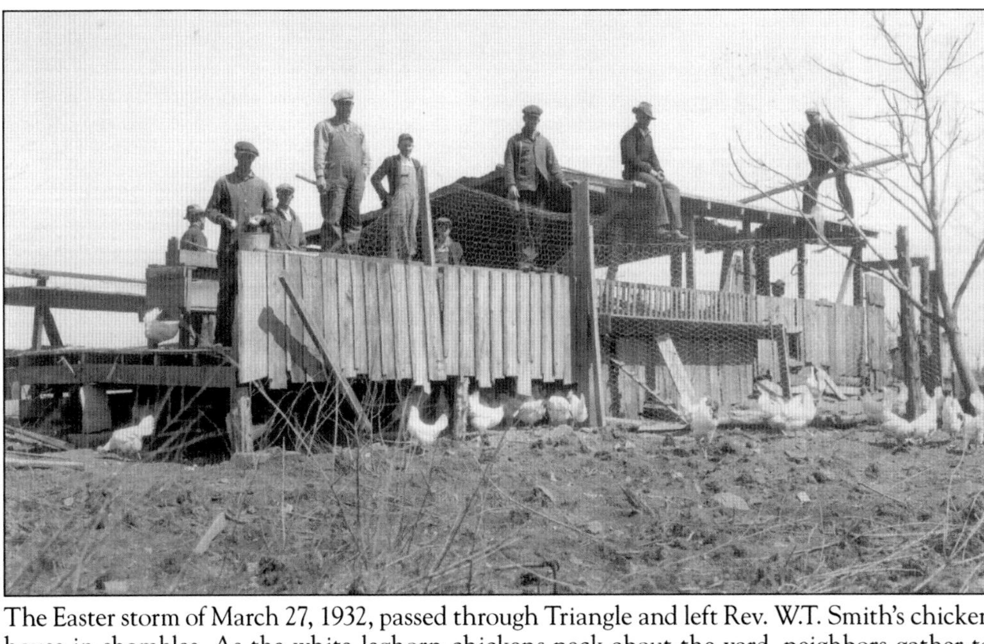

The Easter storm of March 27, 1932, passed through Triangle and left Rev. W.T. Smith's chicken house in shambles. As the white leghorn chickens peck about the yard, neighbors gather to help put things back in order. One man holds two eggs to show that not all is lost. (Courtesy of Ann Smith.)

Reminiscent of Tom Sawyer and Huck Finn, these boys pause after putting in hard work while painting Rev. W.T. Smith's chicken house. Smith raised white leghorn chickens to supplement his income as the pastor of Unity Presbyterian Church. The boys are, from left to right, Jim Smith, Bobby Aiken, and Ted Smith. (Courtesy of Ann Smith.)

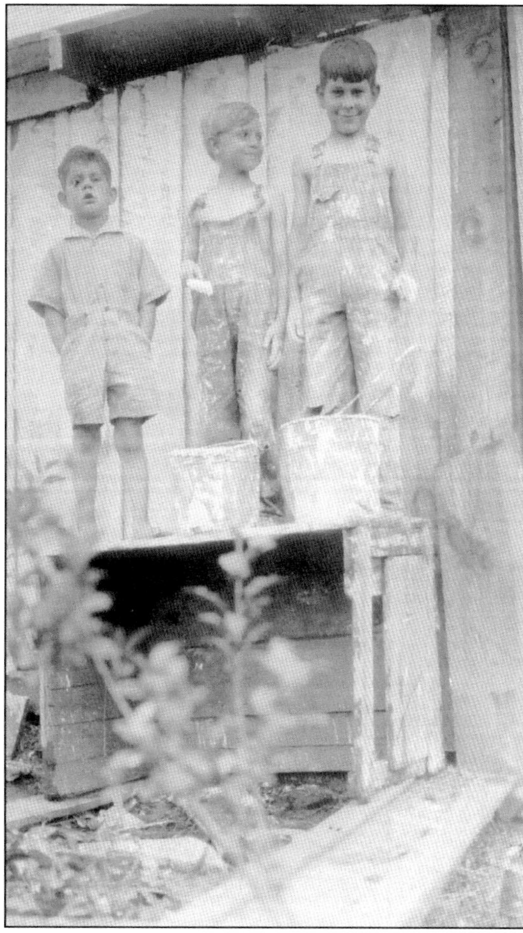

Hard work in the fields will yield a great harvest. These men from Triangle in this 1930s photograph were recruited by Unity's pastor, Rev. W.T. Smith, to plant an apple orchard on land near the church. They are, from left to right, Robert Cherry, Gray Kelly, Graham Long, Ivey Kelly, Ted Smith Jr., Bill Long, Charlie Weatherman, and "Doc" Cherry (in front). (Courtesy of Ann Smith.)

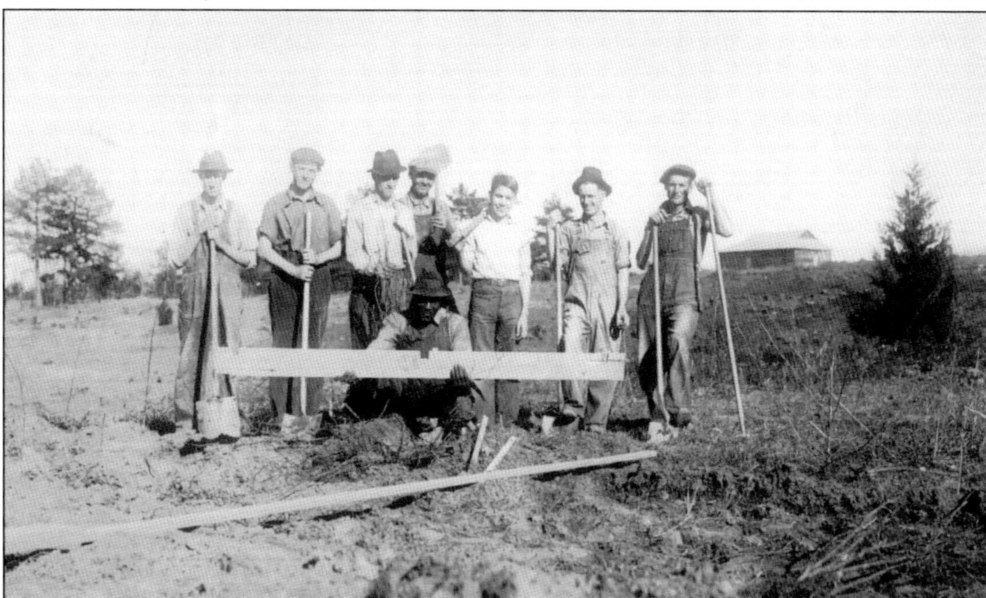

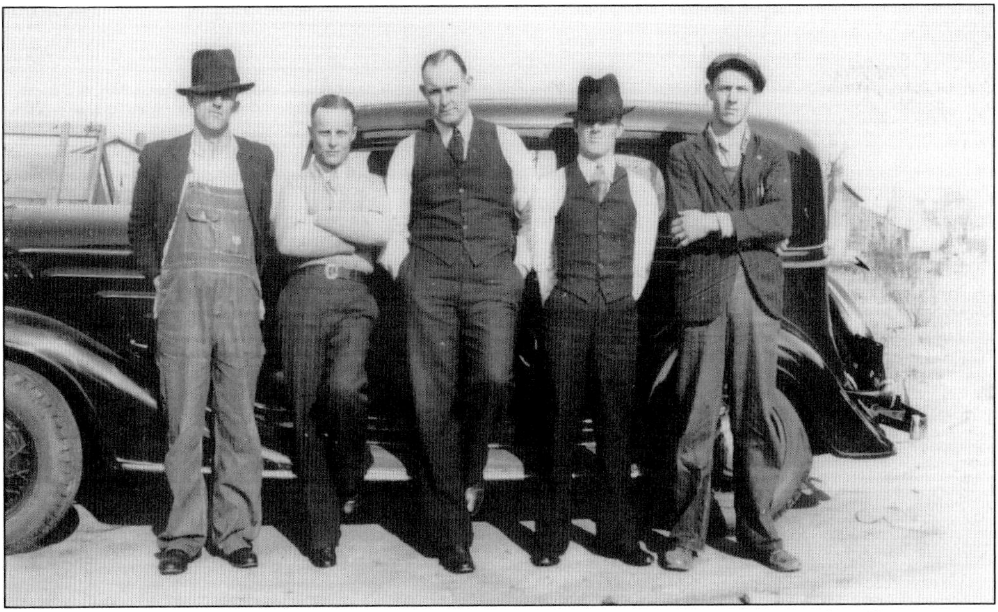

As if in a movie from the time, with their getaway car as a prop, men from Triangle offer a pensive gaze for this photograph. The dapper gentlemen are, from left to right, Graham Long, Henry Graham, Houston "Huse" Nixon, Bill Long, and Grey Kelly. (Courtesy of Ann Smith.)

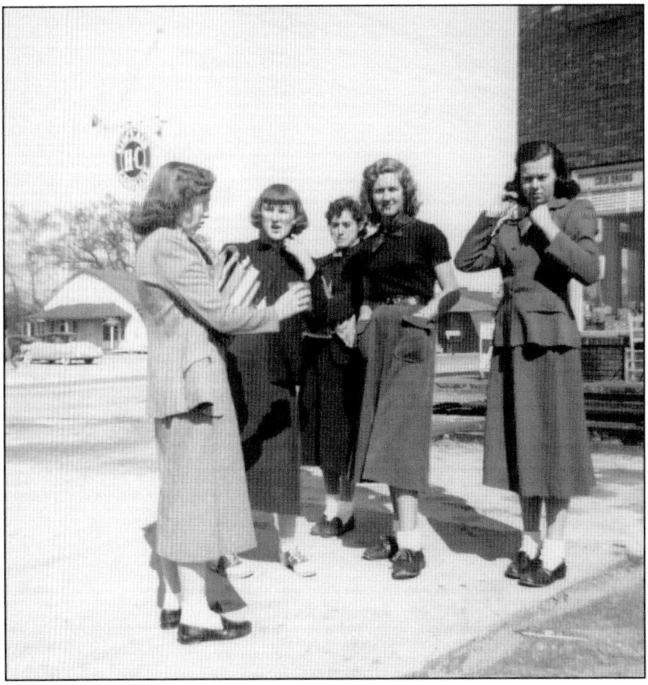

Commiserating in 1951 outside of the Denver Shopping Center on their way to school, Betty Joy Shellem (Bailey), Billie Mae Shellem (Sorter), Peggy Lawing (Morrison), Shirley Little (Mull), and Virginia Ruth Abernethy (Harris) pay little attention to Manson Jones's furniture store and the Denver Post Office in the background. Denver United Methodist Church held services in the furniture store while its new church was being built in the early 1950s. E.F. Killian owned the building and had a grocery in the post office beside it. (Courtesy of Shirley Mull.)

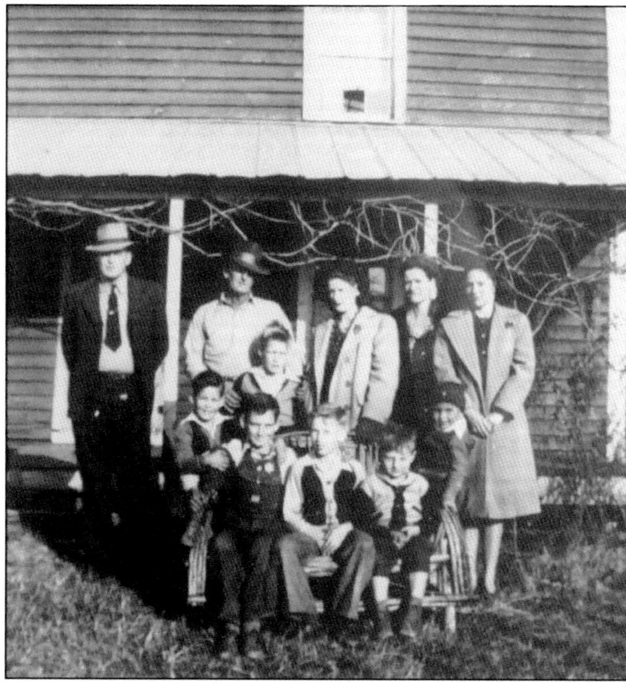

Members of the Barkley and Beal families stand out front of the Barkley house off Keistler Store Road in the Mountain Creek area for this c. 1940 photograph. Family members are, from left to right, (first row) Gene Beal, Bill Barkley, Bob Beal, Kermit Beal, Henry Barkley, and Jerry Barkley; (second row) Henry Barkley Sr., Garland Barkley, Edith Barkley Beal, and Dolly McCaul Barkley. Henry Barkley (1777–1869) built the house during the 19th century on the Barkley plantation, once owned by his father, Robert Barkley (1753–1813). (Courtesy of Henry Barkley.)

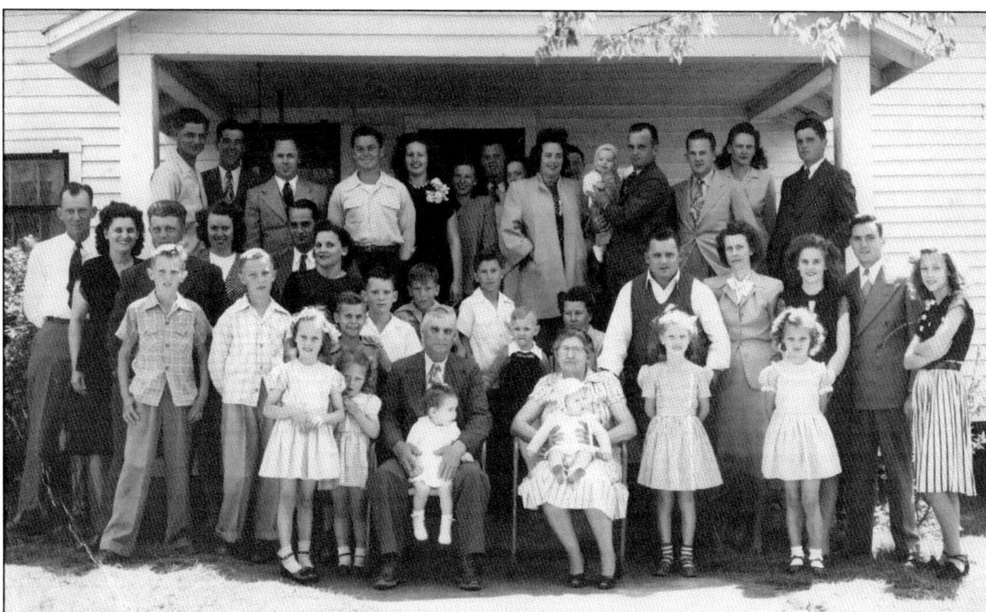

Members of the Boone Sherrill family are, from left to right, (first row) Karen, Dianne, Boone Sherrill holding Fondra, Beulah Sherrill holding Tony, Barbara, and Brenda; (second row) Richard, Joyce, Forrest McIntosh, Jimmy Mundy, Jim, Murrey, Nicky, Jessie, Warren, Mozelle, Billie Dove, Newton Smith, and Merriel; (third row) Asbury Mundy, Helen McIntosh, Ralph, Vivian, Kermit, and Mary Mundy; (fourth row) Aumon, Vaness Barker, Carroll McIntosh, Herman, Gaynel, Joy, Jack, Darwin, Ruby, Kenneth Brown, Larry (baby), John Roland, Dewey, Ann, and Rodney. The Sherrill home stood at the southeast corner of Webb's Road and Highway 16. (Courtesy of Merriel Mundy Lawing.)

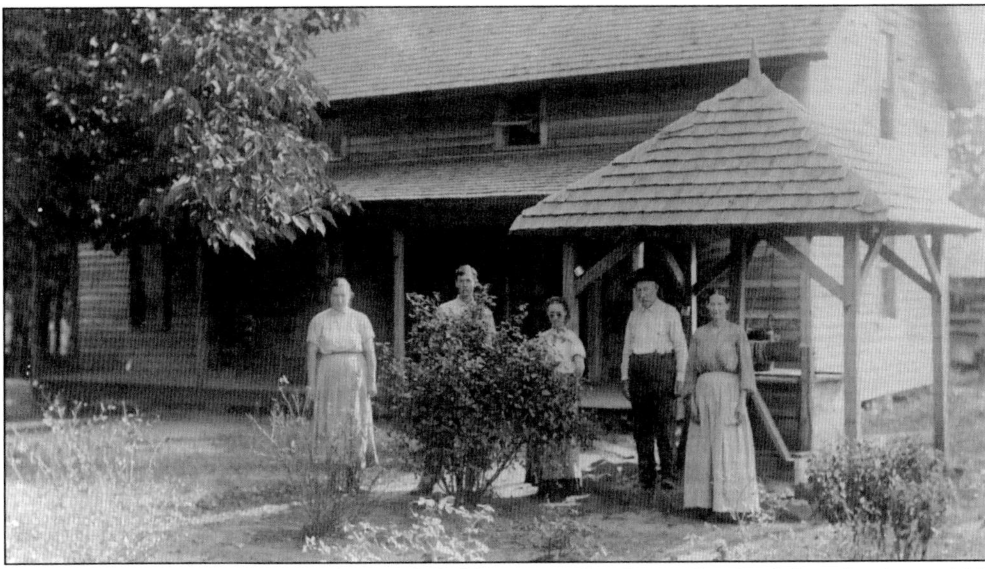

The home and well house of James Archibald Nixon offer the perfect backdrop for this c. 1910 family portrait in Triangle. From left to right are Eva Jane (1891–1963), David Carl (1887–1947), Rosa Lee (1884–1967), James Archibald (1848–1913), and Sarah Catherine Cherry Nixon (1851–1934). Not pictured is son Samuel Jasper Nixon. J.A. Nixon was described as a genial man. He was a farmer, businessman, and merchant in Triangle for many years and served as a registrar and justice of the peace, performing many marriages. Following in his footsteps, his son David Carl, known as Carl, ran the recently restored store that still stands in front of the home of Jimmy Nixon in Triangle. (Courtesy of Frances Nixon Sigmon.)

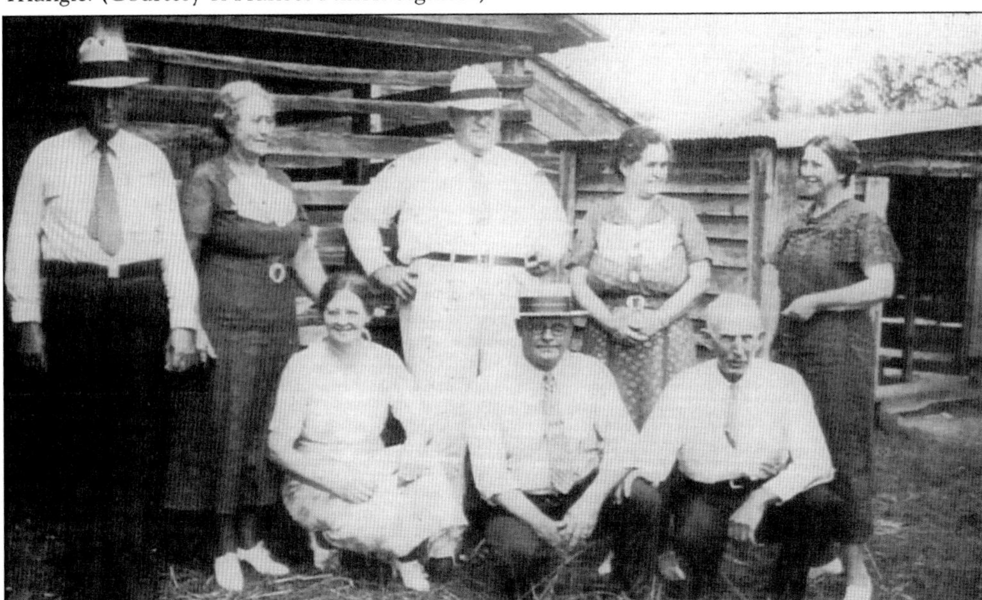

So many family portraits have been taken over the years at Rock Spring Campground. This group took part in this tradition in the early 1930s; they are, from left to right, (first row) Fannie Gabriel, Mr. Brown, and Charles Gabriel; (second row) Early Sherrill, Lucy Sherrill, Cleve Gabriel, Essie Brown, and Pearle Gabriel. (Courtesy of Janet Sigmon Jones.)

With an armful of tomatoes, Georgia Dellinger Jetton looks up from her work for a photograph while picking tomatoes in Lowesville. Georgia, wife of Kenneth Jetton, was born in Lincoln County on April 11, 1884, the daughter of Leroy and Sarah "Sallie" Nixon Dellinger. Kenneth and Georgia moved to Charlotte at some point, and she died on November 16, 1959. She is buried with her husband at Hills Chapel United Methodist Church in Lowesville. (Courtesy of Bernice Luckey Nixon.)

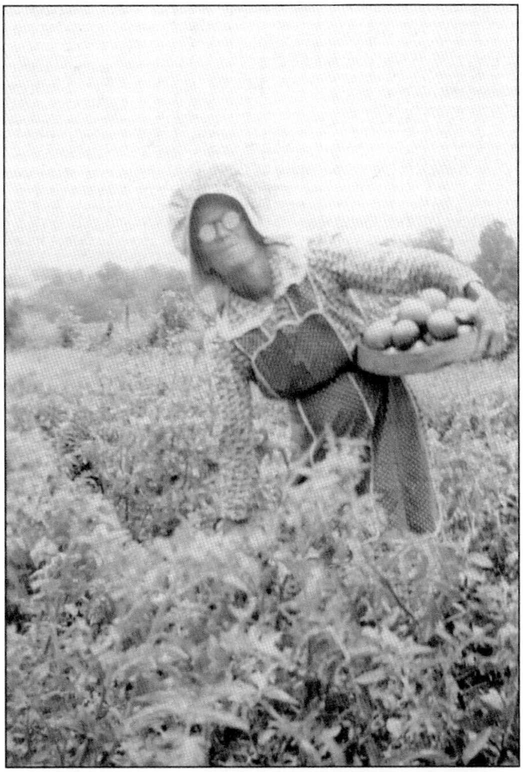

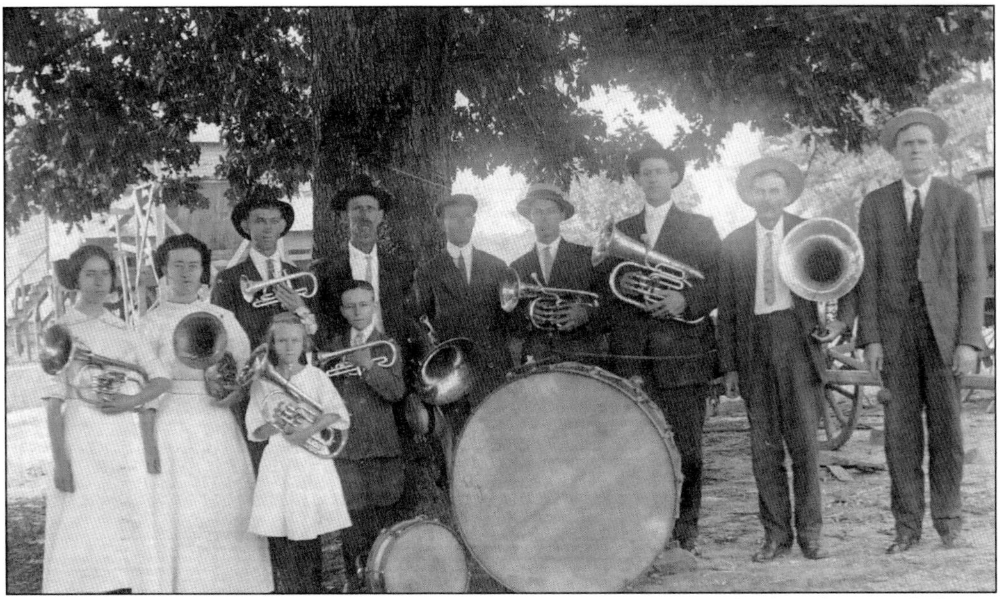

Members of the Dellinger Family Band of Triangle brandish their brass for this photograph during the 1920s. The band played at speaking engagements, school functions, farmers' union picnics, and fairs throughout Lincoln County. From left to right are Birdie Dellinger Beatty, Bessie Dellinger Cherry, Ellis Dellinger, Alba "Alby" Dellinger (father), Laddie Nixon, Ernest Cherry, Boyd Cherry, Jim Sifford, and Charlie Dellinger. The two youngest are not identified, but the little girl is believed to be Nettie Dellinger. (Courtesy of Doris Jean Keever.)

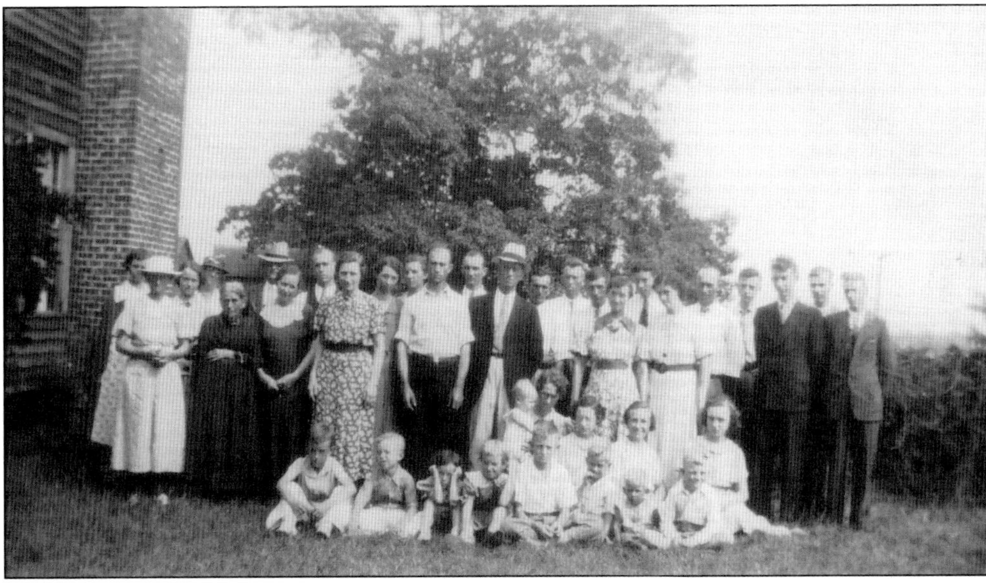

The large family of Alba Conway Dellinger (1867–1951) and Ada Magnolia Dellinger (1873–1957) assembles beside the family house with anxious children for this 1930s photograph. His family was well known for their Dellinger Family Band. Purchased in 1917, the Dellinger house once served as the manse for Unity, Machpelah, and Castanea Churches. The house still stands in Lowesville near Hills Chapel United Methodist Church. (Courtesy of Doris Jean Keever.)

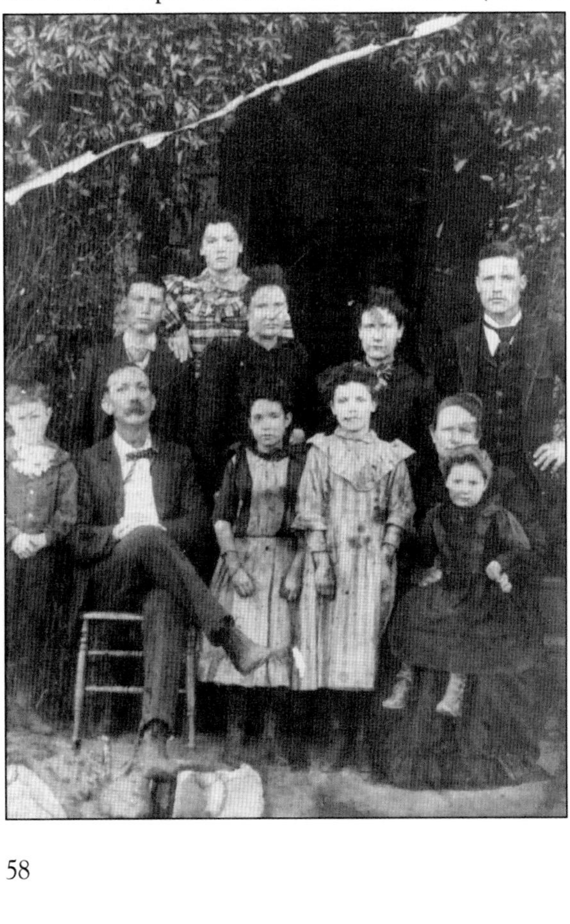

The family of Rufus Milton "Doc" and Frances Anne Rebecca Killian Mundy are pictured in this c. 1899 photograph in front of their ivy-draped front porch in Denver. From left to right are (first row) James Patrick Mundy, Rufus Milton Mundy, Vera Killian Mundy, Julia Pearl Johnson Mundy, Frances Anne Rebecca Killian Mundy, and Lura Boone Mundy; (second row) Charles Marion Mundy, Eva M. Mundy, Cynthia Caroline Mundy, and Robert Osborne Mundy; (third row) Mattie Brown Mundy. (Courtesy of Julia Fields.)

Dr. James Elmer Dellinger was born on November 3, 1862, to James Monroe and Belzie Nance Dellinger near Lowesville. He attended the medical school at Shaw University in Raleigh and received his medical degree within three years. When the Spanish-American War broke out, Dellinger joined the 3rd North Carolina Infantry Regiment as chief surgeon and attained the rank of major. In his professional life, Dellinger built the largest black physician's practice in the Greensboro area. He was a leader in business, and working alongside well-known president of North Carolina A&T, James B. Dudley, he served as the president of the Pioneer Building and Loan Association, providing banking needs to the black community. (Courtesy of the Library Company of Philadelphia.)

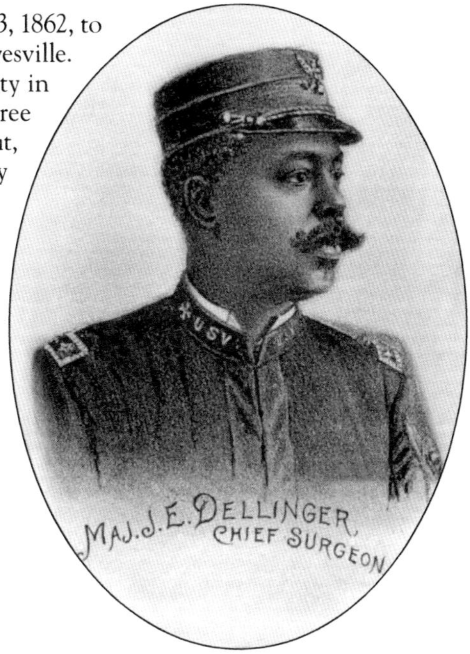

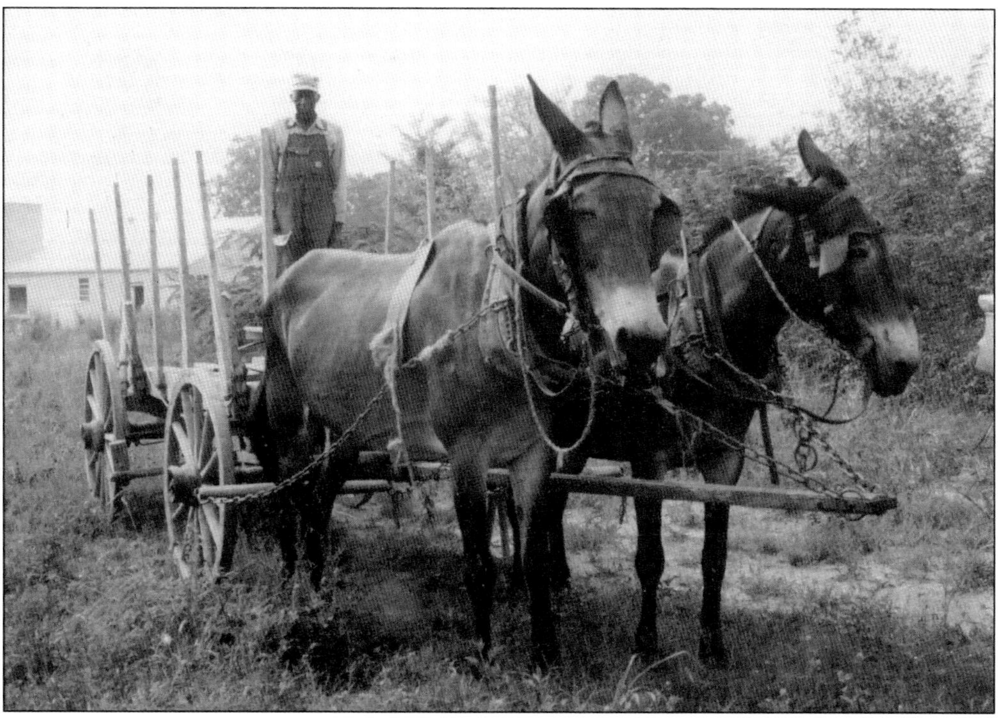

Robert Hilberta Clark, seen here commanding his wagon and mule team, plowed fields in eastern Lincoln County in addition to making oak-split baskets for a variety of uses. He was born on February 20, 1890, in the Little Egypt community. He was a farmer, a well-respected basket weaver, a World War I veteran, and a member of Brevard's Chapel United Methodist Church in Denver. Clark died on April 25, 1980, and is buried at St. James United Methodist Church. (Courtesy of Terry Brotherton.)

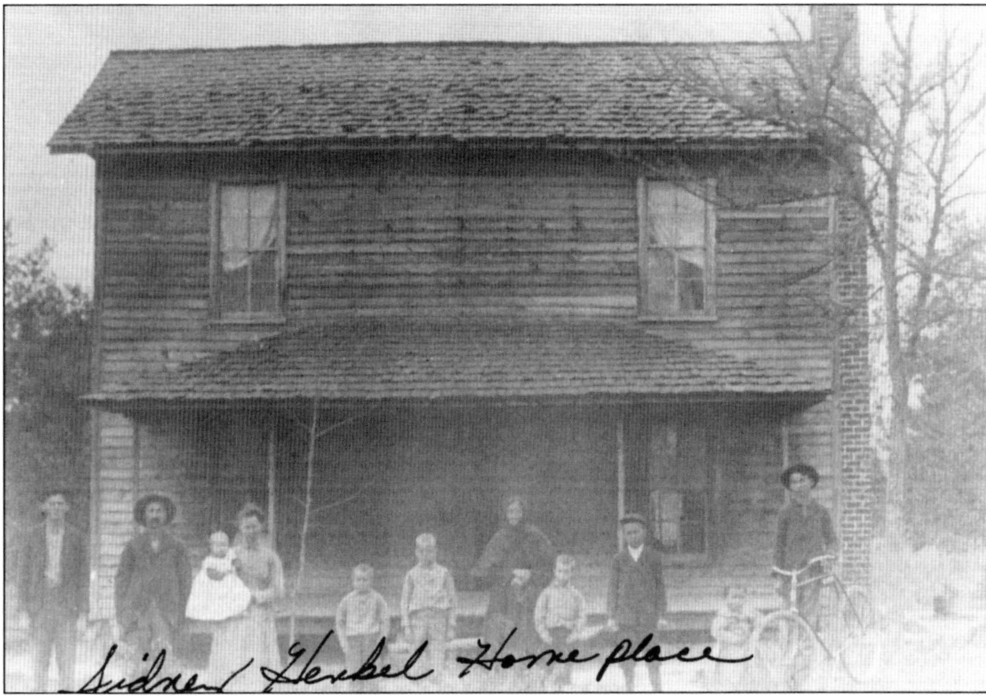

Sidney Coulee Henkle (1864–1950) and Jane Elizabeth Barker Henkle (1870–1946) worked their farm in the Lowesville community. In 1909, he was a road supervisor in the Catawba Springs Township at a time when citizens were encouraged to maintain the roads near their home. The family of Sidney Henkle pose in front of their home in Lowesville in 1905. Henkle's son Freeman Isaac Henkle would later serve as a private in the 103rd Machine Gun Company in World War I. He died from wounds received in France on October 23, 1918. (Courtesy of Doris Jean Keever.)

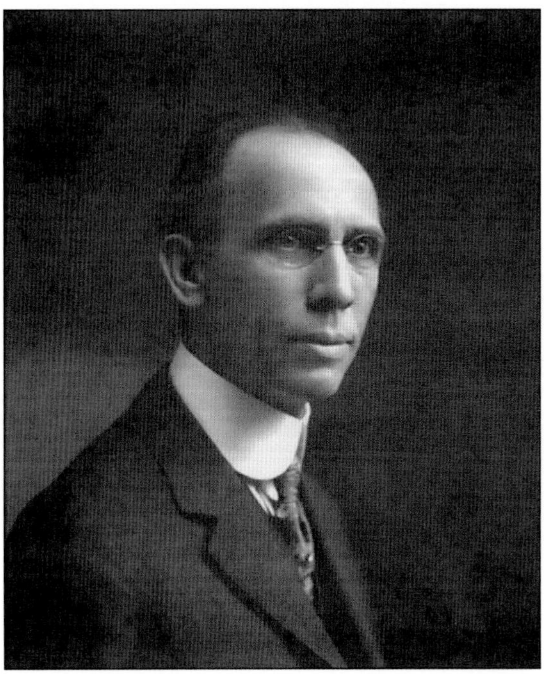

Leroy Long was born in Lowesville on January 1, 1869, the son of William Thomas Long (1837–1903) and Mary Burch Long (1838–1913), and married Martha Downing on August 29, 1896, at Atoka, Choctaw Nation, Oklahoma. He received his primary education in Lincoln County and at the age of 20 learned anatomy from Dr. Robert McLean of eastern Lincoln County. He graduated from the Louisville Medical College in 1893. After running a successful private practice and serving as a surgeon, Dr. Long helped form the Oklahoma State Medical Association and was appointed the dean of the University Medical School in Oklahoma City. (Courtesy of LCHA.)

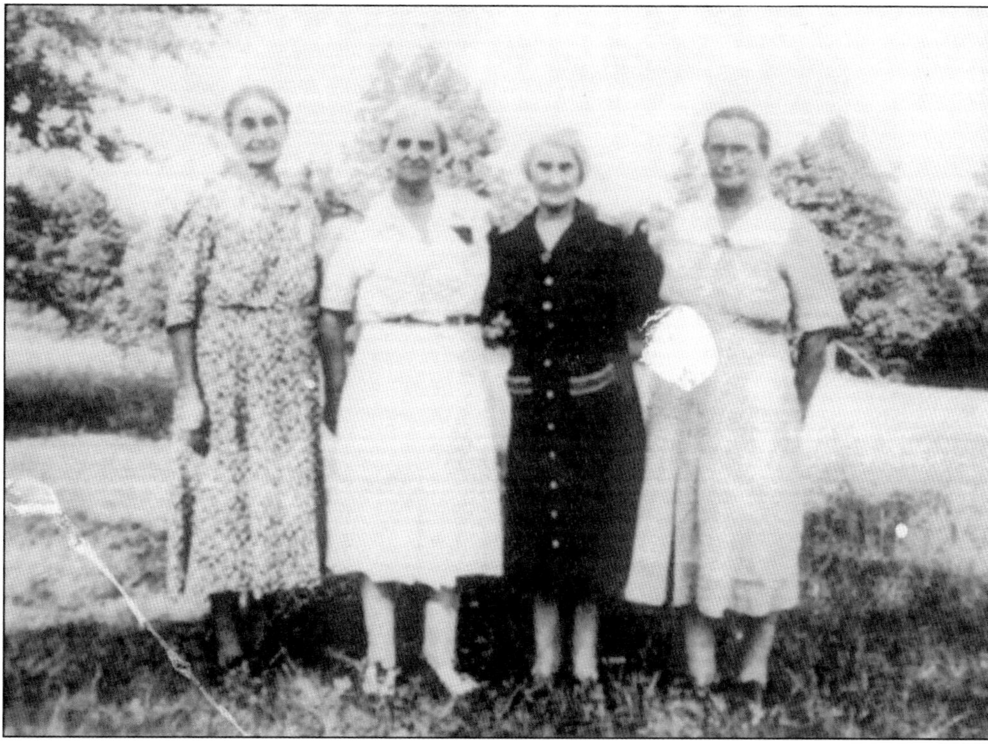

William Francis Sherrill (1852–1904) and Mary Jane Little Sherrill's (1850–1926) marriage in 1872 led to the birth of seven children. The four daughters of this union pose here in the 1940s. They are, from left to right, Anna Eliza (1872–1960), Corine Alda (1876–1953), Martha Mannie (1879–1961), and Cora Jane (1881–1950). Although the siblings spread over both sides of the Catawba, they at one time owned the land at the end of Unity Church Road, north to Webb's Chapel and what is now Lake Norman. (Courtesy of Anne Eudy.)

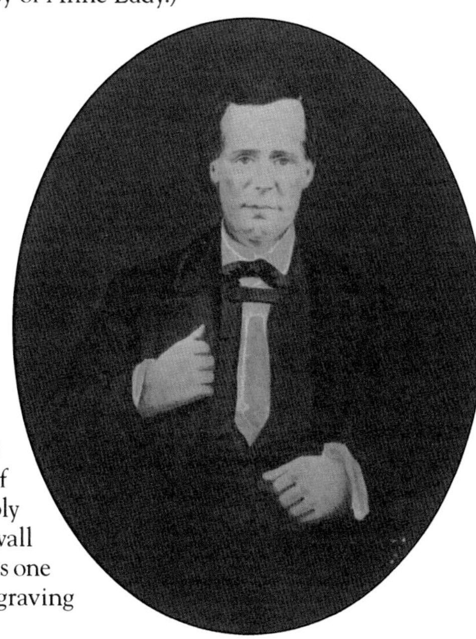

James Madison Smith (1809–1874) operated the Vesuvius furnace and lived in the house of the same name starting in 1857. He married Hettie Rudisill (1812–1891), the great-granddaughter of Lincoln County pioneer Michael Rudisill. With the outbreak of the Civil War, Smith built and operated the Stonewall furnace, named in honor of Maj. Gen. Thomas J. "Stonewall" Jackson, to supply iron to the Confederacy. He operated the Stonewall furnace until his death in 1874. An iron lintel across one of the three openings at the furnace bears the engraving "J.M. Smith." (Courtesy of Jim Smith.)

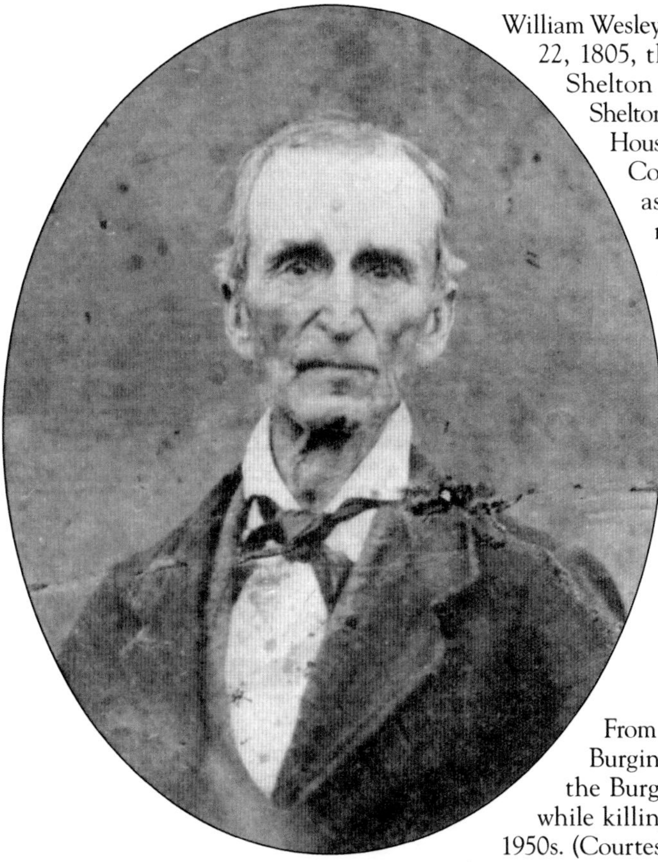

William Wesley Munday was born on September 22, 1805, the son of Jeremiah and Chloe Shelton Mundy, and married Lucinda Shelton. He served in the North Carolina House of Representatives from Lincoln County in 1838 and 1840. He served as the chair of the committee that met in Dry Pond, now Denver, on January 21, 1871, for the purpose of establishing a school at Rock Spring Campground. He died on September 3, 1881, and is buried at Bethel United Methodist Church in Denver. (Courtesy of Jim Smith.)

From left to right, Finley Burgin, Luther Burgin, and an unidentified member of the Burgin family are caught in the act while killing hogs on their property in the 1950s. (Courtesy of Lela Burgin Nixon.)

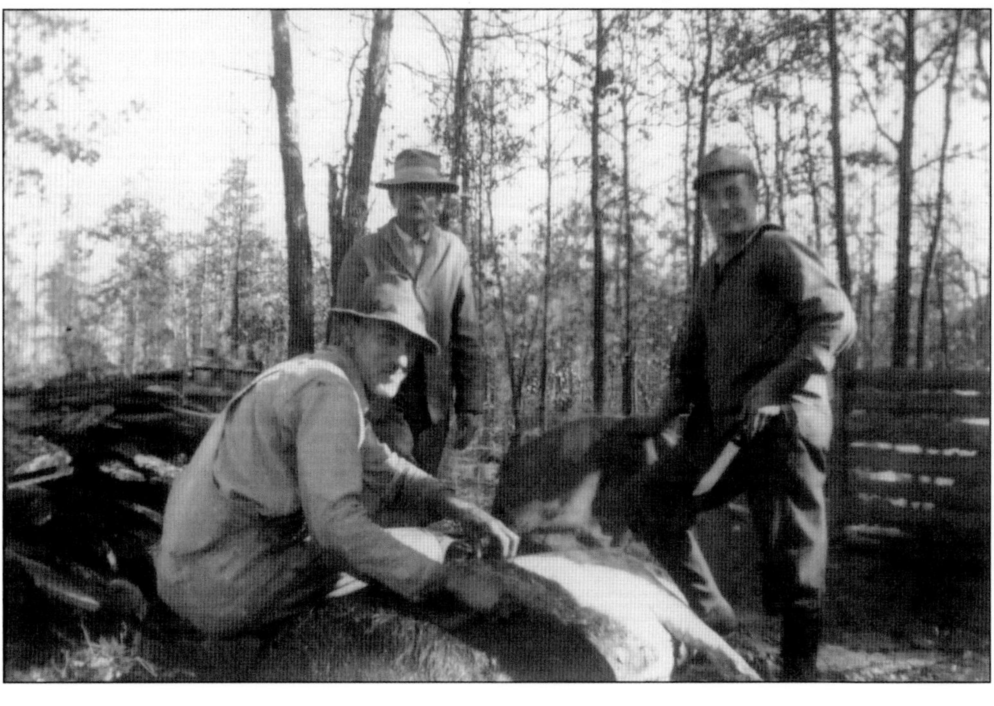

Dressed in their Sunday best, the children of Henry Durant Cherry (1881–1968) and Minnie Iola McIntosh Cherry (1884–1969) pose for this early 1910s portrait in Triangle. Jessie Cherry (center, 1907–1997) married Perry Nixon (1907–1978), and they farmed the land near their home surrounding Unity Presbyterian Church. For a number of years, Perry barbered on the weekends in Denver and in Triangle in the back of Carl Nixon's store. Frank Cherry (right, 1911–1997) became a school teacher in the Catawba County school system and later ran the Sherrill's Ford mail route for 40 years, and Russell Cherry (left, 1909–1989) ran a store on the east side of Highway 16 where South Triangle Circle intersects. Russell ran a race track known as Lakewood Speedway with Bruton Smith as promoter in the early 1950s. (Courtesy of Bill and Lela Nixon.)

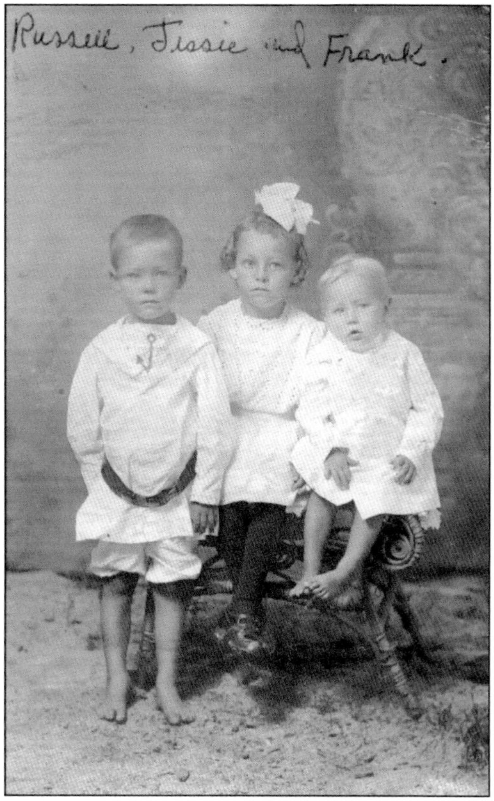

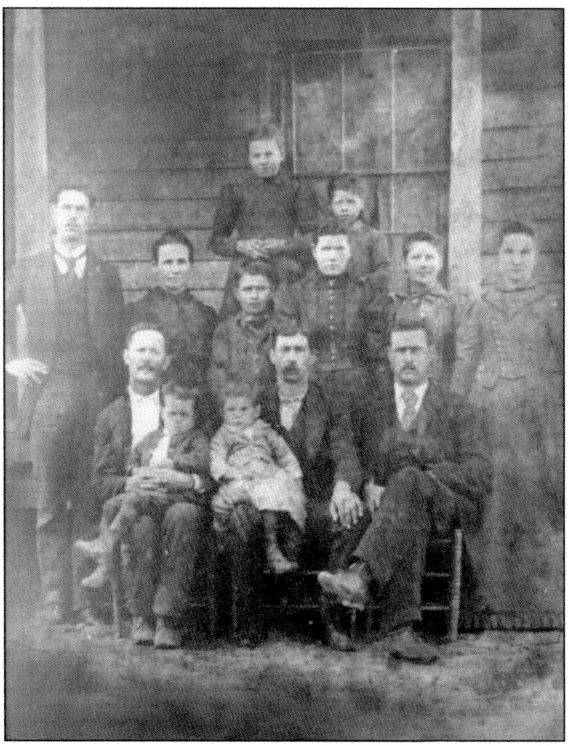

The family of Luther Alexander Killian chose their home in Denver as the backdrop for this 1891 photograph. Members of the family are, from left to right, (first row) Luther A. (father), Ephraim F., Oliver Mack Lawing, Avery, and Jacob F.; (second row) Levi E. "Lee," Emily, John, Nannie E., Blanche E., and Rebecca "Molly," Jacob's wife; (third row) Beulah May and Nora. (Courtesy of the Killian family.)

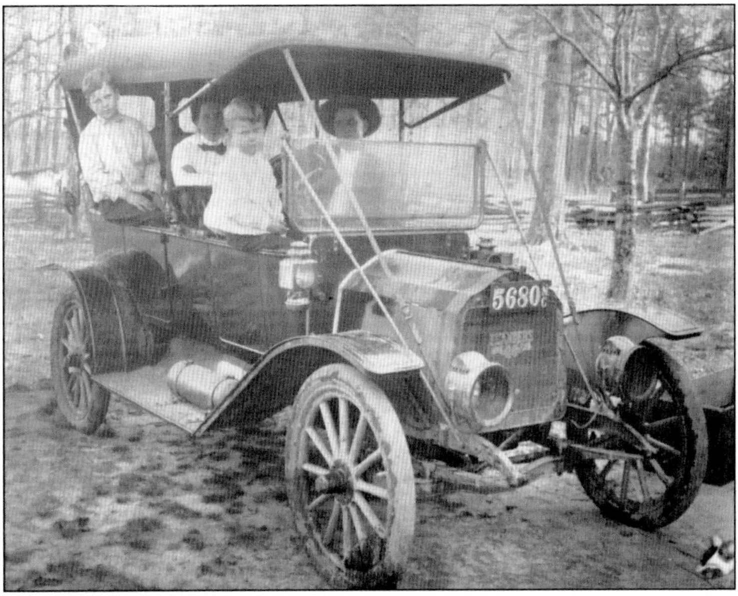

From left to right, Carl Killian, Eunice Killian, Seth Killian, and John Killian sit in their Flanders Model 20 automobile in this c. 1912 photograph in eastern Lincoln County. (Courtesy of the Killian family.)

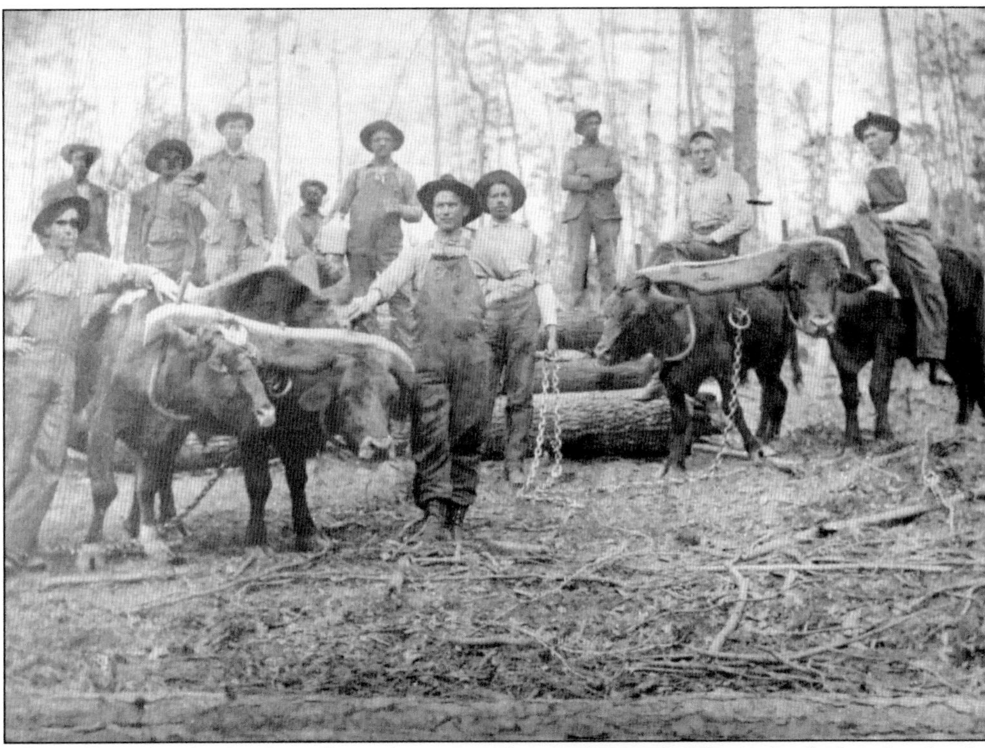

John Killian's hardy crew wrestles with a team of oxen that are hauling a load of timber for the Killians' sawmill. It was said by *Lincoln County News* that "It don't make any difference what John Killian puts his hand to, it has to move and move fast." John Killian and Company threshed wheat and sawed many acres of timber in eastern Lincoln County, and as King Wilkinson, also known as Alpha, reported on July 8, 1910, in the *Lincoln County News*, "For fast work we don't believe this company can be beat in the county." Among those pictured are John Killian, John Shelton, Foss Puntch, and Gaither Gilleland. (Courtesy of the Killian family.)

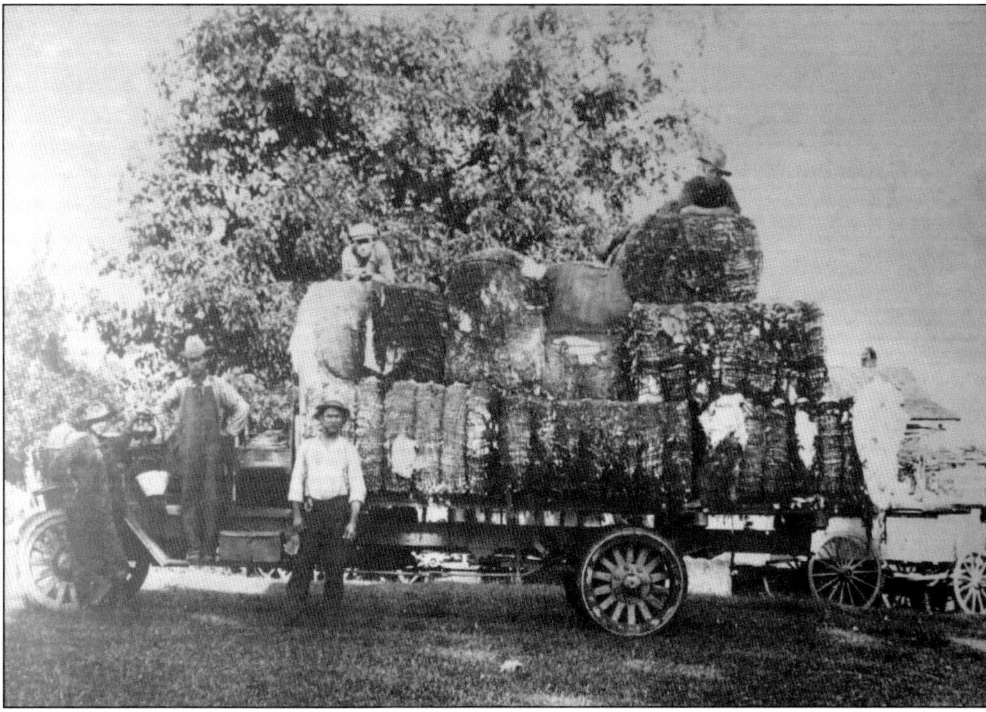

John A. Killian and a small crew are dwarfed by a massive load of cotton as they leave a cotton gin, possibly the Killians' gin. John ran a country store at Killian's Crossroads, what is today the intersection of Highways 16 and 150, where the community purchased groceries, feed, and clothes. He also farmed on his family's land, ran a sawmill where he pulled logs using oxen, and operated a cotton gin. (Courtesy of the Killian family.)

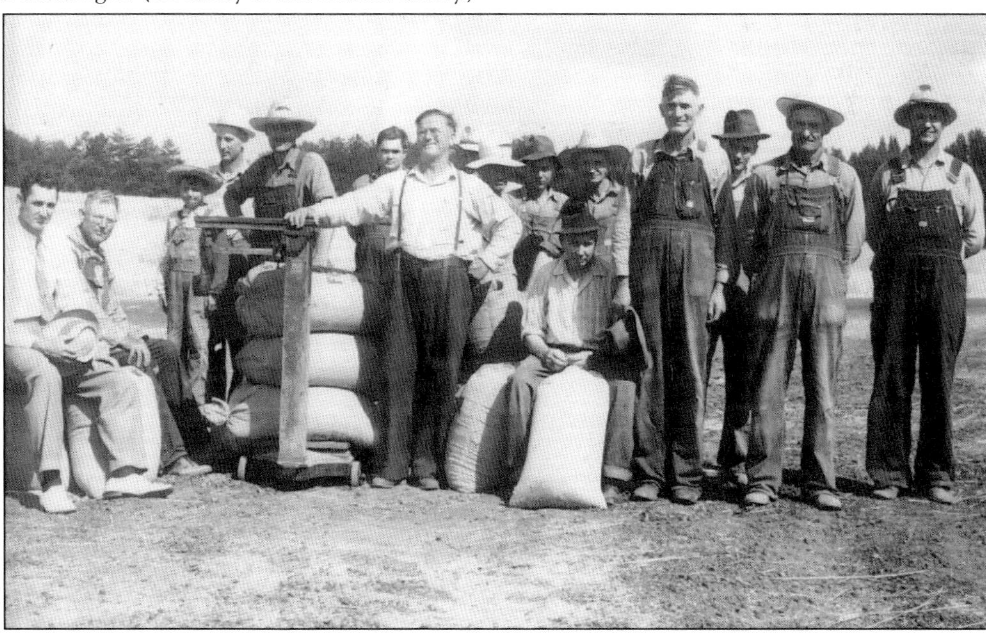

Large bags of wheat are weighed by local men while a farming agent looks on in this photograph from the 1940s. (Courtesy of the Killian family.)

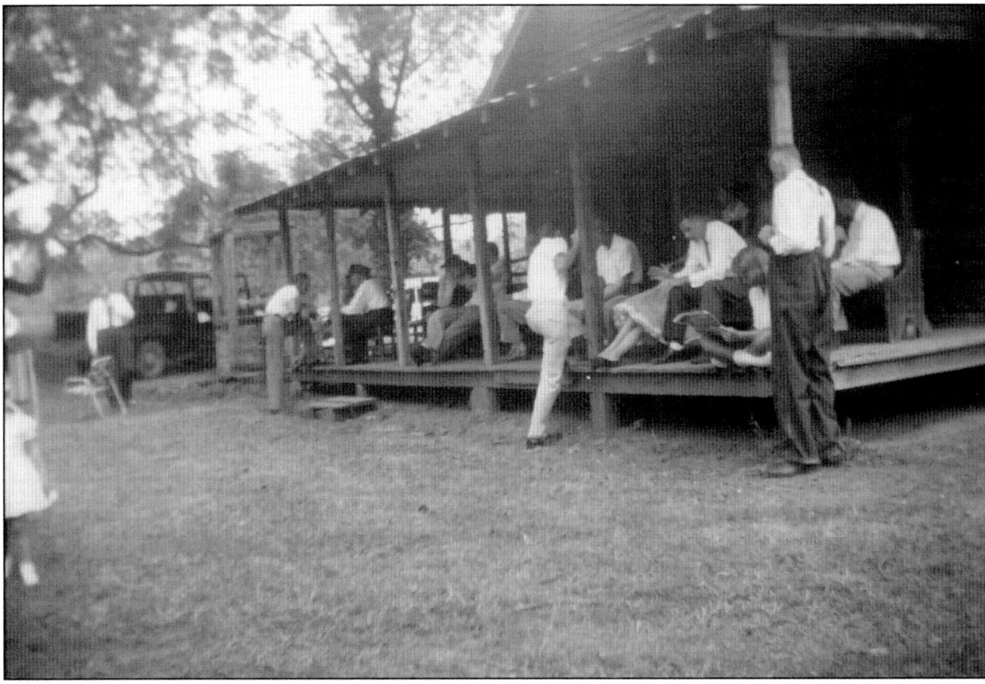

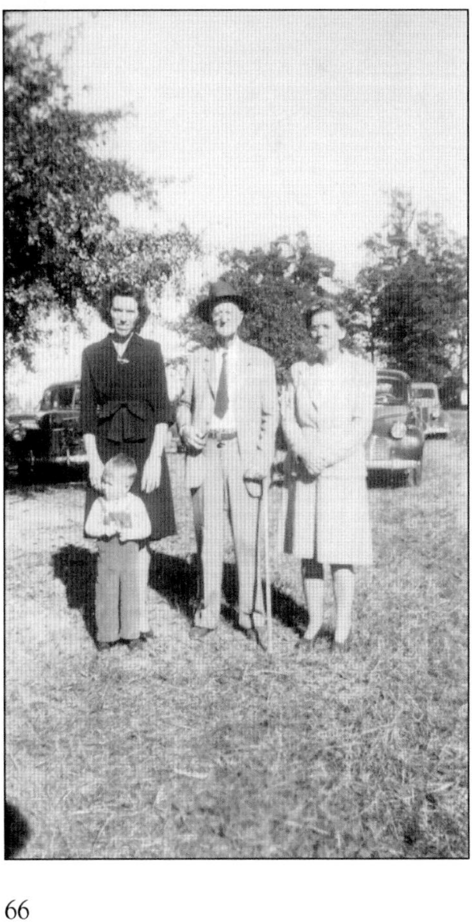

The Luckey family enjoys the large front porch and church pews from the old Salem Methodist Church during a family reunion in the 1950s. The house is the William Davidson Luckey homeplace, which was made out of two one-room school buildings after Lincoln County had purchased property to build the Triangle School. The house was located on Luckey Creek and was moved up the nearby hill from the creek closer to Graham Road by Duke Power before flooding the creek for Lake Norman. The family held reunions at the house before and after it was moved. (Courtesy of Bernice Luckey Nixon.)

The Beatty family held many reunions over the years at their home in Lowesville on the Lincoln-Gaston County border. Four generations come together to capture this moment in time. They are, from left to right, Jerry Nixon, Bernice Luckey Nixon, grandpa Will Beatty (1861–1953), and Clara Beatty Luckey (1898–1979). (Courtesy of Bernice Luckey Nixon.)

The family of Clarence Eulie Nixon is the subject of this photograph in the front yard with their house in the background on the lower end of Hager's Ferry Road, now under water. From left to right are (first row) Otis, Grover, and Roy; (second row) Clarence Eulie and May Dellinger Nixon. Eulie Nixon was born in 1886 and died in 1946, while May Nixon was born in 1892 and died in 1959. They are both buried at Hills Chapel United Methodist Church Cemetery in Lowesville. (Courtesy of Bernice Luckey Nixon.)

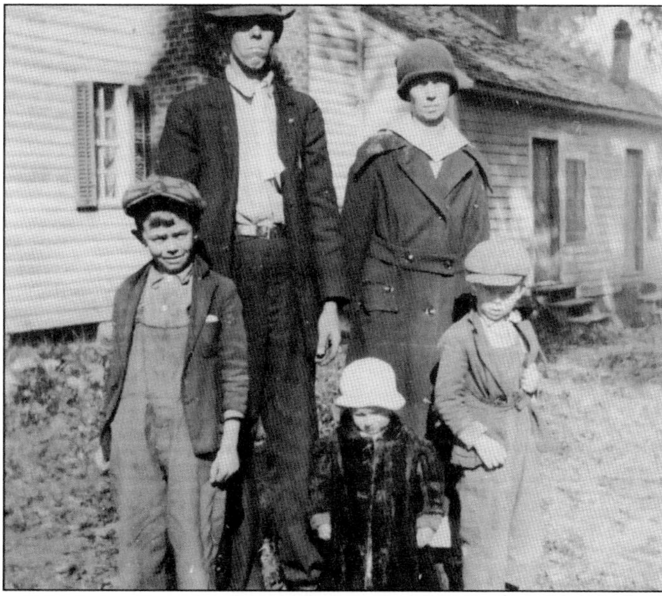

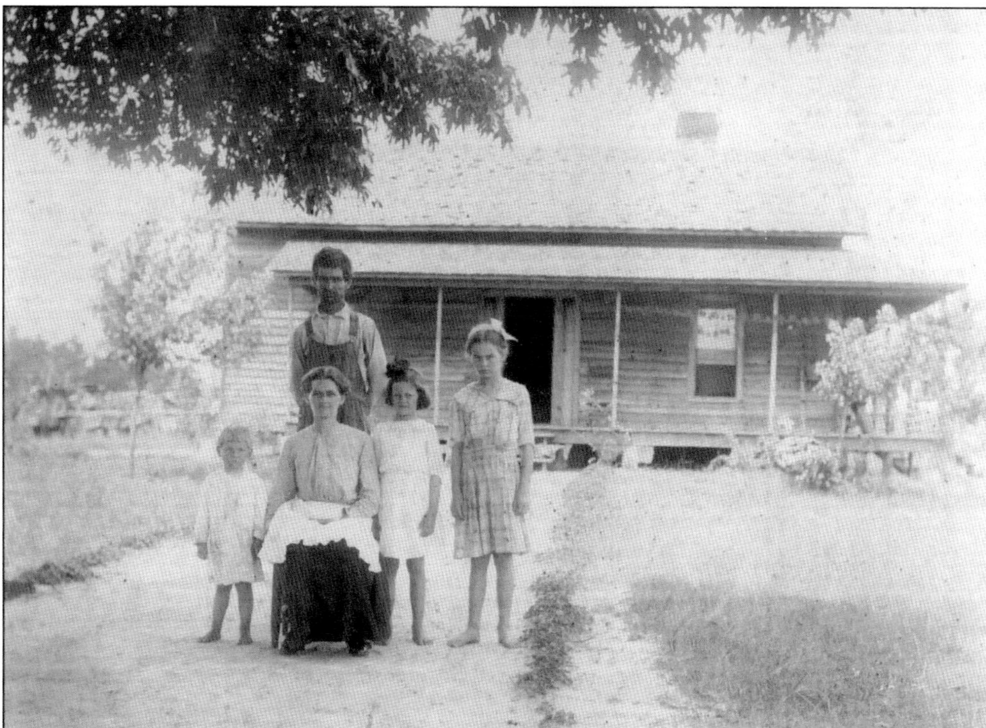

The family of Ivey and Otta King Hager poses with their bare-footed children for this early-20th-century photograph on an unpaved walkway leading to the front porch and central entry of a one-story frame house in Lowesville. Ivey Hager, the son of Julius P. and Annie P. Hager, was a farmer in eastern Lincoln County until his death, and he married Otta King on June 2, 1901. From left to right are Russell Hager, Otta King Hager (1882–1973), Ivey N. Hager (1878–1960), Faulabelle Hager, and Grace Hager. Ivey and Otta Hager are buried at the Denver Community Cemetery in Denver. (Courtesy of Shawn Howard.)

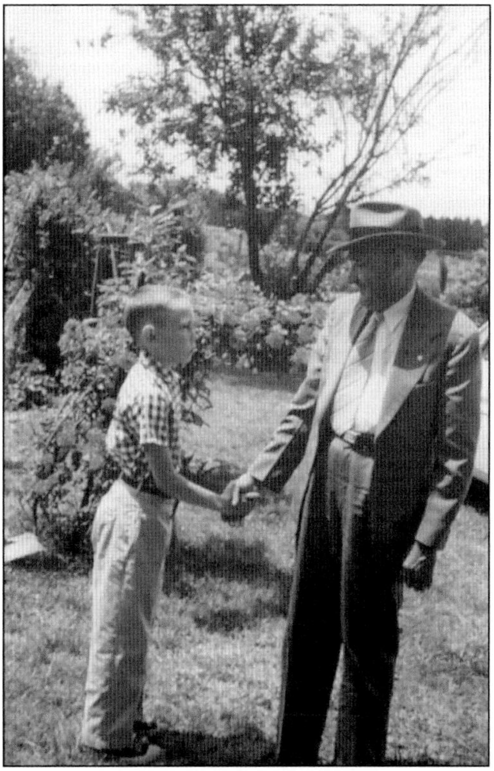

Charles Brower Armstrong (1885–1960) married Nora Jane Coulter (1893–1955), a teacher from Newton, on July 18, 1918. He started as a rural mail carrier on June 1, 1911, and took over as the local mail carrier from his father, James Pinkney Armstrong. Charles, known by many as "Mr. Munn," began carrying the mail by horse-drawn wagon to the Denver Post Office. He would cross the Catawba River into Davidson daily and pick up the mail to be delivered to the Denver Post Office, then would deliver the rural route known as Davidson Route 1. He later transitioned to delivering the mail by car. He delivered mail well into his 70s and retired after 45 years. He and his family lived next to Denver United Methodist Church, across the street from the Beatty house. Charlie and Nora are buried in the Denver Community Cemetery. (Courtesy of Bruce Armstrong.)

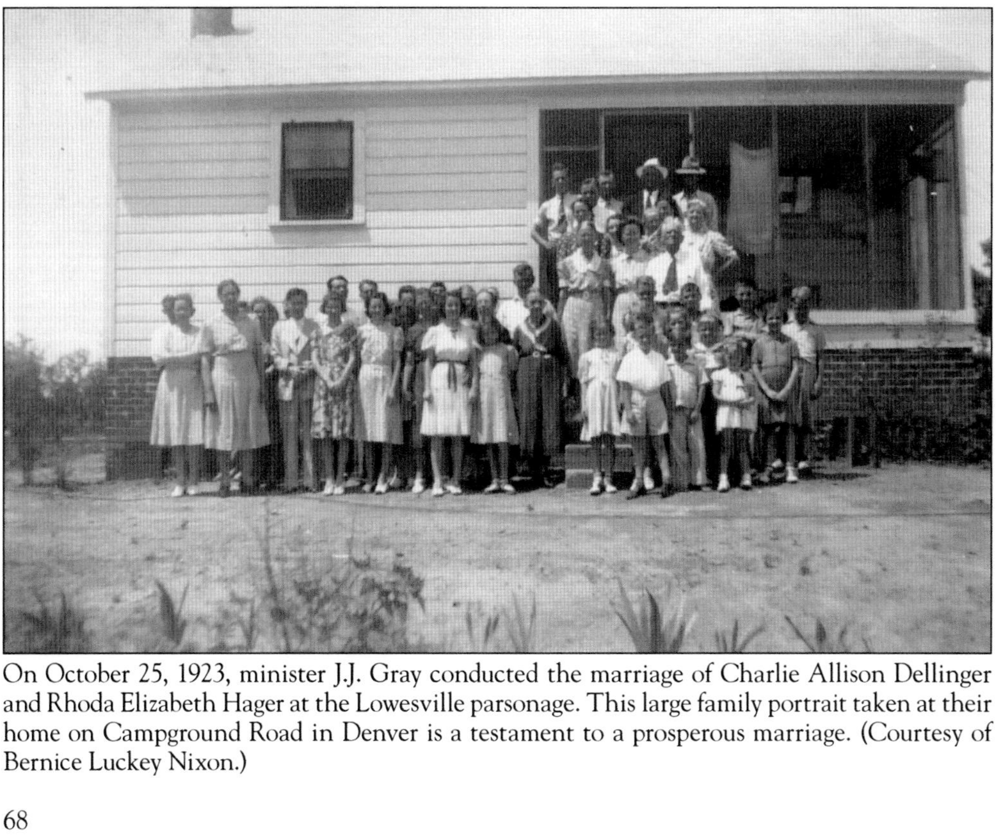

On October 25, 1923, minister J.J. Gray conducted the marriage of Charlie Allison Dellinger and Rhoda Elizabeth Hager at the Lowesville parsonage. This large family portrait taken at their home on Campground Road in Denver is a testament to a prosperous marriage. (Courtesy of Bernice Luckey Nixon.)

Leroy M. Dellinger, of Company G, 52nd Regiment, North Carolina Troops, was born in eastern Lincoln County and enlisted at age 25 on March 23, 1862. He was wounded at Gettysburg on July 3, 1863, returned to duty prior to September 1, 1863, and was promoted to the rank of first sergeant on December 10, 1863. He was captured at or near Amelia Court House, Virginia, and was confined at Hart's Island, New York Harbor, on April 11, 1865. After taking the Oath of Allegiance on June 19, 1865, he was released. Dellinger died on October 29, 1915, and is buried at Hills Chapel United Methodist Church Cemetery in Lowesville. (Courtesy of Bernice Luckey Nixon.)

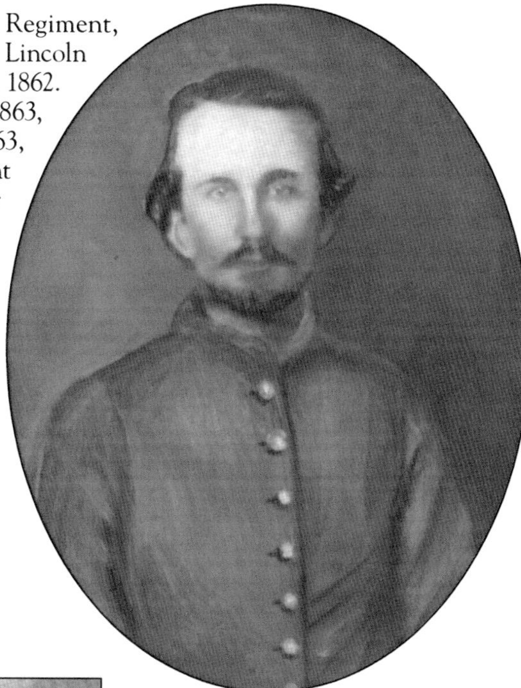

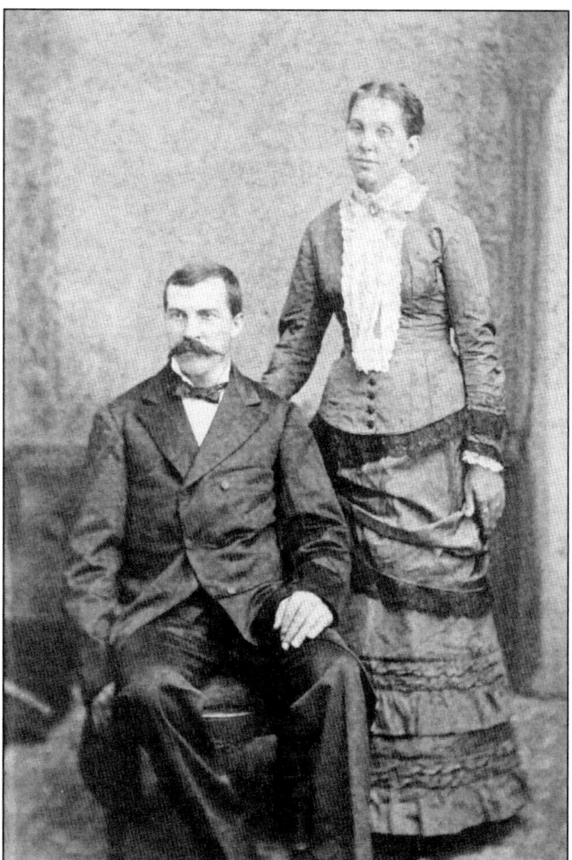

Dressed in their finest at the studio of J.H. Van Ness in Charlotte, Joseph Edgar and Frances "Fanny" Wilson Reinhardt have their likenesses captured during the 1890s. Joseph was born in Gaston County on June 7, 1850, and died on October 2, 1926. He purchased the Phifer Cotton Mill in Lincolnton with his brother R.S. Reinhardt in 1889, and for many years served on the Lincoln County Board of Commissioners. He married Fanny Wilson (1854–1948) in 1874, and they share a granite monument at the Smith-Dellinger Cemetery in Iron Station. (Courtesy of Kirk Bailey.)

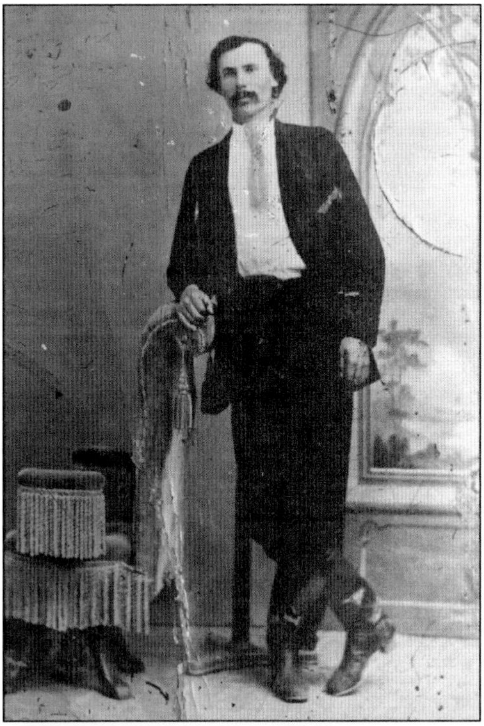

James Coleman Thompson was born on February 17, 1849, the 10th son of Thomas Jefferson and Francis Shelton Thompson, and married Jenny Mundy (1853–1933) on April 3, 1873. He was known locally as Coleman Thompson and was well known for planting a corn field just at the right time every year so that he and all of his friends could have fresh corn for the annual camp meeting at Rock Spring Campground. He was a farmer in Denver and served as a magistrate in Lincoln County for 25 years. He died on August 4, 1924, and is buried at Bethel United Methodist Church in Denver. (Courtesy of Jack Thompson.)

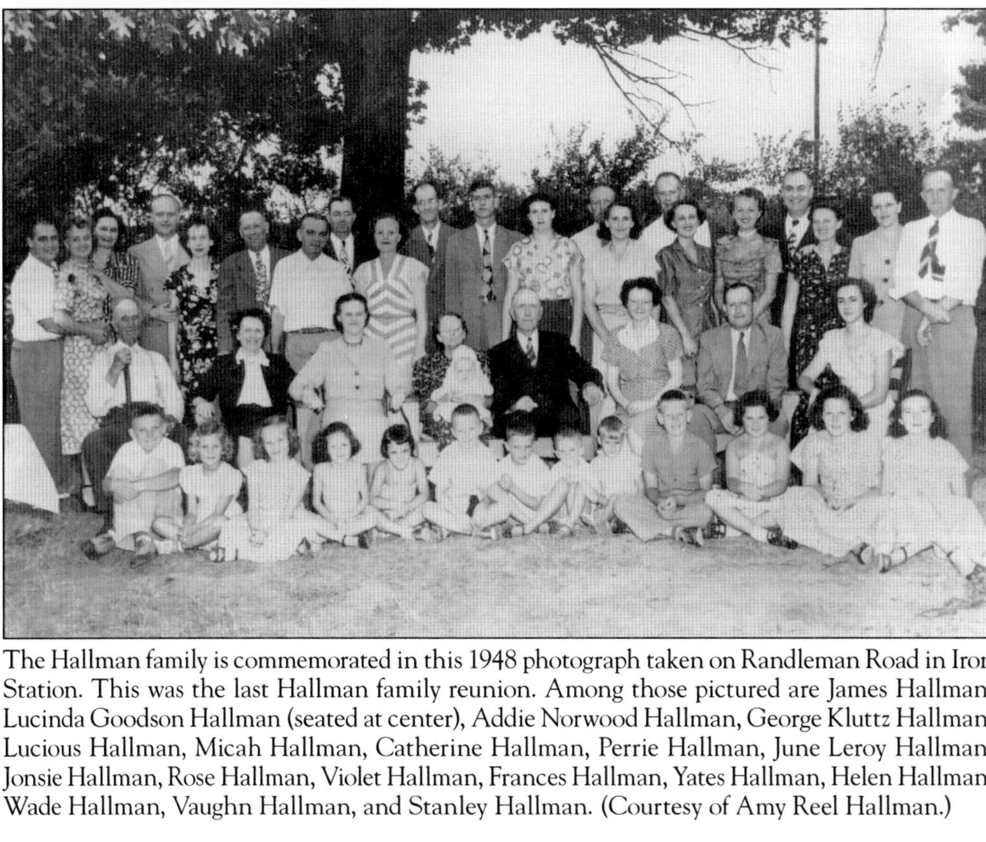

The Hallman family is commemorated in this 1948 photograph taken on Randleman Road in Iron Station. This was the last Hallman family reunion. Among those pictured are James Hallman, Lucinda Goodson Hallman (seated at center), Addie Norwood Hallman, George Kluttz Hallman, Lucious Hallman, Micah Hallman, Catherine Hallman, Perrie Hallman, June Leroy Hallman, Jonsie Hallman, Rose Hallman, Violet Hallman, Frances Hallman, Yates Hallman, Helen Hallman, Wade Hallman, Vaughn Hallman, and Stanley Hallman. (Courtesy of Amy Reel Hallman.)

From left to right, Lester Abernethy, Frank Nixon, Charlie Beal, Roscoe Kincaid, and Houston Thompson stand in the side yard of the Kincaid family house in Lowesville for a Kodak picture by Joe R. Nixon on July 16, 1957. David Kincaid (1830–1908) completed construction on this house in 1907, and his son Roscoe (1878–1964) and daughter-in-law Marguerite occupied the house from 1908 until Marguerite's death in 1971. (Courtesy of LCHA.)

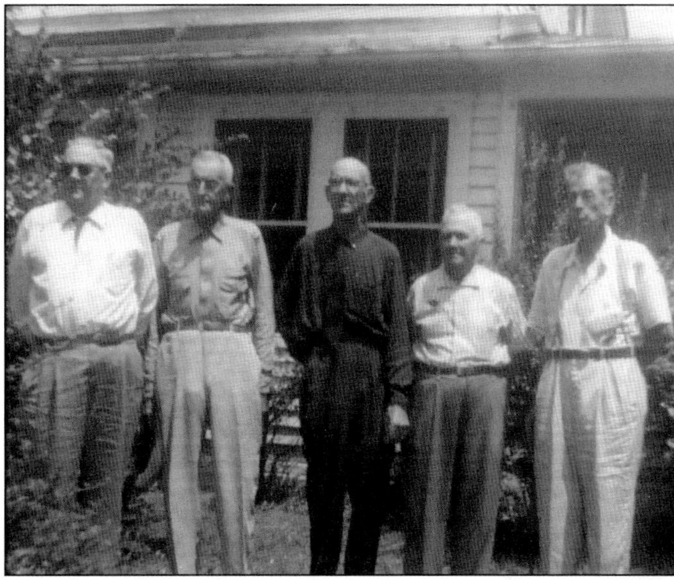

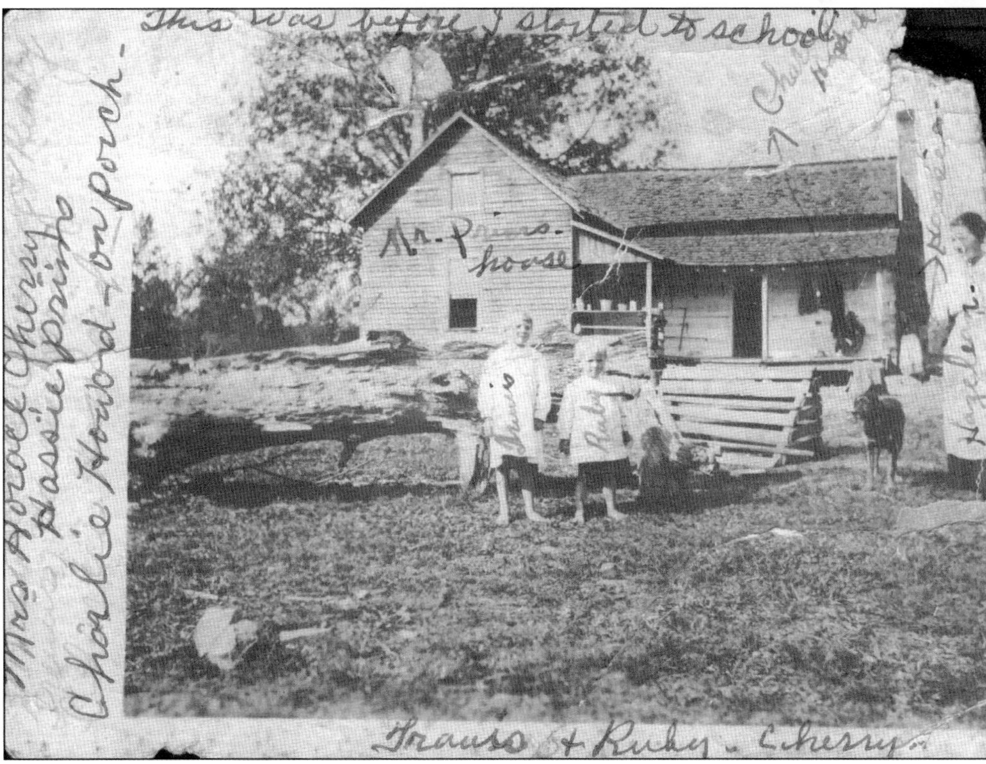

The ink that litters this historic photograph of "Mr. Prim's house" in the Traingle area shows an interest in identifying as many people as possible. Travis and Ruby Cherry stand in front of a downed tree in their long shirt-tails as an unidentified dog looks on near Hazelean Cherry (1895–1962). Clay crocks rest on a rail on the porch of the Primm house's rear ell, and Charlie Howard sits on the side porch as Hassie Mae Primm (1890–1976) leans against the gable end of the house near the chimney. The Primm family home was located on the road that led to historic Elmwood. (Courtesy of Nancy Long.)

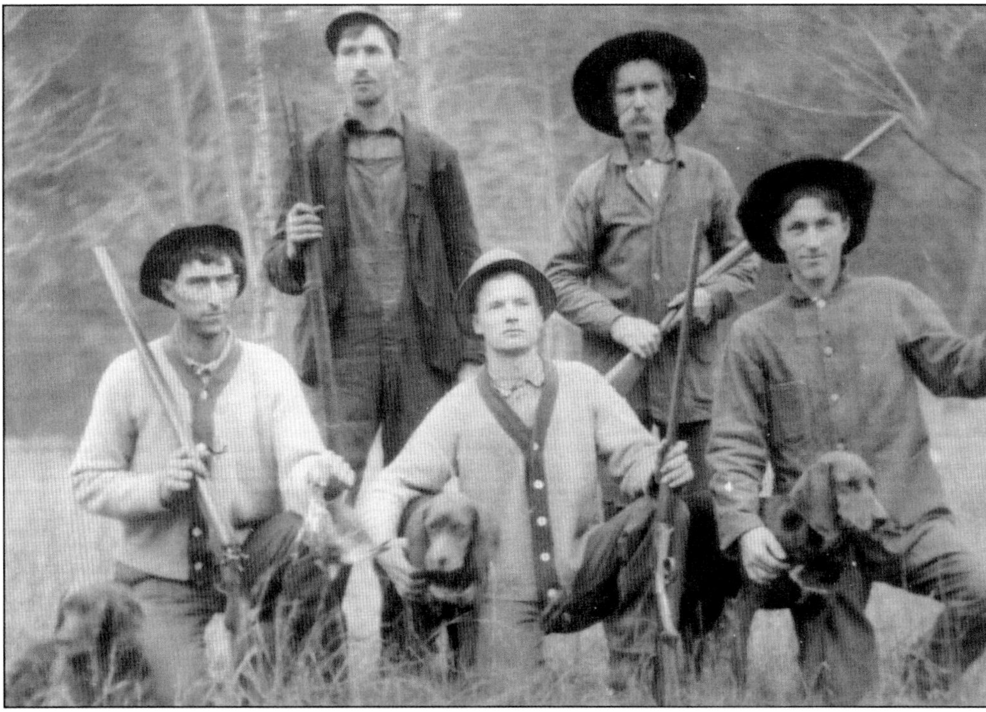

With trusty hounds at bay and a wooded landscape at their backs, men from the Pumpkin Center community of eastern Lincoln County present themselves during a day of hunting in the 1930s on the Vesuvius furnace property. From left to right are (kneeling) Bob Watts, Jessie Williams Jr., and Edd Reel; (standing) Martin Williams and Jesse Williams Sr. (Courtesy of Amy Reel Hallman.)

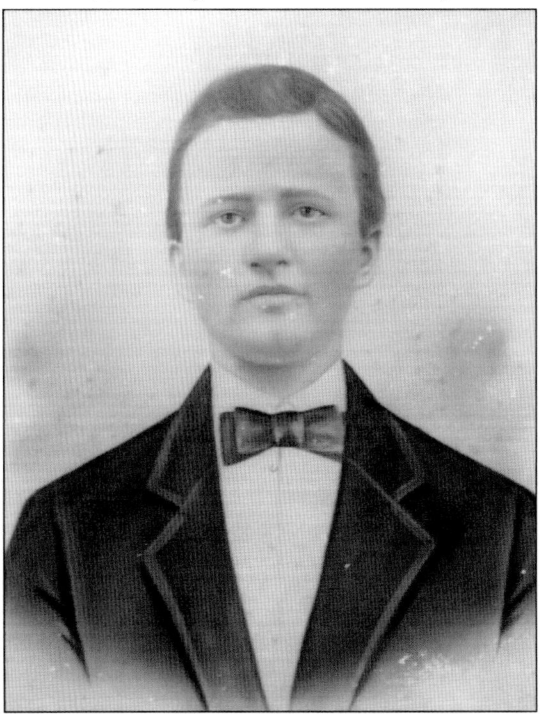

David Calvin King Wilkinson was born in Catawba County, North Carolina, on October 20, 1853. He received his early education in a small one-room school in this area. He taught schools for over 30 years in Lincoln and Catawba Counties, and was a member of the Lincoln County School Board for a number of years. On December 20, 1876, he married Julia Ann Rebecca Lockman, and they had nine children. Wilkinson also farmed, was a magistrate, and was Sunday school superintendent at Lebanon Methodist Church. Wilkinson wrote a weekly newspaper column under the alias "Alpha." In his articles, he discussed farming, education, politics, economics, religion, and life in Lincoln County. He died on Thursday, January 23, 1919, and is buried at Lebanon Methodist Church Cemetery. (Courtesy of Julia [Patsy] Smith.)

In 1950, Russell Cherry constructed Lakewood Speedway on property adjacent to his home on Highway 16. The vertical oak board fence that encompassed the track and made up the bleachers was harvested and milled on the property. From left to right, Scotty, Janet, Scott, and Fabena Phillips take a moment to pose in August 1950 in front of the grandstand on the front stretch of Cherry's racetrack. Only a few weeks earlier, on July 30, 1950, the inaugural race was held at the one-mile dirt track 15 miles northwest of Charlotte. Headed by race director Bruton Smith, a double feature race of stock and modified racers competed for $5,000 in prize money. Leading into the May 6, 1951, race at Lakewood, Hall of Fame driver Buck Baker took his turn as promoter of the race, and as mentioned in the *High Point Enterprise* on May 4, 1951, Bill France and his NASCAR organization was backing the Lakewood race to the hilt. The high speeds that racers achieved caused deep ruts in the turns and made the course hard to maintain. The track was short-lived. (Courtesy of Jan Phillips Hoke.)

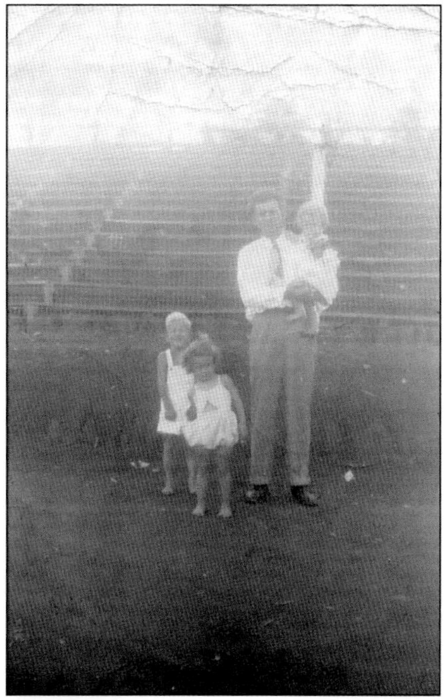

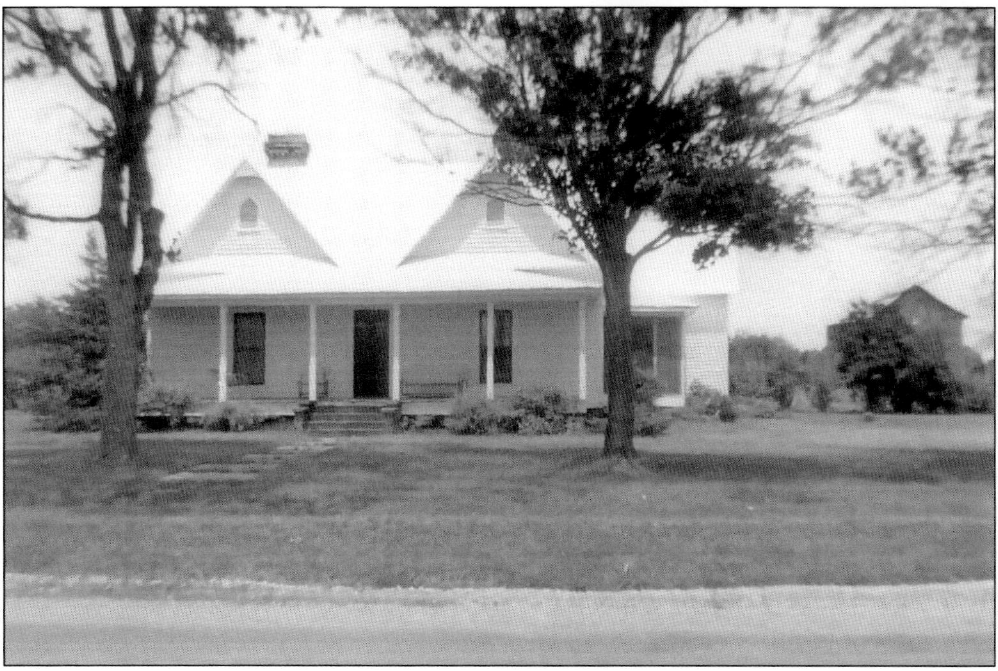

Shaler R. Proctor (1885–1948) built his home at what is today the intersection of Highway 16 Business and Proctor Road in Denver after he purchased the property from R.E. and Marie Proctor in 1915. Shaler was the son of W.C. and Vassie Proctor and husband of Leslie Lowe Proctor (1888–1914). Key Howard purchased the property in 1936. He was a farmer and auxiliary deputy sheriff and worked at the Carbon Plant in Charlotte. He also worked at Eff Killian's store and would routinely go to homes around Denver to remove bodies for Warlick's Funeral Home where cars or wagons could not go. The house was razed in the early 2000s. (Courtesy of Shawn Howard.)

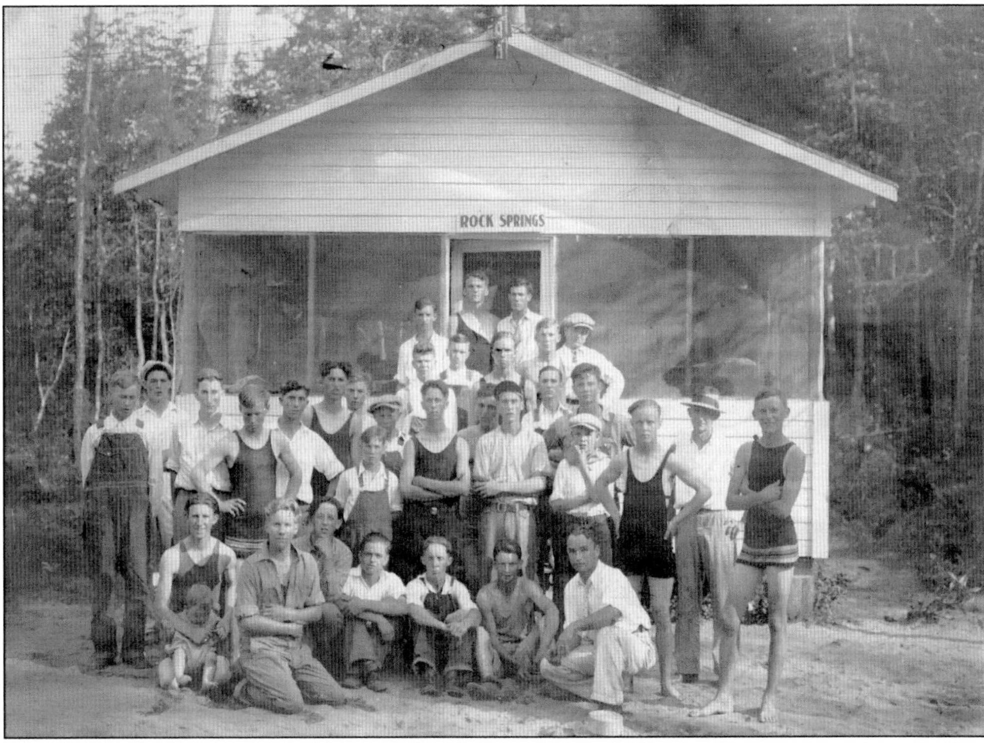

Rock Springs High School's vocational agricultural class, with their teacher, J. Alvin Wilson, attended the Young Tar Heel Farmer's Camp at White Lake in the 1930s. The 30 boys and guests in attendance were Hadley Wilkinson, Yates Wilkinson, Howie Keever, Auston Goodson, Roland Ballard, Lensie Sherrill, Blair Sigmon, Loyd Abernethy, Walter Canipe, Joe Morrison, Junius Morrison, Clyde Dellinger, George Brotherton, Henry Graham, Harold Graham, Wilson Graham, Bennie Graham, Wilburn Kelly, Dan Cherry, James Nixon, Franklin Williamson, Johnnie McIntosh, Ernest Nixon, Grady Jones, Paul Henkle, Claude Henkle, Joe Nixon, Yates Rogers, James Hager, Wilbur Sherrill, Sidney Henkle, and Yates Edwards. (Courtesy of Nancy Long.)

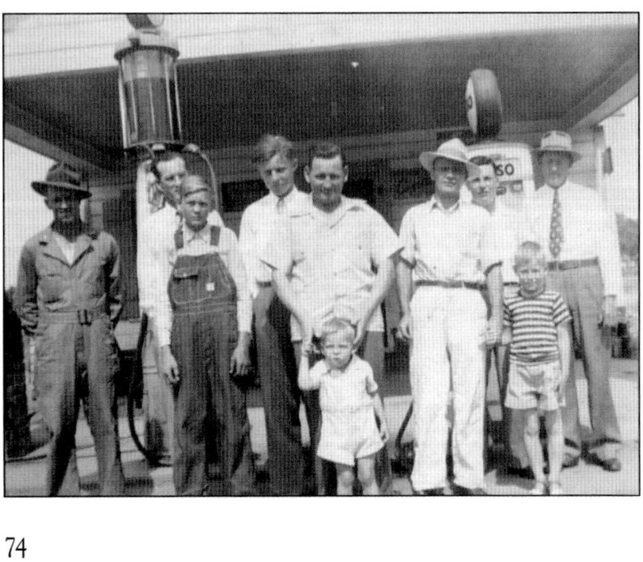

The home and store of Russell Cherry were at the intersection of present-day Highway 16 and Triangle Circle. Stores such as his were the gathering place for men to socialize and take a break from their daily tasks in the fields. In this photograph, Graham Long (far left, 1906–1983), Frank Cherry (center, 1911–1997), and Charles Black (beside Cherry, 1909–1979), stand among a group of men in Triangle around 1940. (Courtesy of Mary Abernathy.)

Three

"Inseparable Parts of the Same River" Historic Places of Eastern Lincoln County

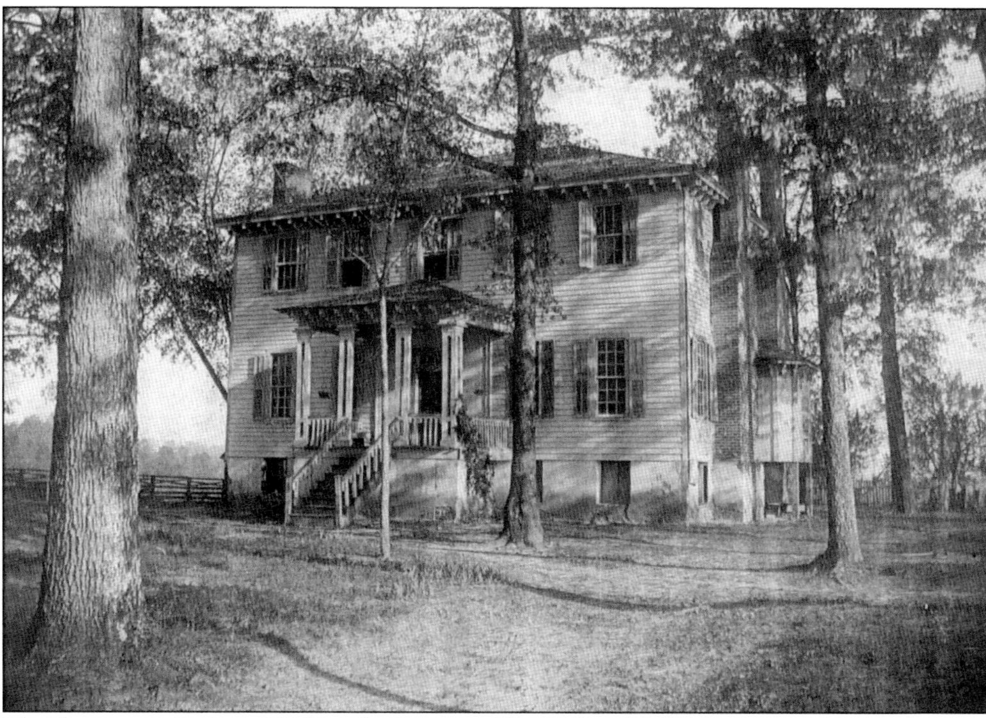

This house was built in 1840 by the Reverend Dr. Robert Hall Morrison and his wife, Mary, on land that they acquired from her father, Gen. Joseph Graham. The imposing three-story, 12-room plantation house was modestly named Cottage Home. The weddings of six daughters took place here: Isabella to Lt. Gen. Daniel Harvey Hill, Harriett to James Patton Irwin, Eugenia to Brig. Gen. Rufus Barringer, Mary Anna to Lt. Gen. Thomas "Stonewall" Jackson, Susan to Maj. Alphonso Calhoun Avery, and Laura to Maj. John Edmunds Brown. This stately Lincoln County landmark burned in 1908, and in 1912, Joseph Graham Morrison replaced it with a brick residence. In 1989, the brick residence was razed to become part of the site of Duke Power Company's Lincoln Combustion Turbine, on the Old Plank Road near Lowesville. (Courtesy of the Stonewall Jackson Foundation, Lexington, Virginia.)

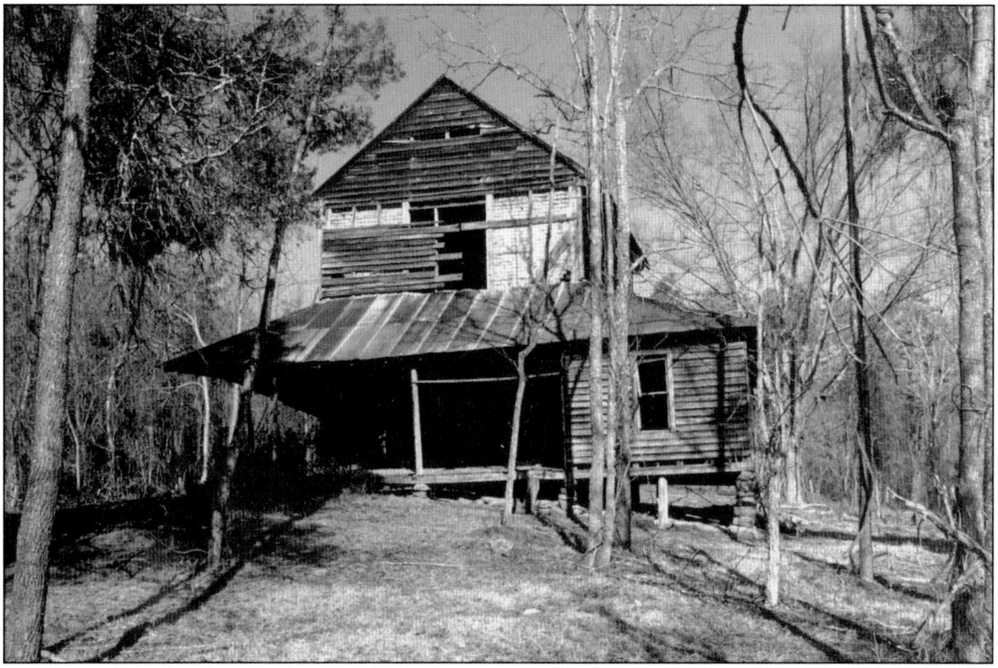

The Catawba Springs Hotel was located in eastern Lincoln County on what is today Kidville Road near Verdict Ridge. The hotel was situated strategically on the old stagecoach line between Salisbury and Asheville and began its operations during the 1790s, with Capt. John Reid (1766–1821) as its earliest documented proprietor. Reid was a veteran of the American Revolution, a state legislator, and an elder at Unity Presbyterian Church in Triangle. Upon the death of Captain Reid, the 600-acre property including "two two-story framed houses, well fitted up for the accommodation of single gentlemen, and a sufficient number of cabins" was sold. One of the frame houses is shown here and is one of the only remaining buildings in Lincoln County with brick nogging. (Courtesy of LCHA.)

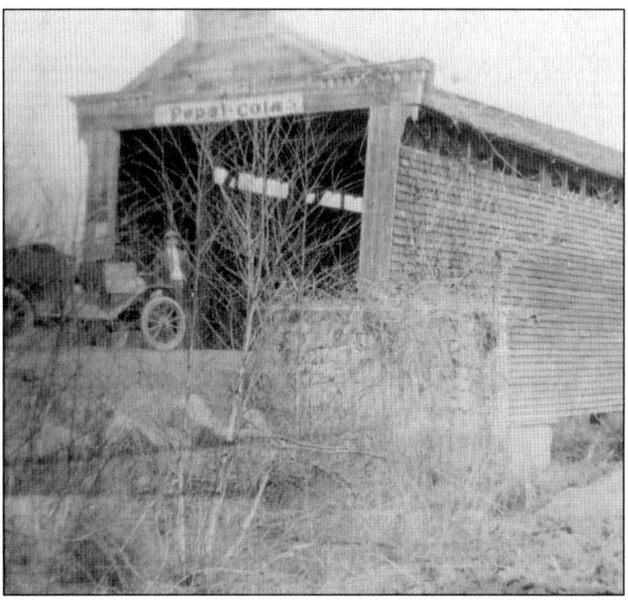

Both Pepsi-Cola and Coca-Cola, as well as dentil modillions, welcome an unidentified man and his car to Hunter's Bridge. The bridge, possibly named for Cyrus Lee Hunter or the Hunter family, spanned Killian's Creek on the plank road from Lincolnton to Charlotte. Built before the Civil War, it was one of only a few bridges to survive the swollen rivers and creeks of the great flood of 1916. Covered bridges offered travelers a safe haven from the elements when very little safety was available. This bridge was in use until the one-lane road became obsolete. (Courtesy of LCHA.)

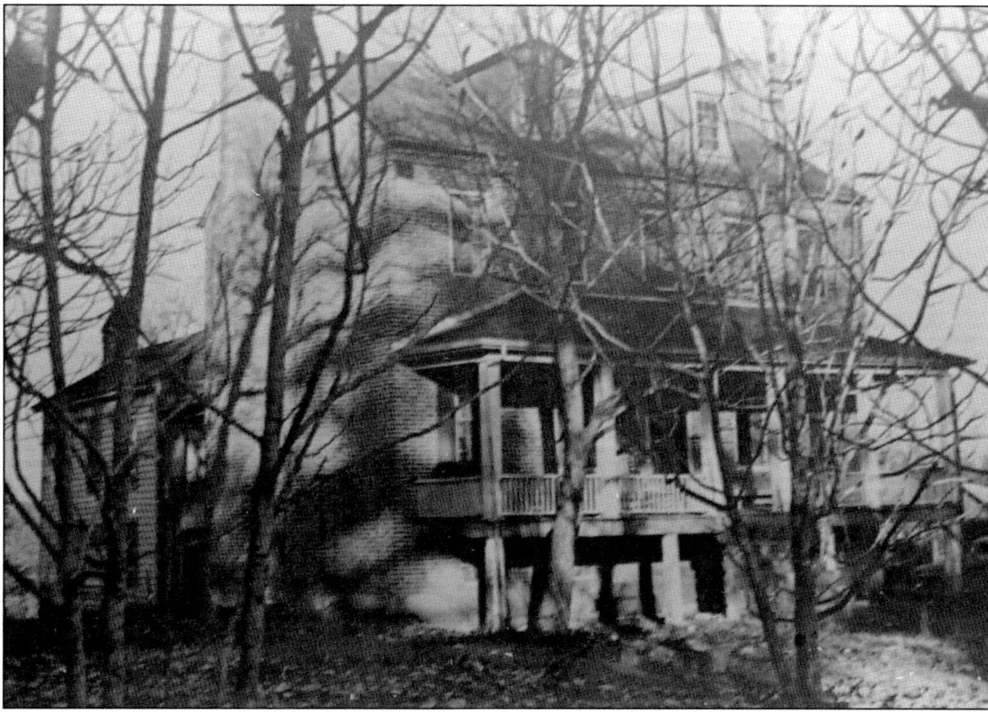

As one of a few brick houses in Lincoln County from the early 19th century, Magnolia Grove exhibits a traditional three-room Quaker plan with Federal-style interior and exterior architectural details. Only later was a partition added to create a center hallway, which the house still retains. Aptly named for the grove of magnolia trees that surround the estate, the house was built in 1824 for David (1787–1874) and Elizabeth Arends Smith, the daughter of the late-18th-century clergyman Rev. Johann G. Arends, along the former Tuckaseegee Road between Charlotte and Lincolnton. Visible below under the large tree in the front yard is a rectangular stepping stone that visitors would use to step out of their carriages when they arrived at the estate. (Both, courtesy of LCHA.)

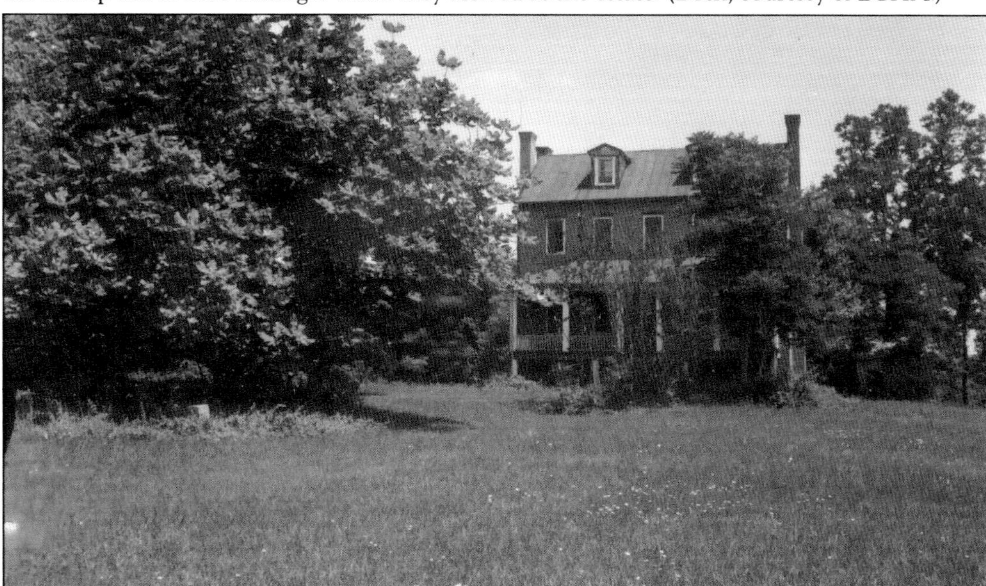

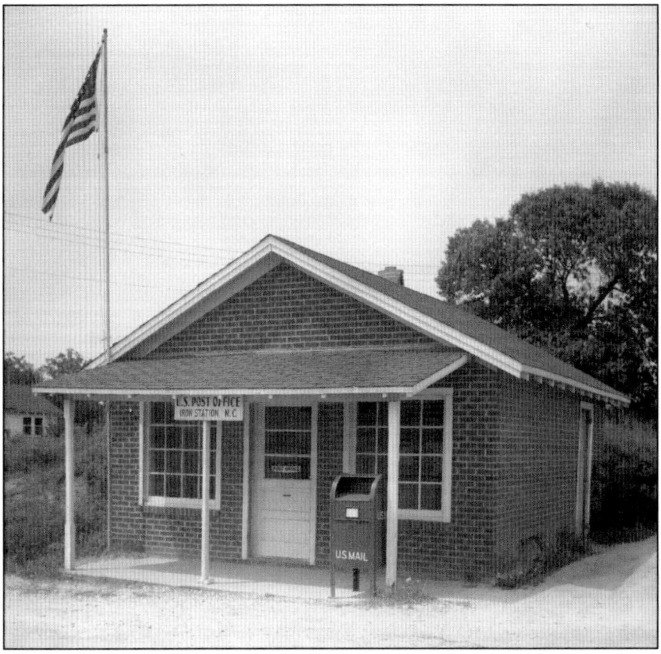

An American flag flies high during the 1940s at the Iron Station Post Office. Located in southeast Lincoln County, Iron Station was settled around 1789 and was incorporated in 1909. The first post office in Iron Station was established on December 17, 1867, with William Miller as the postmaster. The area is named for the iron mines and forges that operated within a 10-mile radius around the area from the time that the iron industry started during the 1790s until the industry's demise during the 1880s. (Courtesy of the North Carolina Office of Archives and History.)

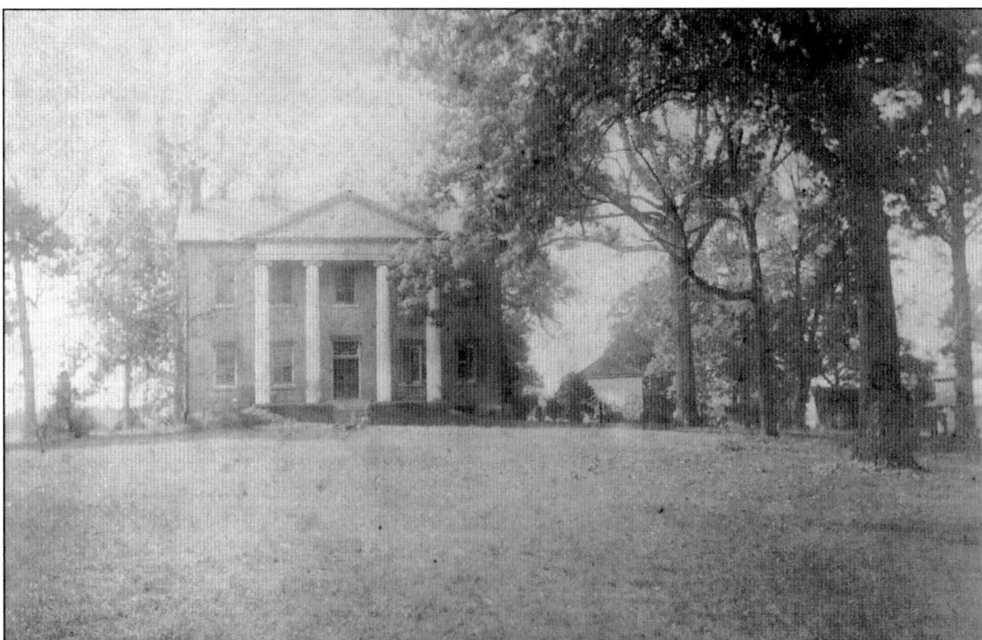

This beautiful and elegant Federal-era residence stands as a testament to a time of grandeur and mystique that once existed in Lincoln County. The home was built for Daniel M. Forney about 1817, after Forney's marriage to Harriet Brevard, on the land of his father, Gen. Peter Forney. Ingleside was the name given to the house during the time that the Hall family owned it around the 1890s. It is the earliest example of a central hall plan in the county. Attributed architecturally to Benjamin Latrobe, the designer of the US Capitol in Washington, DC, the house's pedimented portico and 30-foot-tall Ionic columns convey an overwhelming brilliance. Ingleside is listed in the National Register of Historic Places and is a local historic landmark. (Courtesy of LCHA.)

An unidentified elder and two small children, possibly from the Reel family, enjoy quality time in the stately and monumental drawing room of Ingleside. The fluted colonnettes, rope molding, and elliptical sunbursts of the Federal-style mantel are hints to the grandeur of this room's detailing. Rooms throughout the house have fully ornamented Federal-style motifs. (Courtesy of Amy Reel Hallman.)

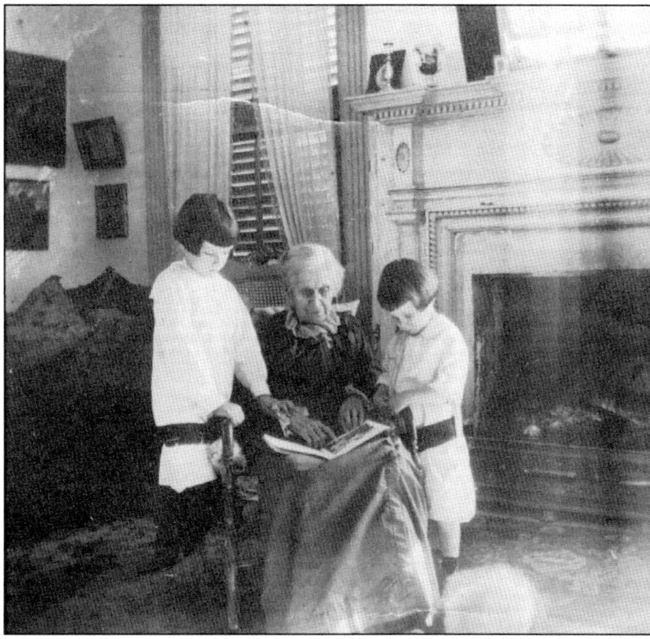

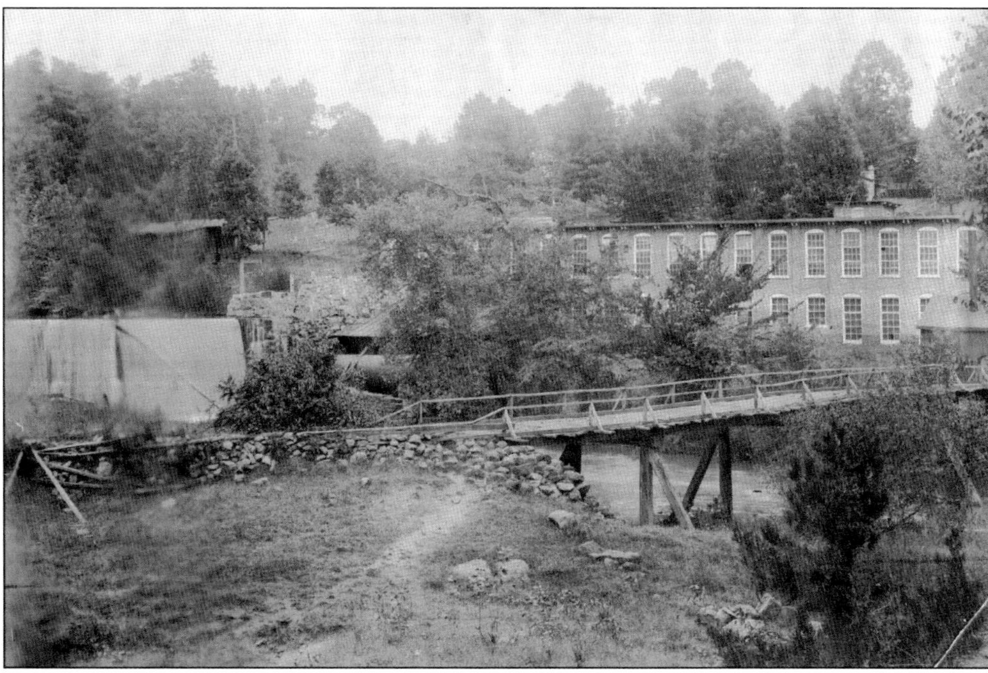

An article published in the *Lincoln Courier* on February 22, 1889, stated that "a new cotton mill will at once be built at the Johnson homestead, Leeper's Creek, Lincoln County, by Messrs. Reinhardt and Morrison . . . Dimensions 160 x 48 ft., spindles 2000, water power." Capt. Joseph Graham Morrison began production at the Mariposa mill in 1902 and gave it its name after a visit to Mariposa, California. The Mariposa Cotton Mills were incorporated on September 19, 1911, and Morrison secured the machinery for Mariposa Mill from the Mountain Island Mill in Gaston County, North Carolina. The Mariposa Mill was later known as Lloyd Cotton Mills and Alba Twine Mills. (Courtesy of the Russell and Dot Cornwell family.)

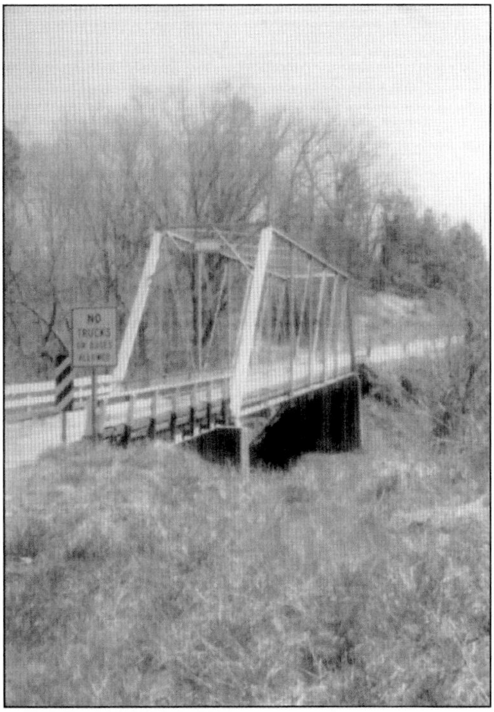

The Mariposa Road Bridge, located on old Mariposa Road in southeastern Lincoln County, is a well-preserved and representative example of early-20th-century bridge construction using the Pratt through truss form. Spanning Leepers Creek near the Lincoln-Gaston County border, the bridge served the Mariposa Mill and mill village from 1912 until vehicular traffic was suspended in 1979. The Mariposa Road Bridge was built of rolled steel with riveted connections, A-frame portals of angles and back-to-back angles, concrete abutments, and rolled floor beams that stand suspended by U-shaped hangers from lower chord pins. (Courtesy of LCHA.)

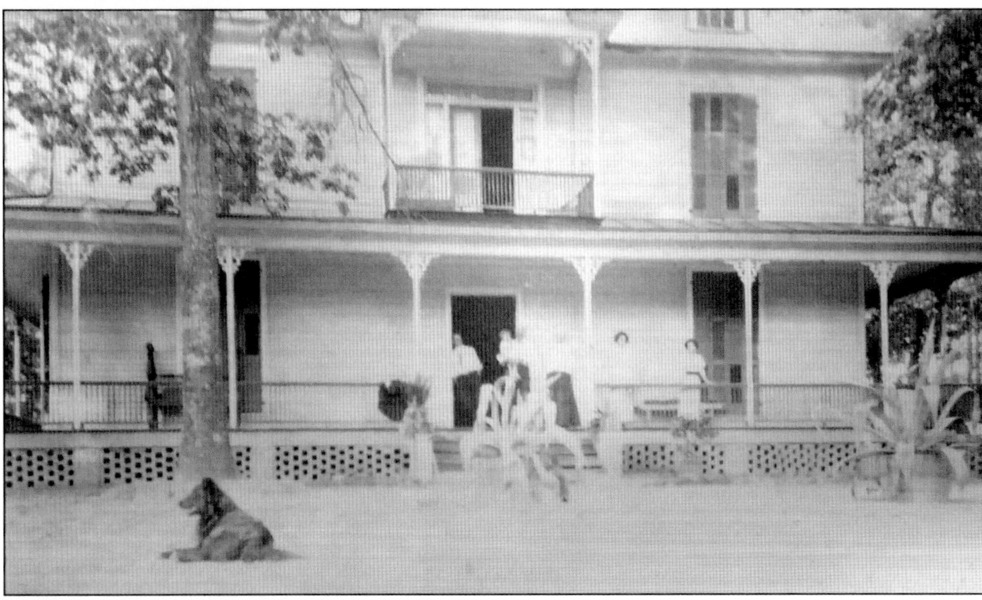

The beauty, spaciousness, and picturesque setting of the J.E. Reinhardt house and property on Reinhardt Circle in Iron Station allow for lounging by both the family and their canine companion. Thomas A. Edison stayed at this house in 1906 and spent time with J.E. Reinhardt while searching the Piedmont of North Carolina for deposits of minerals containing cobalt to use as the filament for his electric light bulb. Reinhardt was an amateur geologist, and his family had operated the Rehoboth/Reinhardt furnace, located less than a mile from the family's house, from the 1850s through the 1880s. Additionally, Reinhardt knew the locations of other iron ore deposits in Lincoln County. The Reinhardt house burned in 2014. (Courtesy of Fran Goins.)

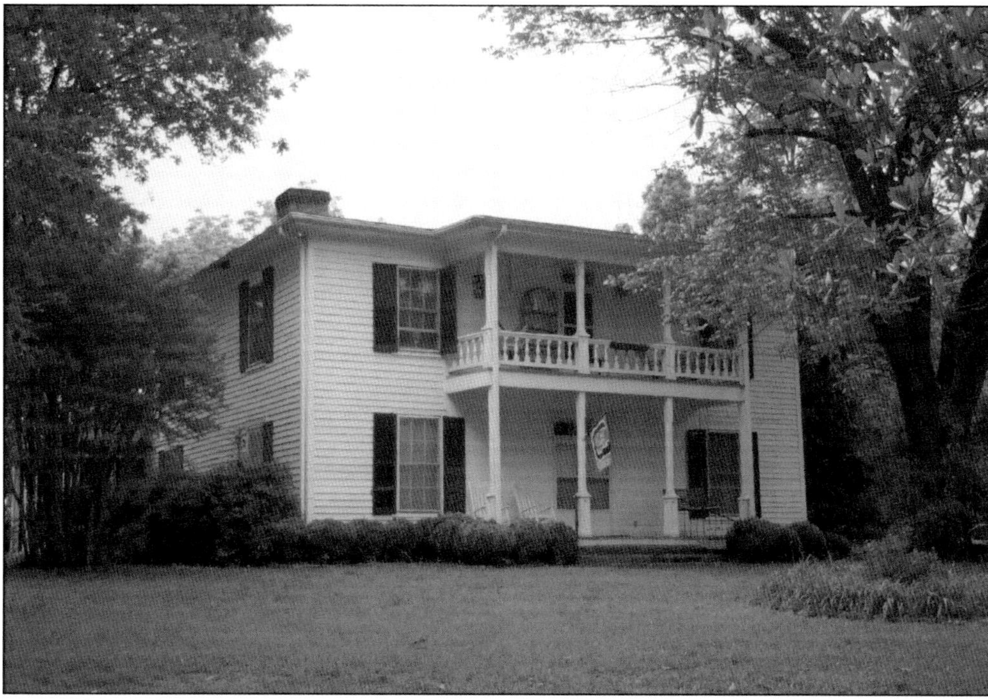

Situated near the intersection of Old Plank Road and Mariposa Road in eastern Lincoln County, the Reinhardt house, or Mount Welcome, occupies historic grounds that harken back to both the iron and agricultural heritage of Lincoln County's past. Built between August and December 1885, this two-story double-pile frame house replaced the Bartlett Shipp house, which was badly deteriorated when John Franklin Reinhardt bought the property in 1876. Reinhardt did retain a small one-story block of the Shipp house that is now the ell of the present house. Under Reinhardt's management, this farm had many agricultural outbuildings that are no longer standing. The house is listed in the National Register of Historic Places. (Courtesy of Matt Boles.)

Built in 1811, the Burton Plantation sits atop a bluff in an area now part of Lake Norman known as Governor's Island. Robert Burton, attorney and cousin of Gov. Hutchins Burton (1824–1827), owned the plantation. During the 1850s, Col. John H. Wheeler, author of *Wheeler's History of North Carolina*, lived at the plantation. (Courtesy of the Library of Congress.)

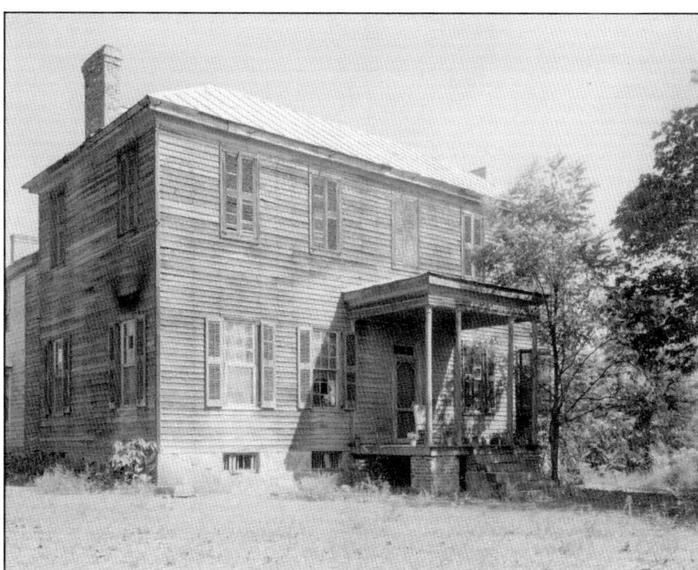

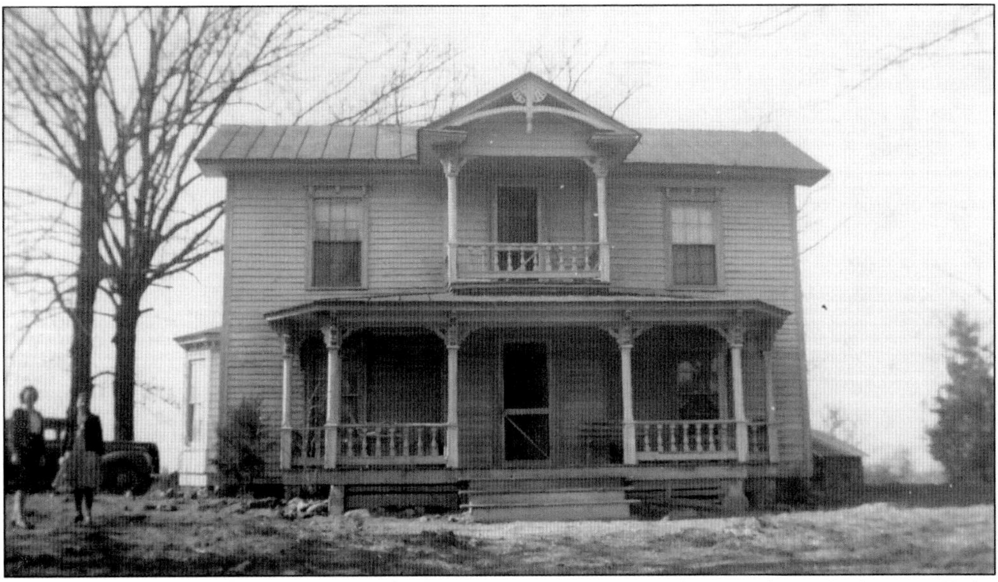

Bernice Luckey Nixon and Velma Rea Duckworth Nixon, daughters-in-law of Clarence Eulie Nixon, barely get themselves in this rare photograph from the 1940s of a stately Victorian house. Bernice married Eulie's son, Otis Nixon, and Velma married another of Eulie's sons, Grover Nixon. This house was located on what was known at the time as the River Road, today's Hager's Ferry Road. (Courtesy of Bernice Luckey Nixon.)

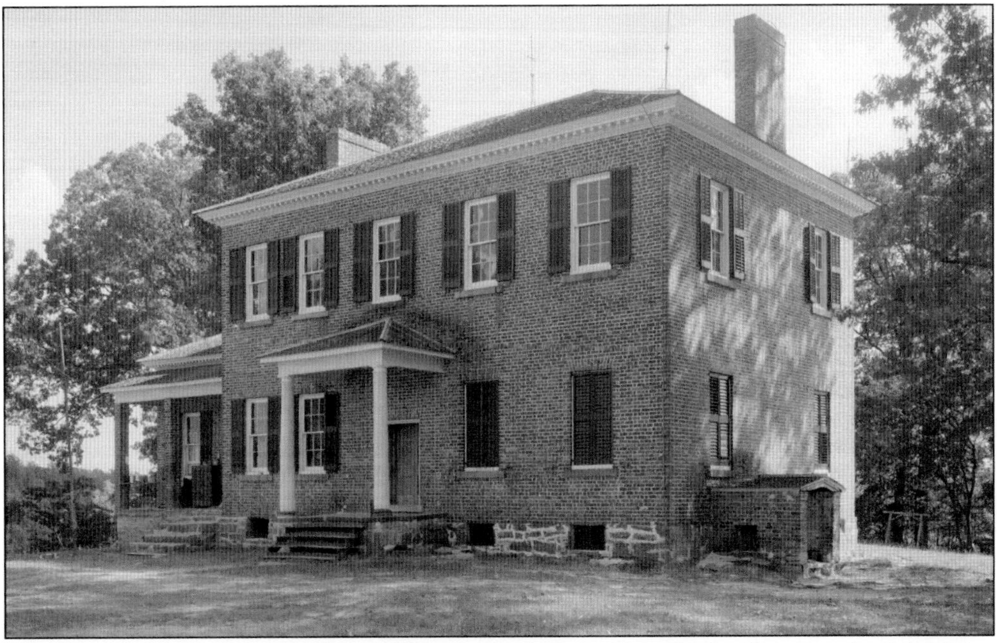

This stately, two-story Flemish bond brick Greek Revival–style dwelling was built by John Davidson Graham on the banks of the Catawba River in eastern Lincoln County during the 1820s. According to family tradition, Graham started construction on the house in 1822 but did not finish until 1827. The house had eight rooms, and the walls were two feet thick with very deep windows. The house was known locally as both Elmwood and Riverview. (Courtesy of the Library of Congress.)

John D. Graham built this two-room brick office on his property to be used as living quarters for the family while he built his home, Elmwood. John D. was a son of Joseph Graham, Revolutionary War general and iron manufacturer, and his family helped start the iron industry in eastern Lincoln County. The house and office were the site of many social gatherings during the 19th and 20th centuries. (Courtesy of the Library of Congress.)

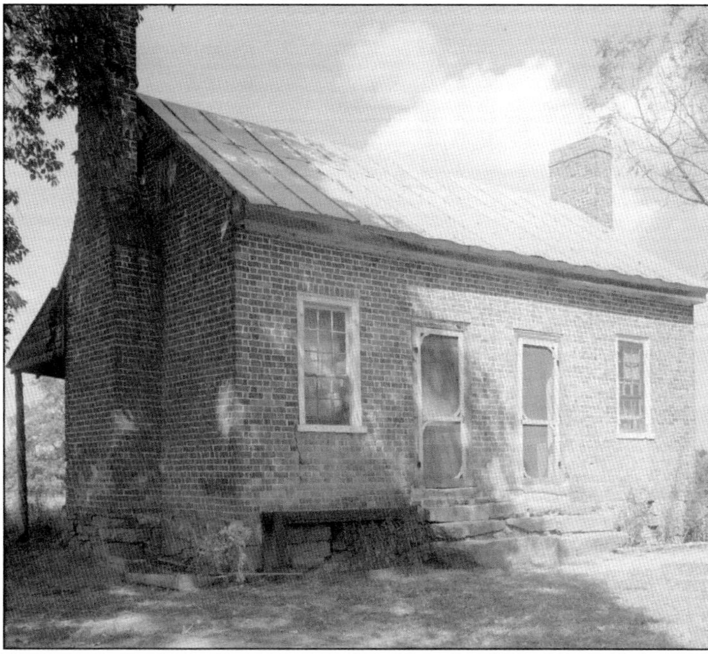

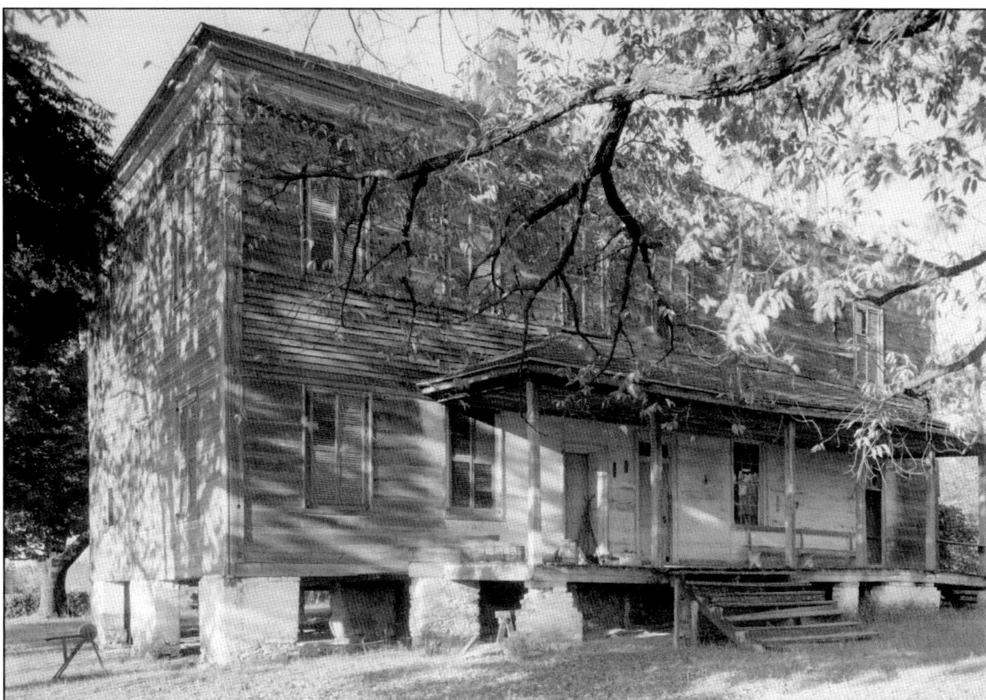

Once a stately plantation home of the Brevard family, Mount Tirzah stood the test of time until it fell victim to a fire during the 1950s. The house was named after the Mount Tirzah forge, built by John Davidson, Alexander Brevard, and Joseph Graham in 1795 on Leeper's Creek as part of their iron works operations at Vesuvius furnace. The forge and house remained in the Brevard family for nearly 100 years, and Brevard Place Road in Iron Station is named for this family. (Courtesy of the Library of Congress.)

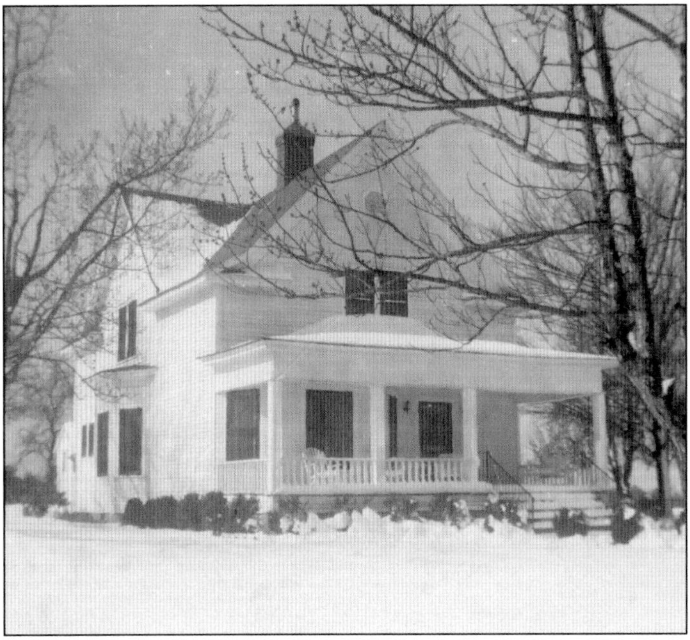

Known locally as the Beatty House, this house was built by E. Johnston "E.J." Nixon (1877–1950), the son of James and Mary Proctor Nixon, after he purchased the property on Highway 16 from J.E. and Lelia Bolick in 1911. E.J. and Katie Boovy Nixon (1884–1974) sold the house and property to Blanche B. Rhodes in 1945, and it was sold to Warlick Funeral Home in 1983. (Courtesy of Dorothy Beatty Maiers.)

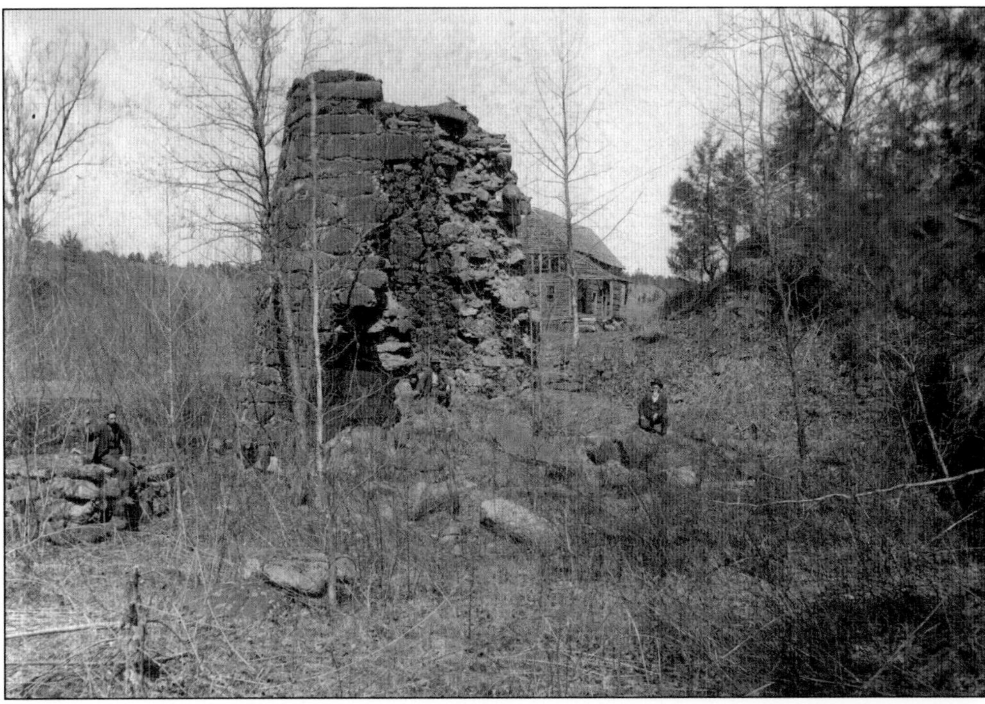

The historic remains of Vesuvius furnace provide a reminder of Lincoln County's first industry in this photograph from the late 19th century. Peter Forney, Alexander Brevard, Gen. Joseph Graham, and John Davidson formed a partnership around 1790 to establish Vesuvius furnace in what is today known as Iron Station. The partners were motivated to build the furnace by an act of North Carolina General Assembly in 1788 that directed the granting of large amounts of free land to persons who successfully established iron works and produced bar and pig iron. (Courtesy of the Robinson-Spangler Carolina Room, Charlotte-Mecklenburg Library.)

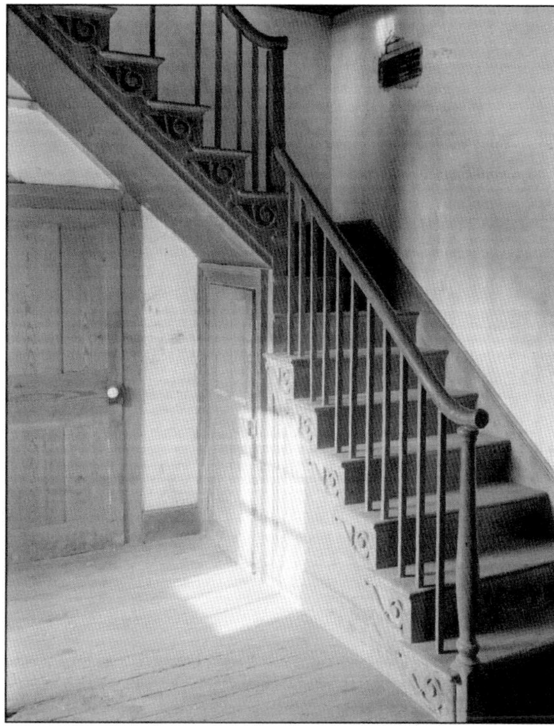

Natural light shines through the window at Vesuvius to show the wooden doors, tulip-bracketed stair ends, and plaster walls of the earliest part of the house, built in 1792 by Gen. Joseph Graham. Graham built additions to the west of the original house in 1810 and 1820. From the Graham family, the house passed to a variety of owners, such as Graham's nephew Ephraim A. Brevard and James Madison Smith. In 1945, B.C. Lineberger acquired the house and added the two-story portico that can still be seen today. The house is listed in the National Register of Historic Places. (Courtesy of the Library of Congress.)

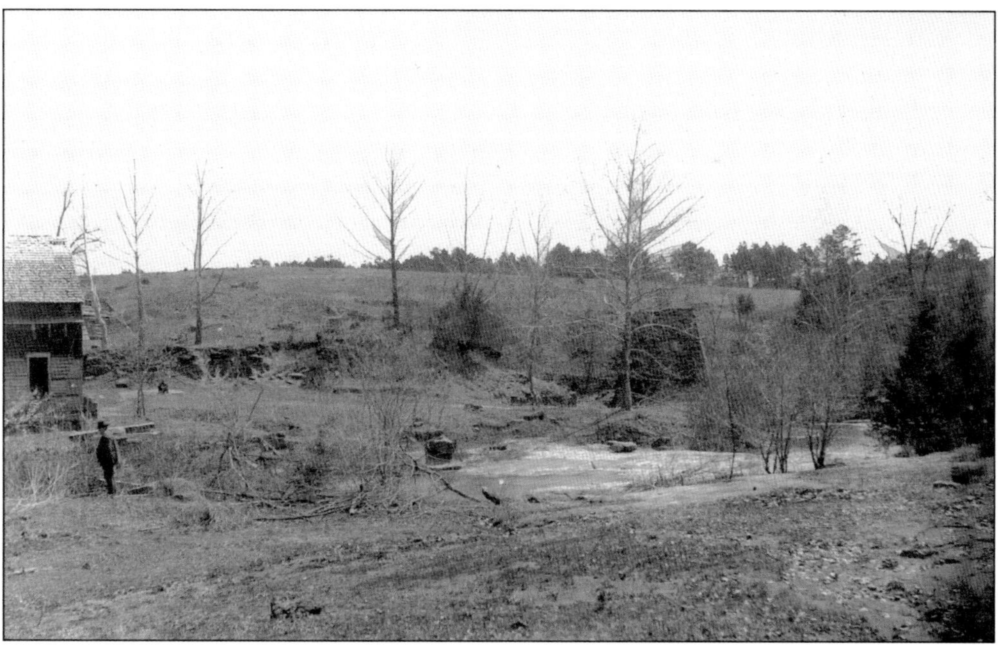

In a rare photograph of the property at Vesuvius, a man at the bottom left near an abandoned building peers into the creek that ran by the iron furnace, seen on the right. Unlike the lush landscape that visitors enjoy today at Vesuvius Vineyards, at the time of this photograph, nearly all of the trees on the property were gone. During the nearly 100 years that owners of the property operated the furnace, the timber provided charcoal, one of the essential products needed to fuel the furnace. (Courtesy of the Robinson-Spangler Carolina Room, Charlotte-Mecklenburg Library.)

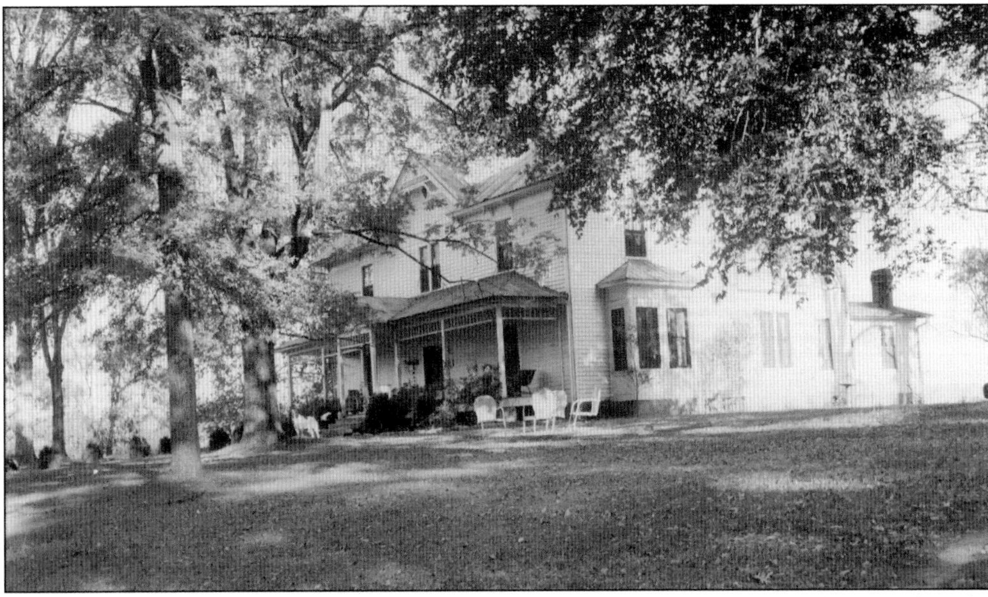

Maj. William A. Graham Jr. built this two-story frame late Victorian house on the site where his grandfather, Gen. Joseph Graham, had built a house in 1834 after retiring from the iron industry and moving from Vesuvius. General Graham's house burned in July 1894, and the *Charlotte Observer* reported on September 22, 1895, that William A. Graham Jr. "has just about completed a splendid residence" known locally as Forest Home. Graham used local materials in the construction, and the house's ceiling originally used 14 kinds of wood. Major Graham left the house, barns, and outbuildings to his son William A. Graham III in 1923, and in 1943, his grandson Joseph sold the property to David Clark. The property is listed in the National Register of Historic Places. (Courtesy of Lincoln Soil and Water Conservation District.)

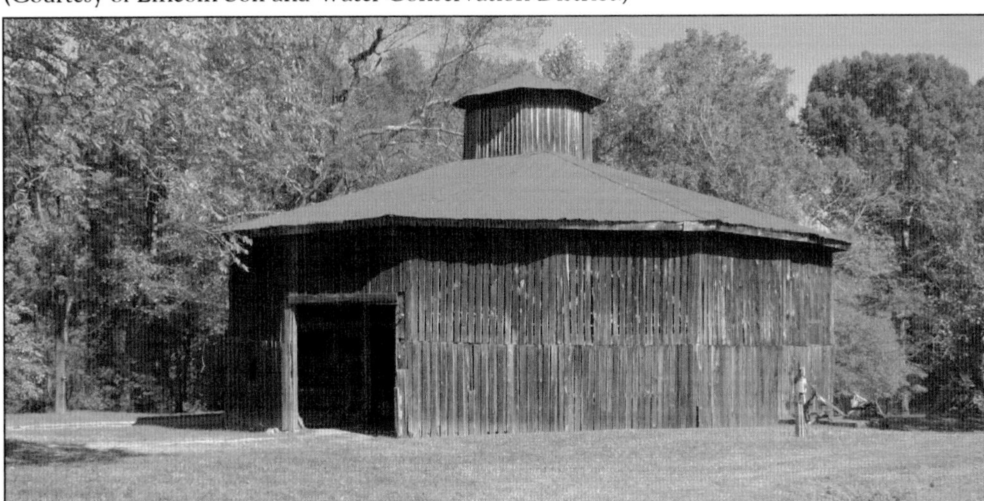

William A. Graham Jr. built this round barn around 1895. The two-story, 16-sided frame barn rests on a low stone foundation with vertical board walls and is an innovative agricultural design. The building has an eight-sided blind cupola from which a low, polygonal roof extends. The Graham Round Barn was listed with the William A. Graham Jr. house and two outbuildings in the National Register of Historic Places in 1977 and is also a local historic landmark. (Courtesy of the Lincoln Soil and Water Conservation District.)

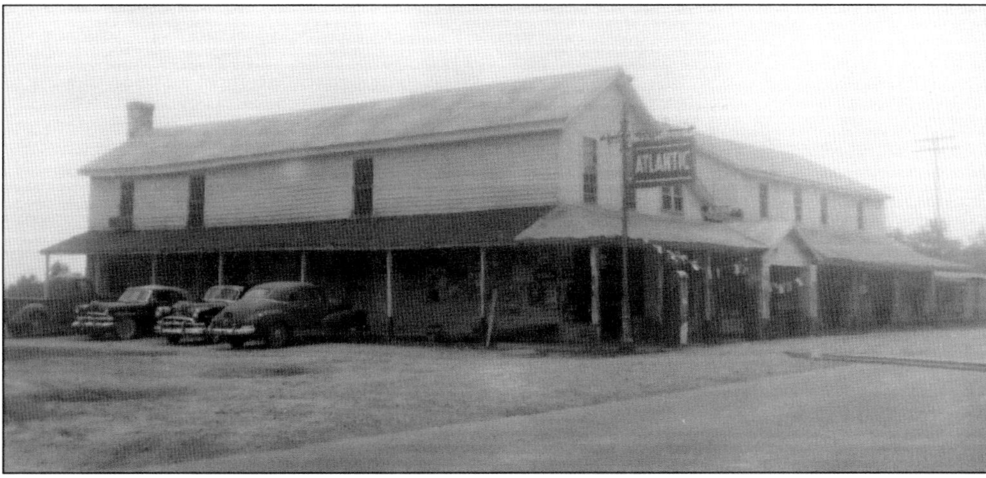

Lowesville in eastern Lincoln County was named for the Lowe family. They built a mercantile store in the 1870s, and it served the community for over 100 years. Caroline Shipp bought Rough on Rats poison at this store in 1891 and used it to kill her son James Shipp, who was nearly one year old at the time of his death. Shipp was convicted of the murder and hanged at the courthouse in nearby Dallas, North Carolina, on December 18, 1891. She was the last woman hanged in North Carolina. (Courtesy of LCHA.)

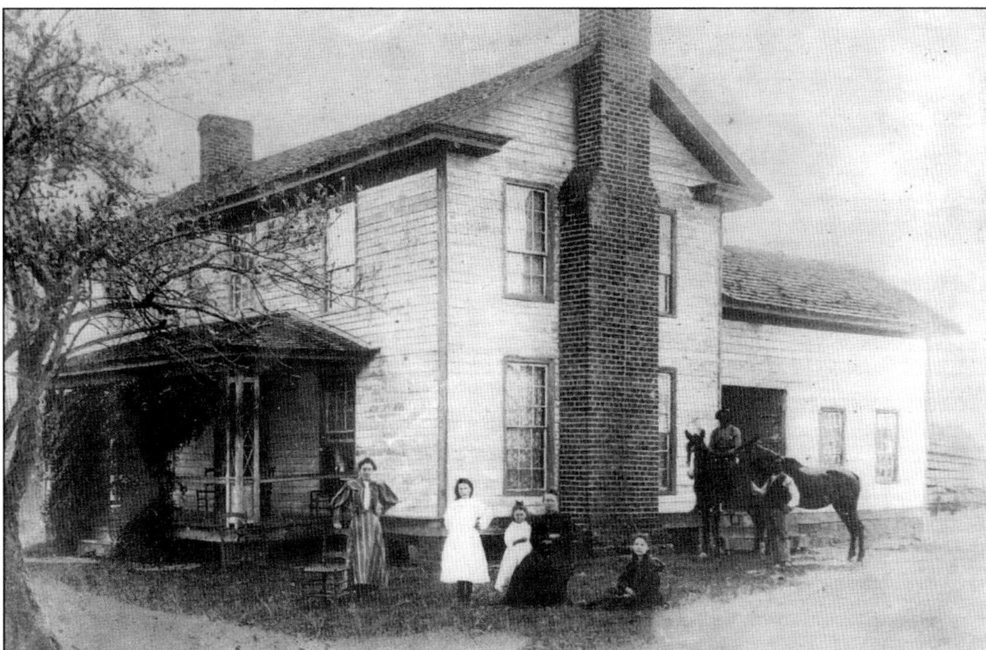

The Mundy House is one of the few remaining historic houses in eastern Lincoln County. This central-hall I-house retains much of its original architectural integrity and dates to the mid-19th century. R.O. and Maggie Allen Mundy and their family of nine children continued ownership of the house until the 1990s, and the Lincoln County Historical Association acquired the house and property in 2014. From left to right are Mattie Brown Mundy, Vera Mundy, Lura Mundy, Frances "Fannie" Killian Mundy, Pearl Mundy, Brucie McCorkle, and Charlie. (Courtesy of Richard Thompson.)

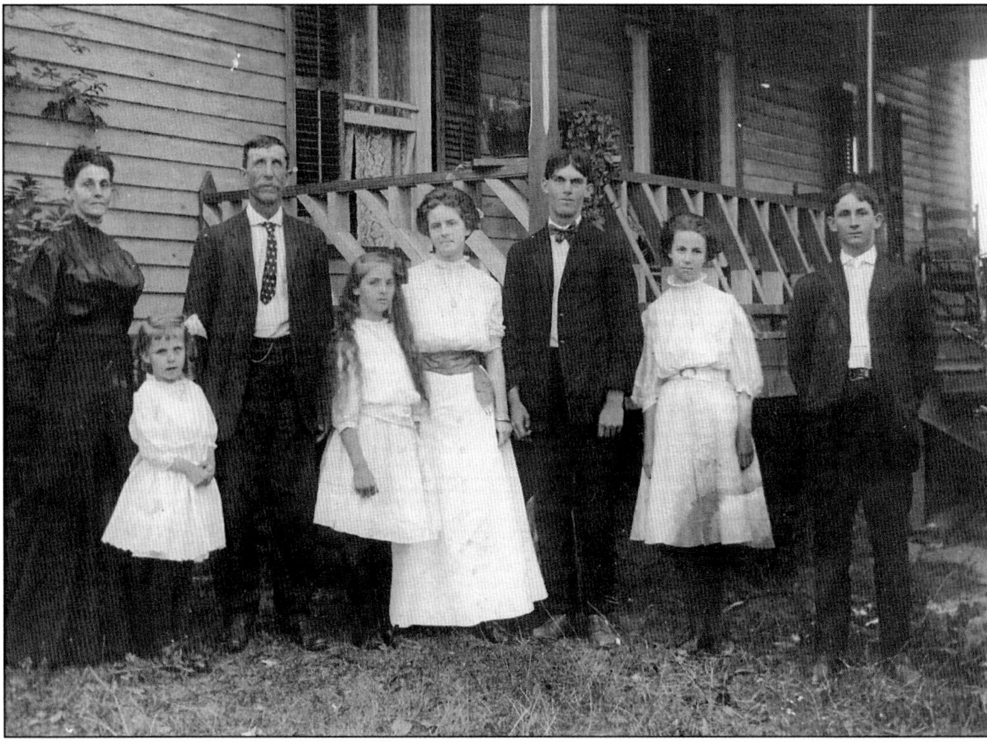

Osburn Wells Mundy (1856–1940) and his family stand outside their house on Beth Haven Church Road in Denver for this c. 1909 photograph. From left to right are Frances Emma King Mundy (1860–1942), Allie Granada Mundy (1904–1985), Osburn Wells Mundy (1856–1940), Violet Elise Mundy (1899–1984), Bertie Lee Mundy (1892–1926), Buford King Mundy (1889–1950), Bettie Graham Mundy (1886–1982), and Sebe Williams Mundy (1894–1978). This house was torn down around 1963, when Victor and Allie Mundy Rhyne built a new house on the site. (Courtesy of Vicki Kopf.)

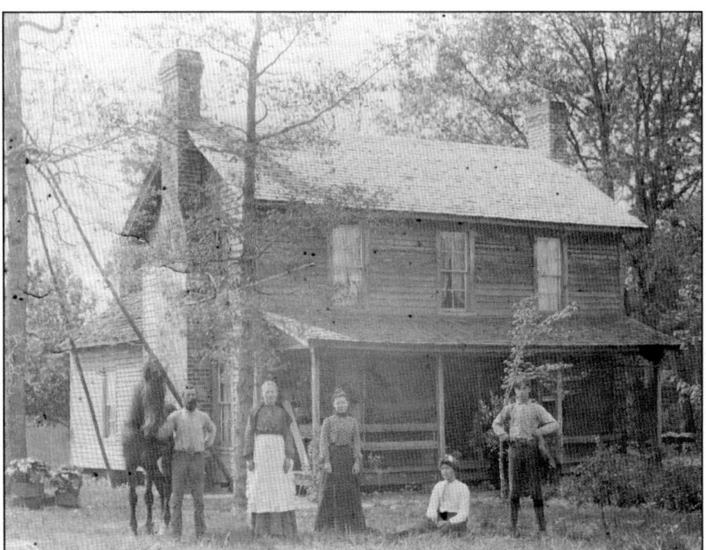

The farming family of Warren Mundy takes a break from their daily activities for this c. 1890s photograph on Campground Road in Denver, near Bethel United Methodist Church. Warren Mundy was born on April 10, 1847, the son of W.W. and Lucinda Shelton Mundy, and died on December 23, 1917, at the age of 73. He is buried at Bethel United Methodist Church in Denver. (Courtesy of Judge Theodore Royster.)

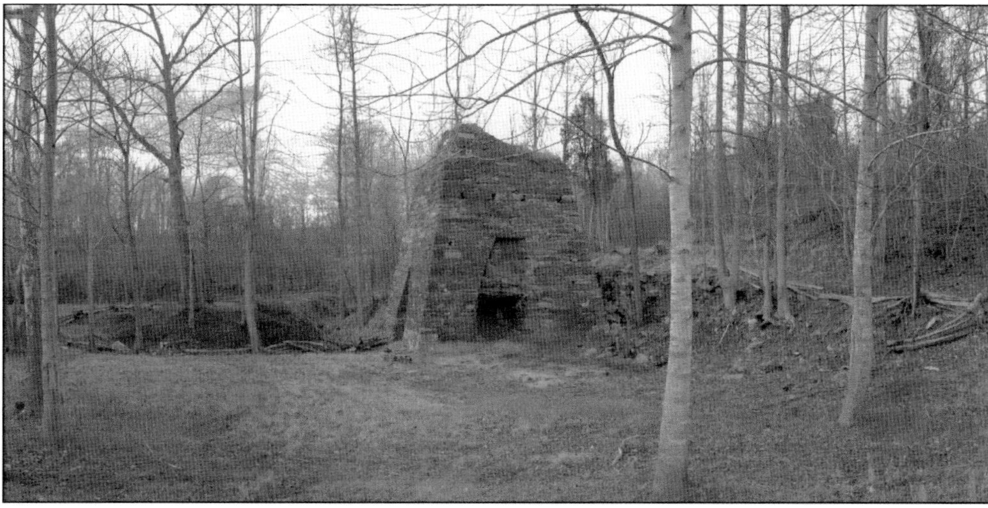

The Madison-Derr iron furnace in Pumpkin Center stands as a monumental stone structure from the 19th century that produced cast iron farming implements, fire backs, cannonballs, and bar iron. Built around 1809 by local iron magnate Peter Forney, this cold-blast stack inhaled iron ore, lime, and charcoal during the iron industry's heyday in Lincoln County from the 1780s to the 1880s. Jonas W. Derr acquired the business and property in the 1860s and operated it until cold-blast iron production in the South became obsolete. The stack and property are currently owned by the Lincoln County Historic Properties Commission. (Courtesy of Matt Boles.)

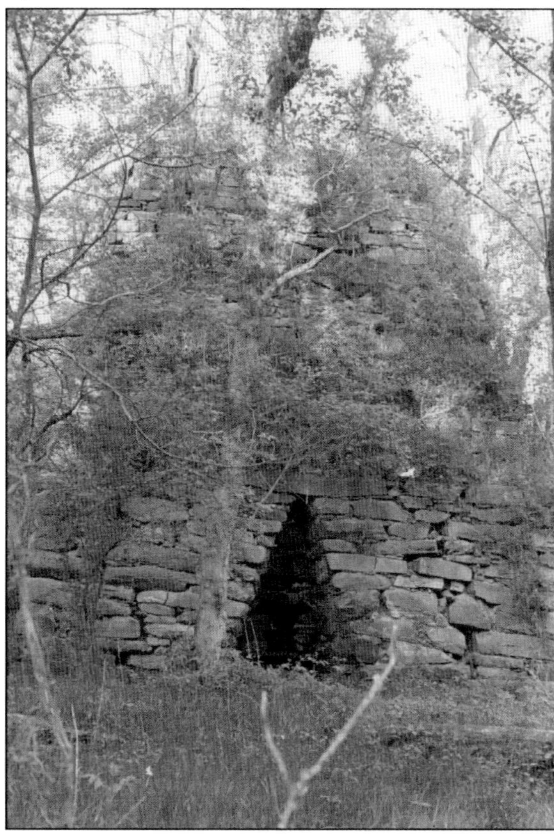

Built of massive cut and stacked granite blocks and rising 30 feet in height, the Rehoboth/Reinhardt furnace rests near Leeper's Creek in Iron Station. Capt. Alexander E. Brevard built this cold-blast furnace in 1814, and at his death in 1829, his son Ephraim continued the business operations. Later, Ephraim sold the furnace operation to Bartlett Shipp and Franklin Reinhardt, who continued the operation as an integral part of this economic engine in eastern Lincoln County until the 1870s. The Lincoln Iron Company rebuilt the furnace stack in 1869 and converted it to a hot-blast furnace. (Courtesy of the North Carolina Office of Archives and History.)

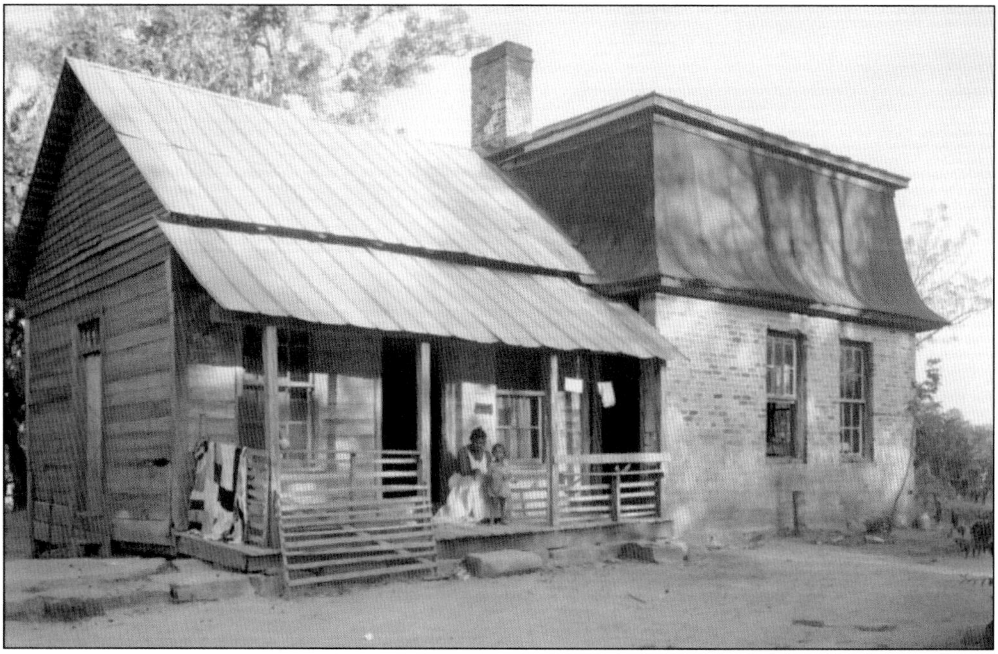

Iron furnaces and forges were built in Lincoln County from the late 18th century through the first two decades of the 19th century, with the exception of the Stonewall furnace, which was built in 1862. Communities formed around these operations included buildings such as the ironmaster's house, workers' dwellings, slave quarters, and a company store. Original ledgers from a few of the furnace operations record products such as tobacco, molasses, coffee, bacon, flour, corn, whiskey, tools, and shoes for sale at the company-operated stores. The ironmaster's house at the Rehoboth/ Reinhardt Furnace (pictured) stood until the 1990s. (Courtesy of the Library of Congress.)

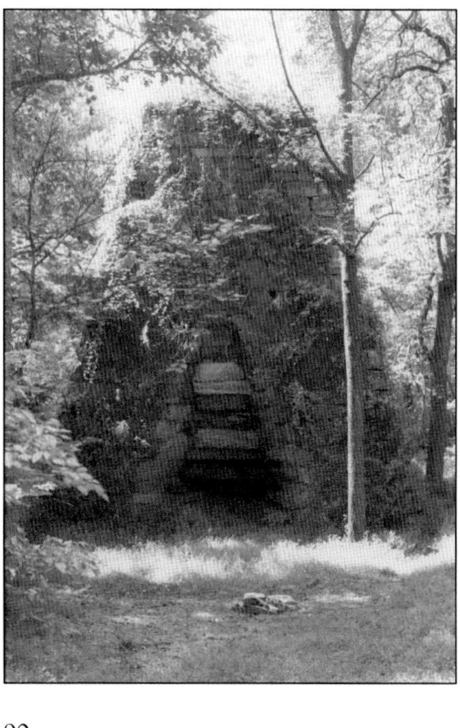

Nearly identical in size and form to the Madison-Derr, Rehoboth/Reinhardt, and Vesuvius furnaces, the Stonewall furnace was the last built in eastern Lincoln County. James Madison Smith built the furnace, named presumably for Thomas J. "Stonewall" Jackson, in 1862 to supply iron for the Southern war effort during the Civil War. The tapered stack stands beside Anderson's Creek in Pumpkin Center, while the remnants of stone dams, foundations of appurtenant buildings, and rock walls are still visible at the site. (Courtesy of the North Carolina Office of Archives and History.)

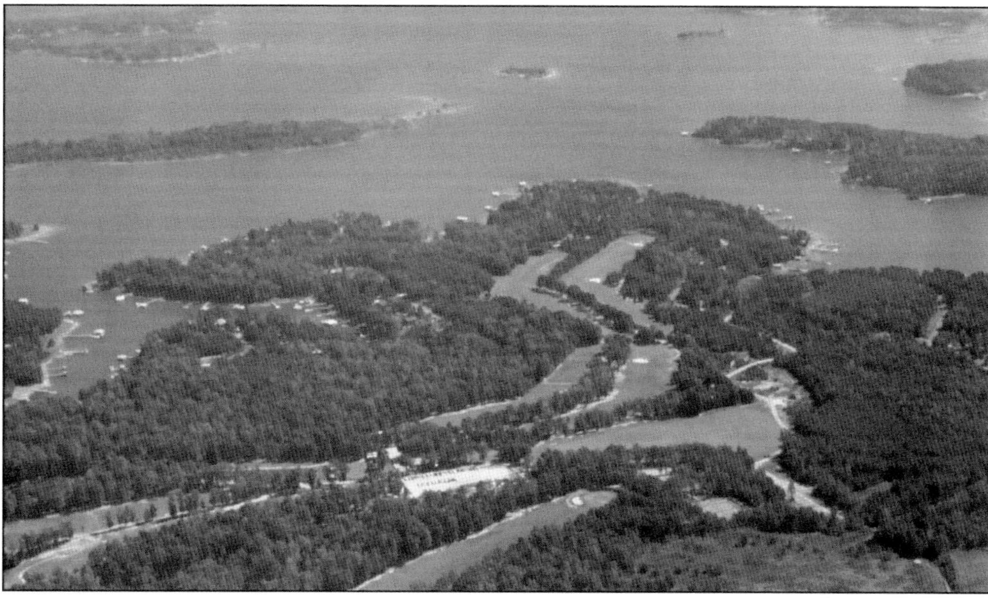

On July 12, 1955, Mary E. Young, a great-granddaughter of Alfred M. Burton, sold 843.9 acres west of the Catawba River to D.L. and Louise Phillips, a real estate developer from Charlotte. In 1965, Westport became the first community on Lake Norman in eastern Lincoln County. The name was selected by Tom P. Phillips, vice president of D.L. Phillips Investment Builders Inc., after being enamored with the town of Westport, Connecticut. (Courtesy of Edgar Smith.)

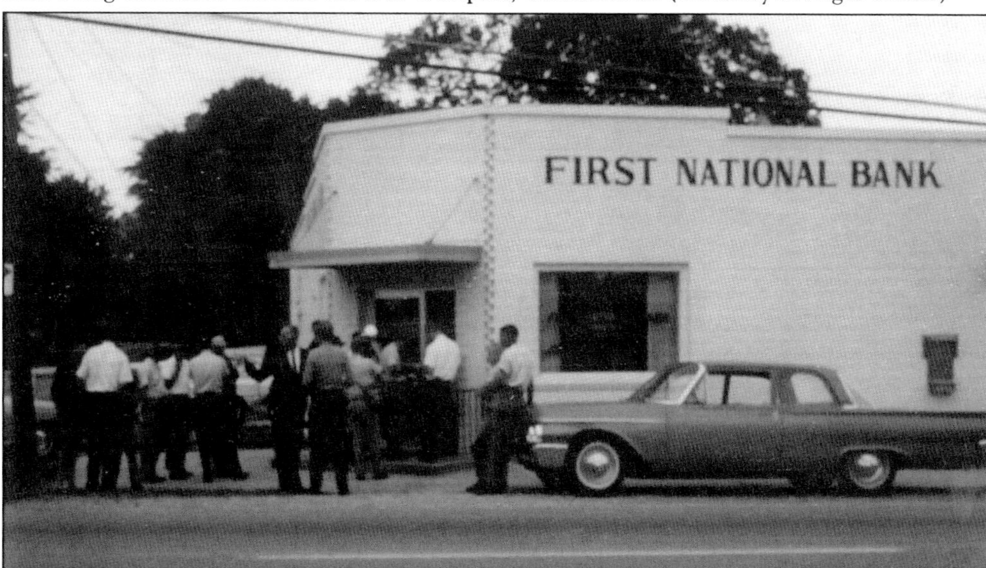

Lily Killian, wife of E.F. Killian, sold the property on which the 800-square-foot bank building was located to North State Insurance Agency, and the First National Bank leased the front one-third of the building. The building was built originally as the Denver Post Office, and Dewey Sherrill, a grocery store operator, leased the back of the building. It was located on what was known as the Denver Square at Highway 16 and Campground Road. The bank was robbed on July 2, 1965, by a young man whom Loy Buff, a salesman from Charlotte, picked up as a hitchhiker at the intersection of Highways 16 and 73. The robber stole $9,121. (Courtesy of Terry Brotherton.)

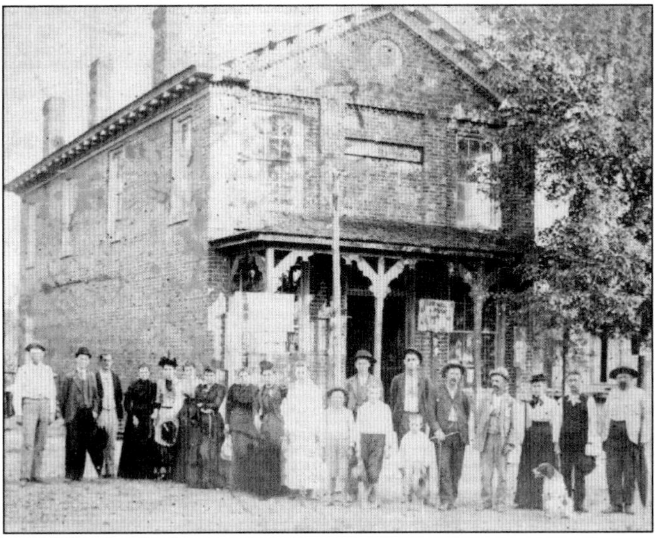

A large group of what could be Proctor family members, members of the Denver community, and store patrons stand in the foreground of Proctor Store in Denver for this 1890s photograph. Three interior brick chimneys with corbeled caps rise from this large two-story, front-gabled brick commercial building that was possibly built by 1893. The *Lincoln Courier* announced on February 24, 1893, that "W.C. Proctor opens a store in Denver to-day." (Courtesy of Terry Brotherton.)

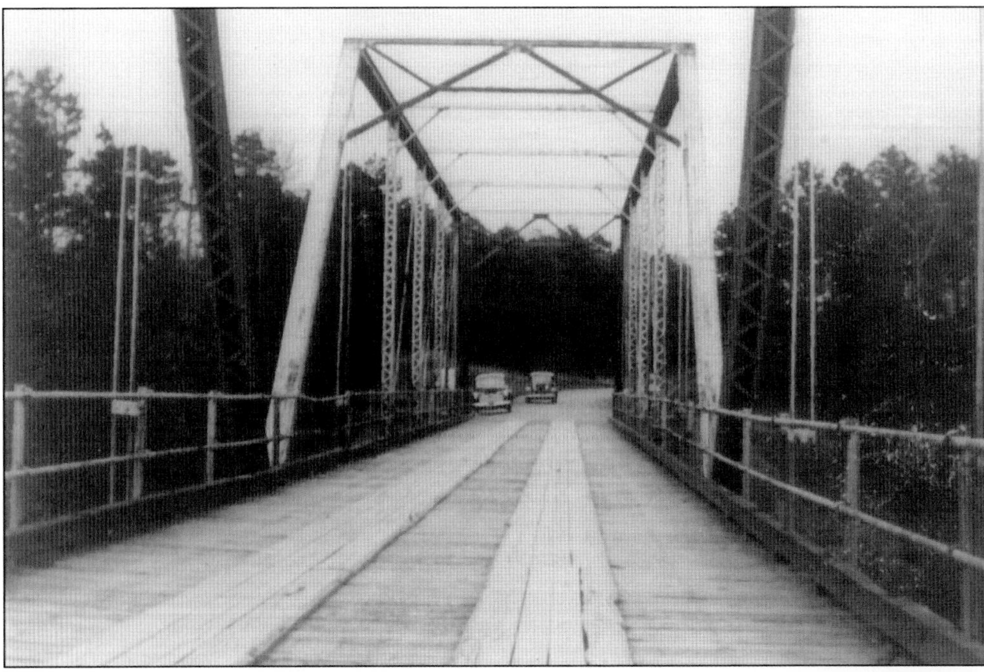

The bridge at Beatties Ford, built after the flood of 1916, was the connection over the Catawba River between eastern Lincoln County and Mooresville, Davidson, Cornelius, Huntersville, and Unity Church Road. It was known as Highway 73. Many eastern Lincoln County residents worked in the mills, shopped in the stores, and worshipped in the churches of their neighbors in Iredell and Mecklenburg Counties. The connection over the river was so close that much of Denver, Triangle, and Lowesville was on the postal service's Davidson Route 1. When the Catawba was dammed to create Lake Norman, the Beatties Ford Bridge was imploded on June 3, 1962. (Courtesy of Mary Abernathy.)

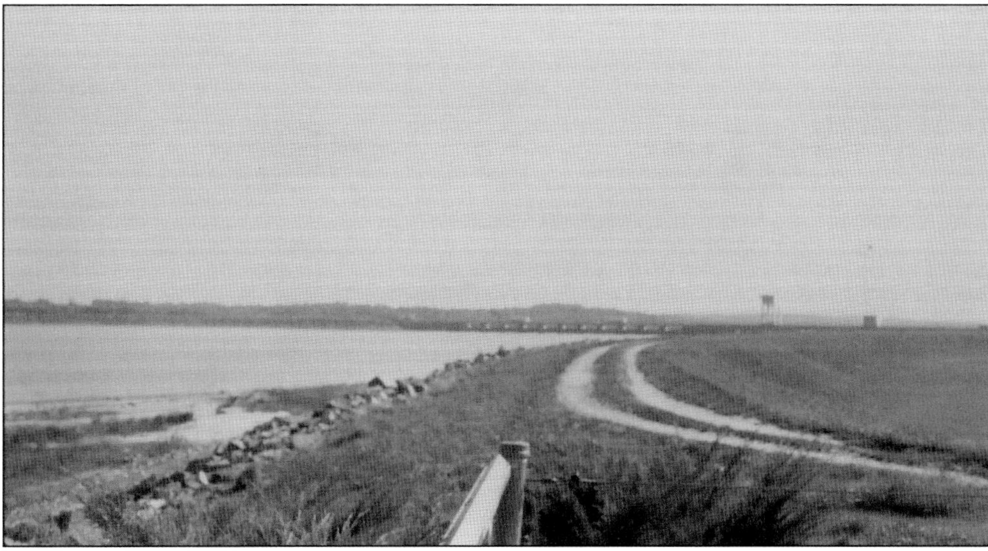

In March 1962, the Duke Power Company completed the Cowan's Ford Dam, and Lake Norman was completely filled by February 1963. Lake Norman, North Carolina's largest man-made body of water, holds 3.4 trillion gallons of water and was created to advance hydroelectric power. (Courtesy of the Lincoln Soil and Water Conservation District.)

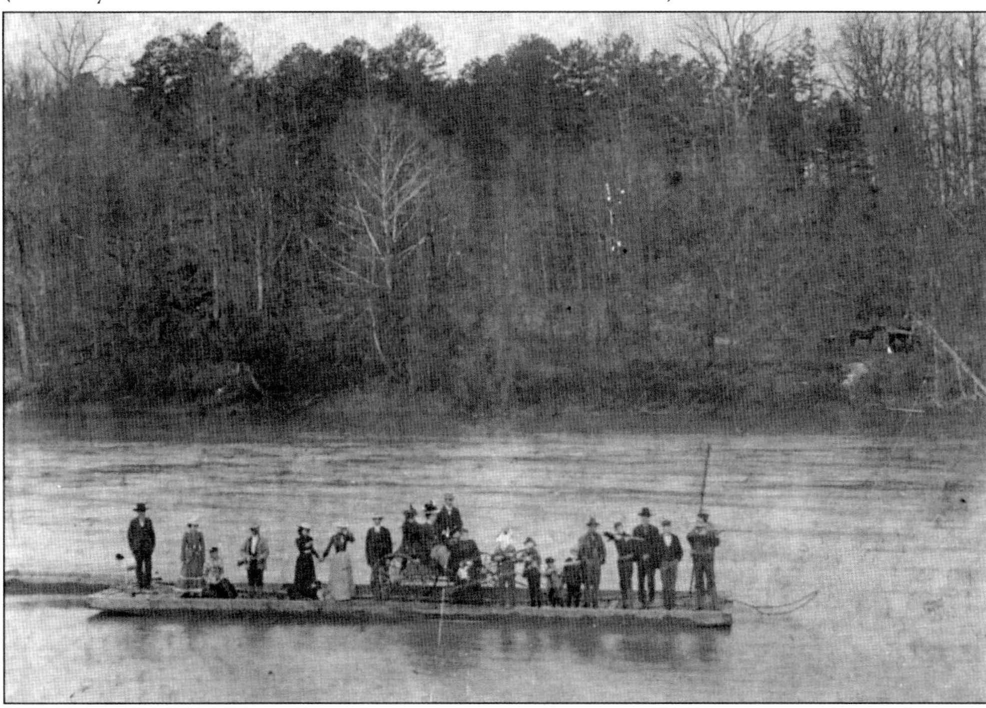

The wooden flat of an unidentified ferry in eastern Lincoln County carries a group of finely dressed women and men bearing firearms for this photograph taken from the riverbank around 1900. Ferries of this type were guided across rivers by a cable that was lowered into the river to afford boats the opportunity to pass. In Lincoln County, numerous ferries operated during the 18th and 19th centuries, such as Hager's Ferry, McConnell's Ferry, and Rozzelle's Ferry. (Courtesy of Terry Brotherton.)

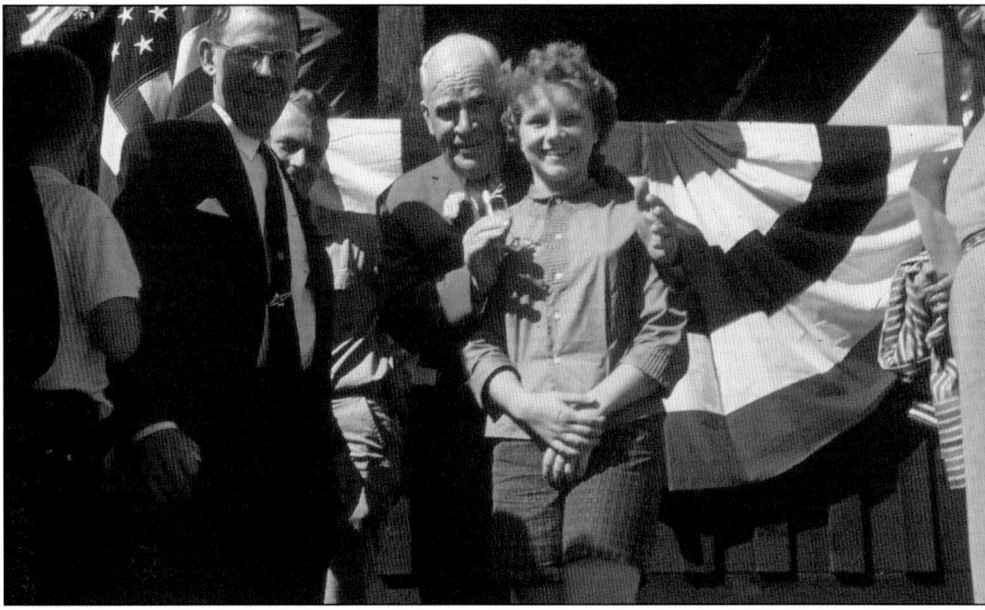

Doris Shuford Little, while an eighth-grade student at Asbury Elementary School in Lincolnton, attended a special event associated with Gov. Luther Hodges's visit to Lincoln County to push the plunger on September 28, 1959, for the explosion on the Catawba River that changed the landscape in Lincoln, Catawba, Mecklenburg, and Iredell Counties. Doris was studying North Carolina history at the time and got an A in the subject for attending the ceremony. (Courtesy of Edward and Doris Little.)

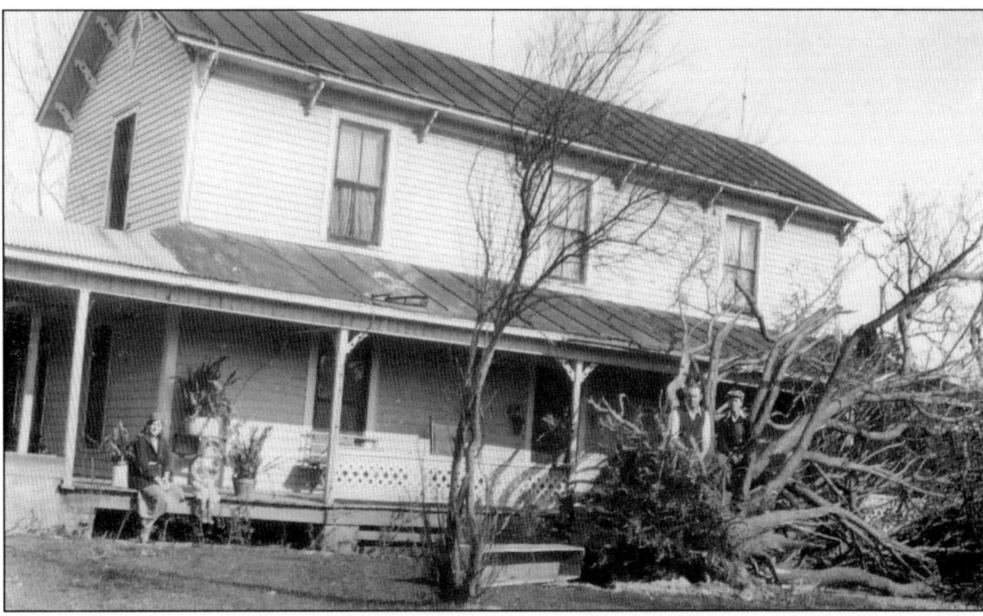

The storm of Sunday, March 27, 1932, devastated the homes and buildings of families living in the eastern part of Lincoln County, so much so that some homes and businesses were not able to be rebuilt. The houses of McLean Cherry, R.P. Aiken, and Robert Nixon Jr. (pictured) were damaged. The *Lincoln County News* surmised that "almost every resident of this section suffered some damage." (Courtesy of Ann Smith.)

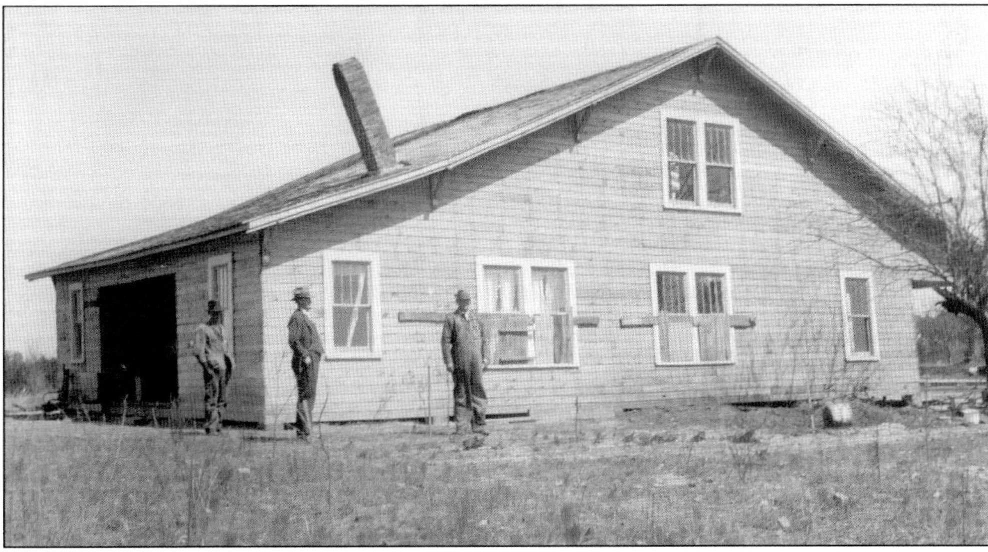

Three men survey R.P. Aiken's house in eastern Lincoln County after what the *Lincoln County News* called "the worst storm which has been in East Lincoln section for a number of years" in its March 28, 1932, edition. The storm occurred on Sunday, March 27, and the newspaper reported that the Aikens' house was too badly damaged to repair. In addition to the Aikens' house, the storm destroyed the Cherry brothers' gin house and J.I. Cherry's cow barn. (Courtesy of Ann Smith.)

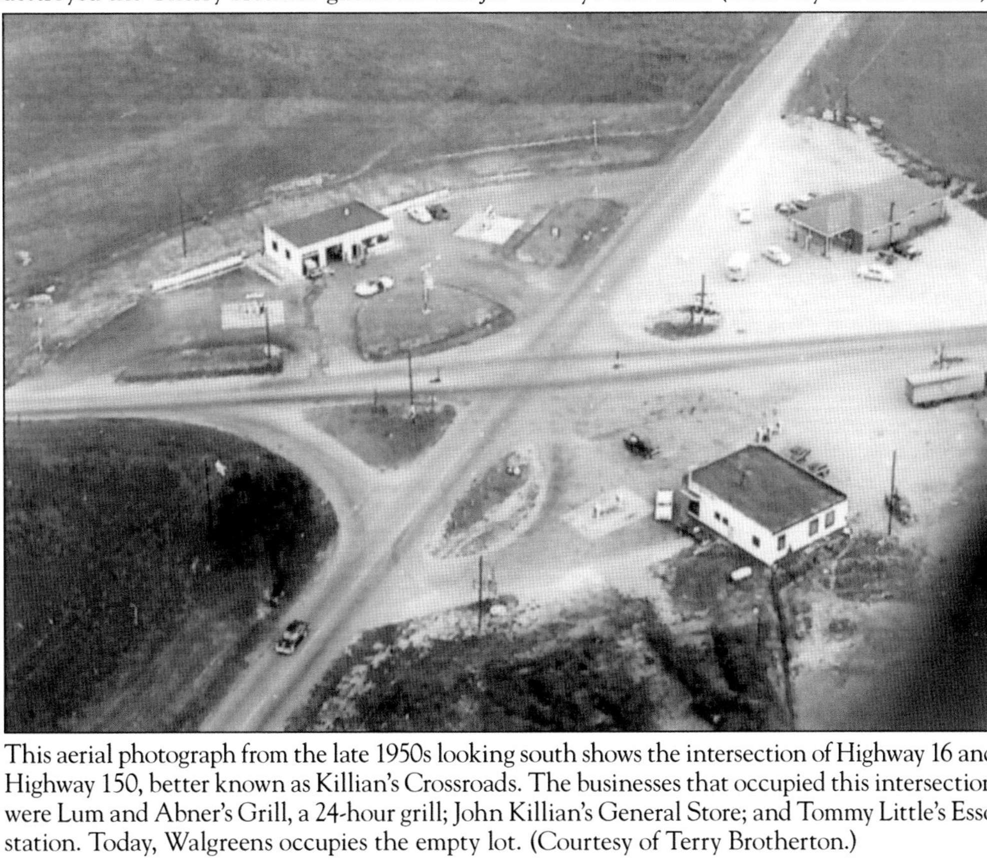

This aerial photograph from the late 1950s looking south shows the intersection of Highway 16 and Highway 150, better known as Killian's Crossroads. The businesses that occupied this intersection were Lum and Abner's Grill, a 24-hour grill; John Killian's General Store; and Tommy Little's Esso station. Today, Walgreens occupies the empty lot. (Courtesy of Terry Brotherton.)

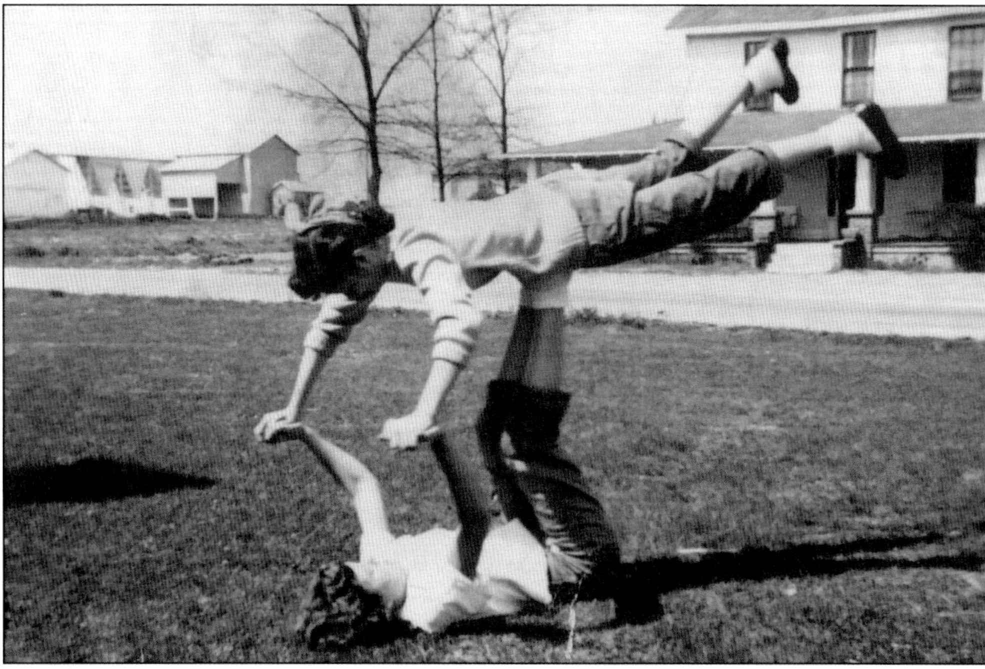

It is all fun and games for these two as Betty Rose Little Howard holds up Dorothy Beatty Maiers in the front yard of H.N. Little. The home of E.F. Killian is seen in the background and stood directly across from the Little home. Cotton was an important crop in eastern Lincoln County for decades, and the Drum Cotton Gin, seen in the far distance, processed much of Denver's cotton. The gin ceased operation sometime in the 1940s. Clinton Drum sold the gin to H.N. Little, and Little used it as a warehouse for his Denver Shopping Center. (Courtesy of Shirley Mull.)

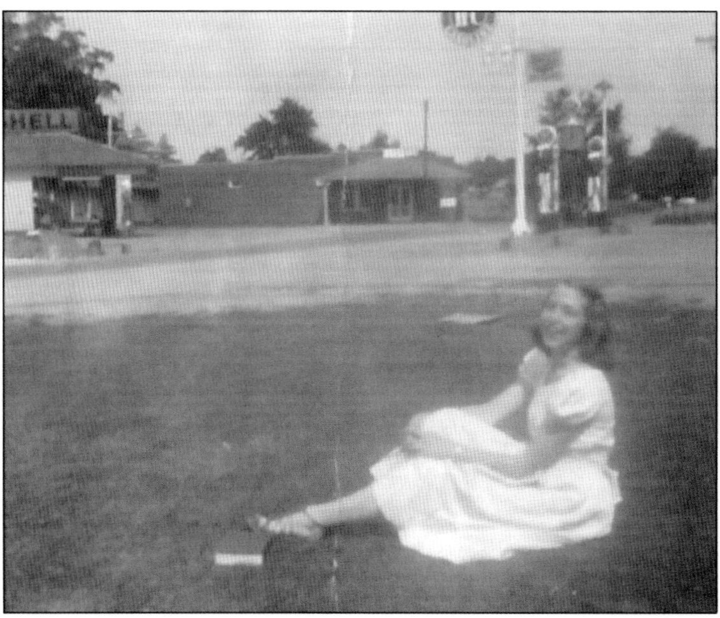

Time stands still in this c. 1950 image captured near the intersection of Campground Road and Highway 16. E.F. Killian Jr.'s Shell station can be seen to the left, where Stacy's Restaurant stands today; the Denver Post Office is in the middle; and the Sinclair gas pumps stood in front of H.N. Little's Denver Shopping Center to the right. (Courtesy of Shirley Mull.)

Dr. Oliver William Shellem (1886–1947), known as O.W., was married to Hattie Mae Rogers Shellem (1897–1971) and lived on Campground Road in Denver. He was born in Wake County, North Carolina, and attended medical school in Davidson and Charlotte, graduating in 1909. He practiced medicine in Ansonville, Lawndale, Lowesville, and, from 1922 until his death in 1947, in Denver. He delivered many babies in eastern Lincoln County during that time. (Courtesy of Shirley Mull.)

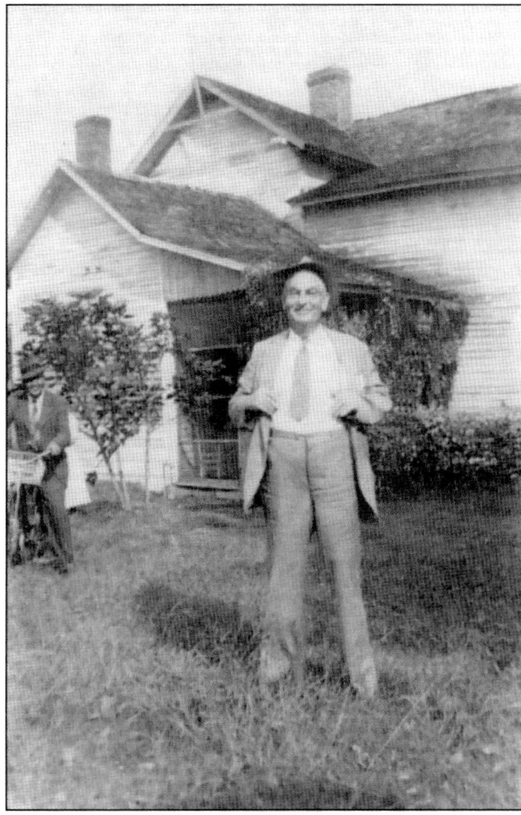

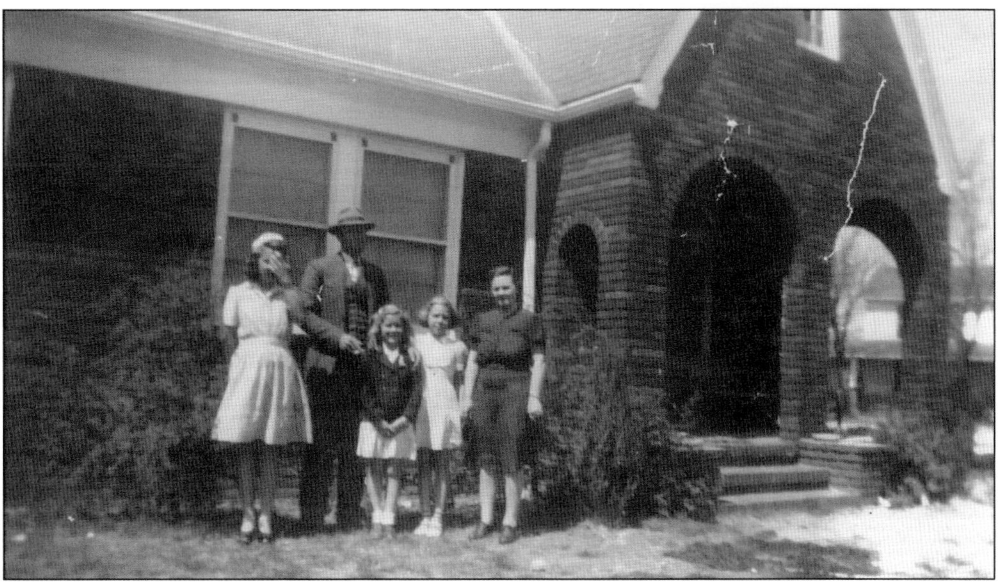

H.N. Little had this home built in 1941 on property adjacent to his Denver Cash Store. It was the first brick home built within the limits of Denver. Here, H.N. (1904–1964) poses with his wife, Callie Greene Little (1906–2010) and his daughters, from left to right, Marjorie Little Best, Shirley Little Mull, and Betty Little Howard. The home of E.F. Killian can be seen in the background. (Courtesy of Shirley Mull.)

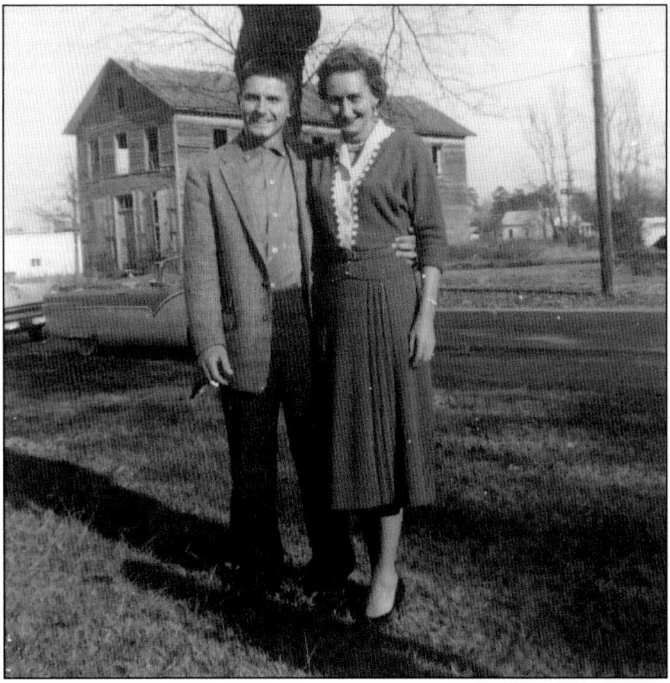

Bobby Hunter and Rosa Beatty pose in front of this building, which served as the Denver Masonic Lodge. The home of Key Howard can be seen in the distance on the right. (Courtesy of Shirley Mull.)

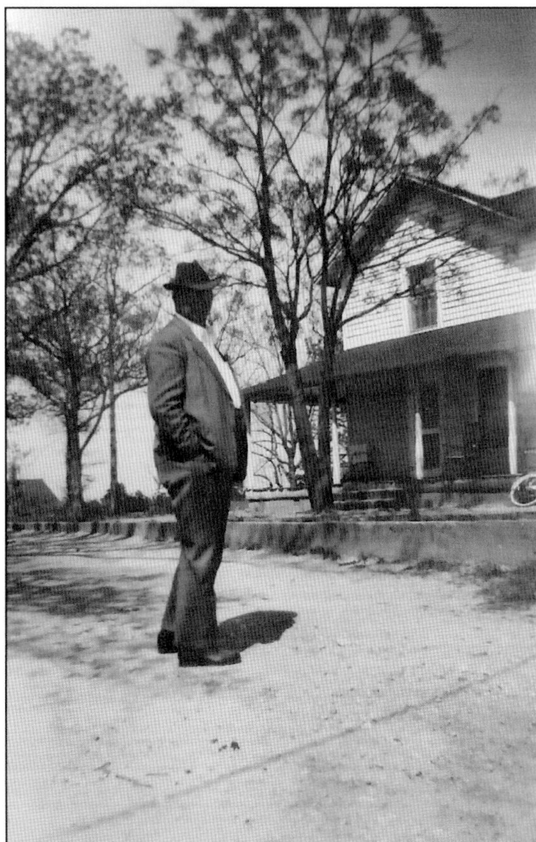

Eddie Clegg Hager (1893–1966) stands in front of the Hager house located on what is now Nellie Circle, off Highway 73, in the Lowesville area. William Julius Peter Hager purchased this property from William J. and Jane B. Cashion in 1882. Family tradition holds that he built his house in 1888, and it is still standing. Hager was a farmer and ran a sawmill, cotton gin, and planing mill. He ran the Hager Post Office out of his house and served as the postmaster in 1892. (Courtesy of Janet McCurry.)

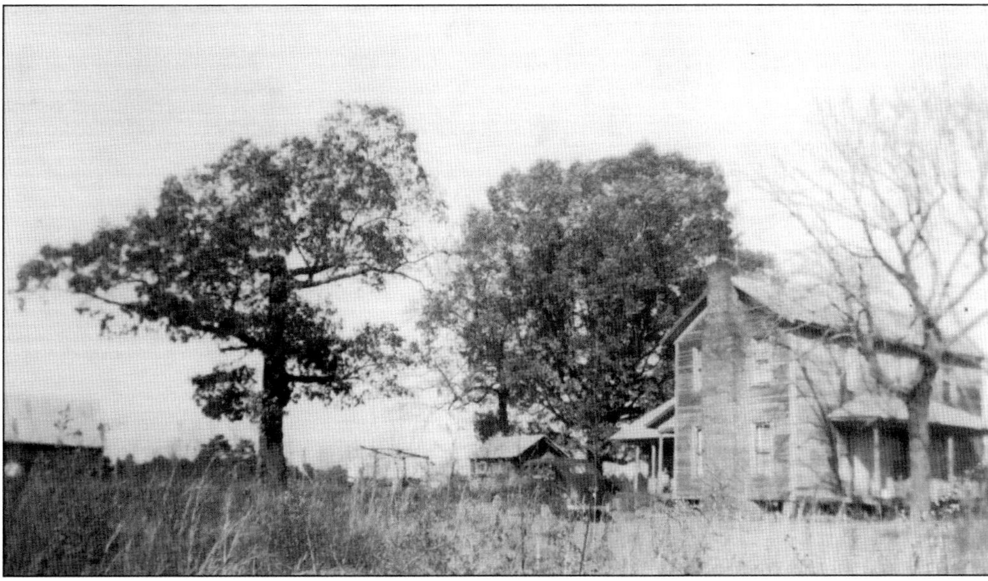

The home of John Hall Nixon (1856–1923) and Harriet Elizabeth "Lizzie" Henkle Nixon (1876–1948) is located on the west side of South Pilot Knob Road heading towards Lowesville. As guests visited the house for Thanksgiving in 1950, they paused to capture this moment in time in appreciation of their hosts' hospitality. F.Y.E. Banning of Arnhem, Holland, took the photograph after being invited by Ernest Nixon, grandson of John Hall Nixon, to take part in the family's annual Thanksgiving Day hunting trip. Ernest carried on the tradition started by his grandfather. Banning worked with Ernest Nixon at the Mount Holly A&P. (Courtesy of Nancy Nixon Little.)

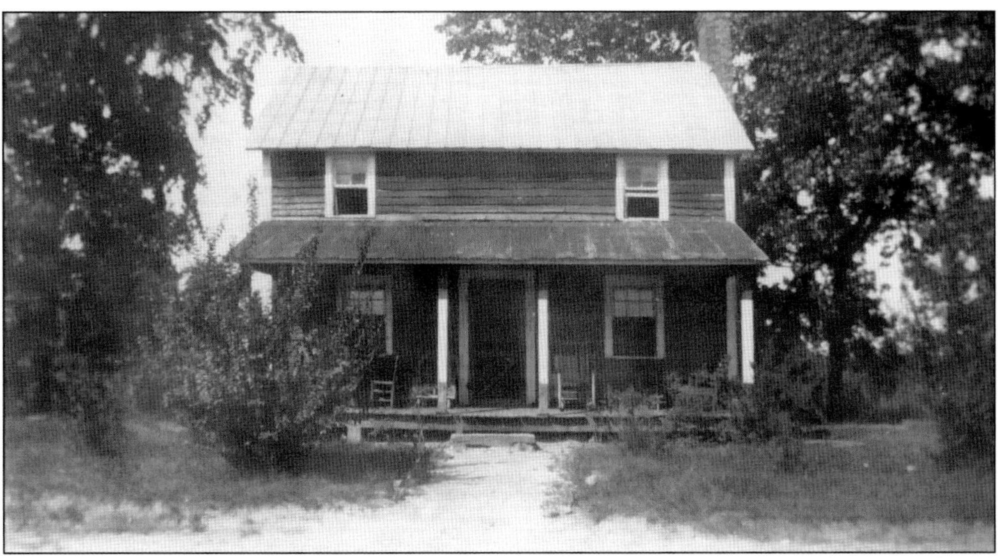

The Duke Power Company built this home in the 1920s, along with others, after it purchased large tracts of land in eastern Lincoln County for what would become Lake Norman. Painted red to denote Duke Power's construction, this house, rented by Ed and Clara Beatty Luckey, was located on the River Road. Today, this road is known as Hager's Ferry Road. Duke Power paid a local man named Mr. Cox to look after all of the houses that it built. (Courtesy of Bernice Luckey Nixon.)

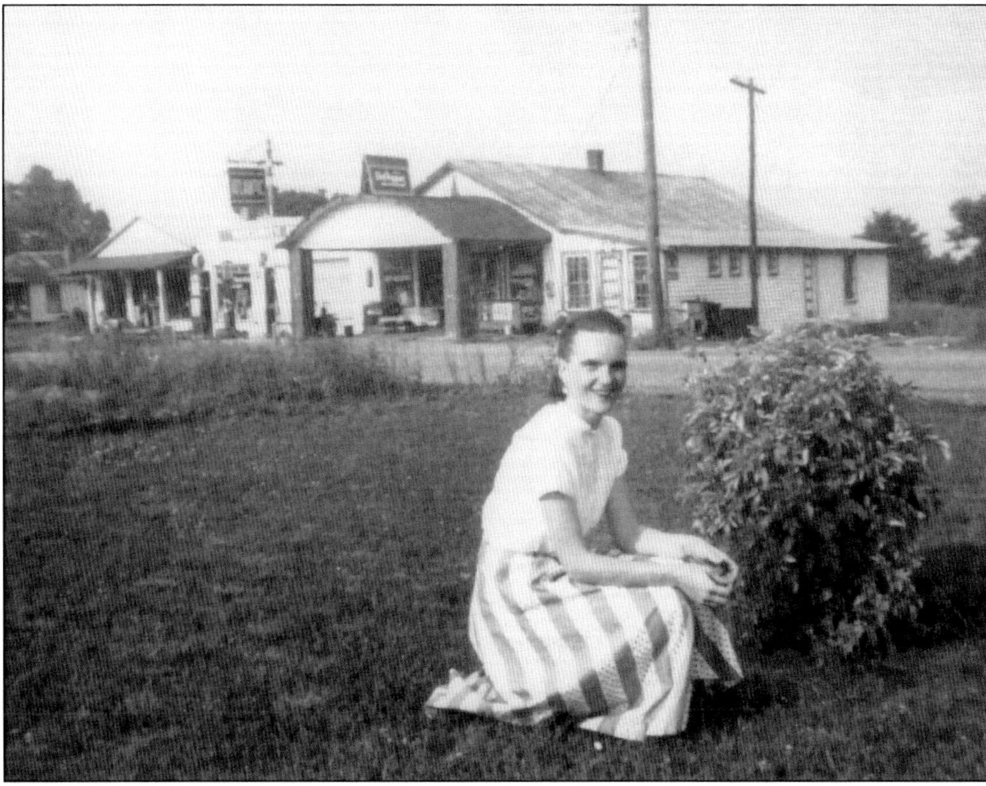

Dennis Bain Dellinger, known as D.B., opened Dellinger Mercantile Company about 1932. The store sold clothes, shoes, seed, fertilizer, hardware, and groceries, and meats were hung in the back. It is said that the store was the largest cutter of meats, and its steaks were popular. Doris McConnell takes time to pose for this 1948 photograph, taken by Paul McConnell across from D.B. Dellinger's store in Lowesville along Highway 16. At some point, the store burned, and members of the community helped rebuild it. This building still stands but has not been in use for many years. (Courtesy of Danny Dellinger.)

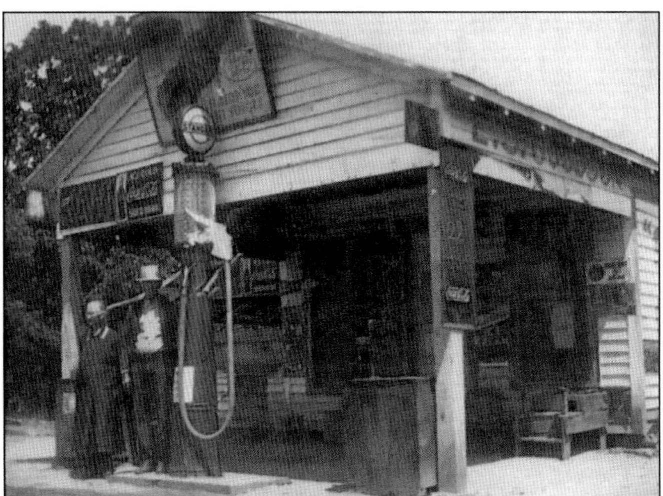

Dovie and E.J. "Jinks" Goodson ran a filling station in Denver at the corner of Campground Road and Proctor Street across from the Rock Spring Campground until the 1960s. During camp meetings, people would cross the road to buy a cold drink or a snack. Goodson built his shoeshine stand under the shed at the right to serve the members of camp meetings who needed a good spit shine. (Courtesy of Terry Brotherton.)

Wearing work clothes of the period, Jesse Claude Killian removed his hat in preparation for this photograph in front of his store in Lowesville during the 1940s. The store of Killian and Price, known locally as "Suge" Killian's store, sat right at the Lincoln-Gaston County line on Killian Farm Road in front of the Killian family's homeplace. Killian's store was started by Killian's grandfather Peter Osborne Alonzo Killian and a partner, James D. Price, in 1901. Suge Killian assumed ownership in 1917, and operated it until 1963. (Courtesy of Frances Hampton.)

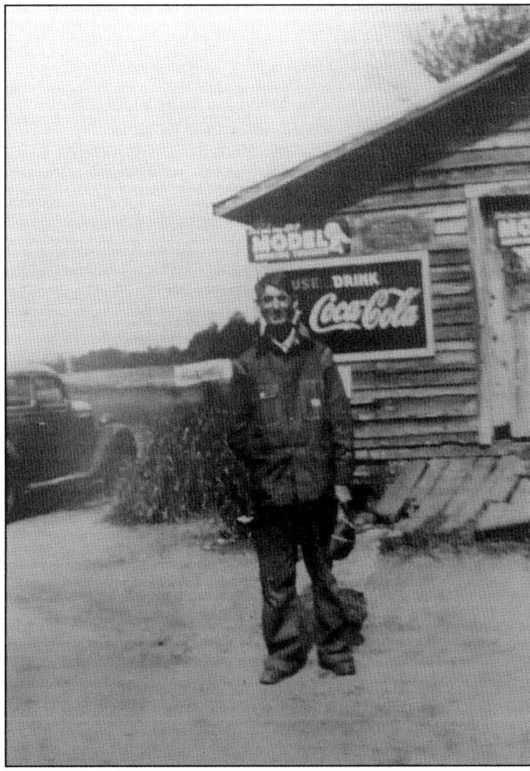

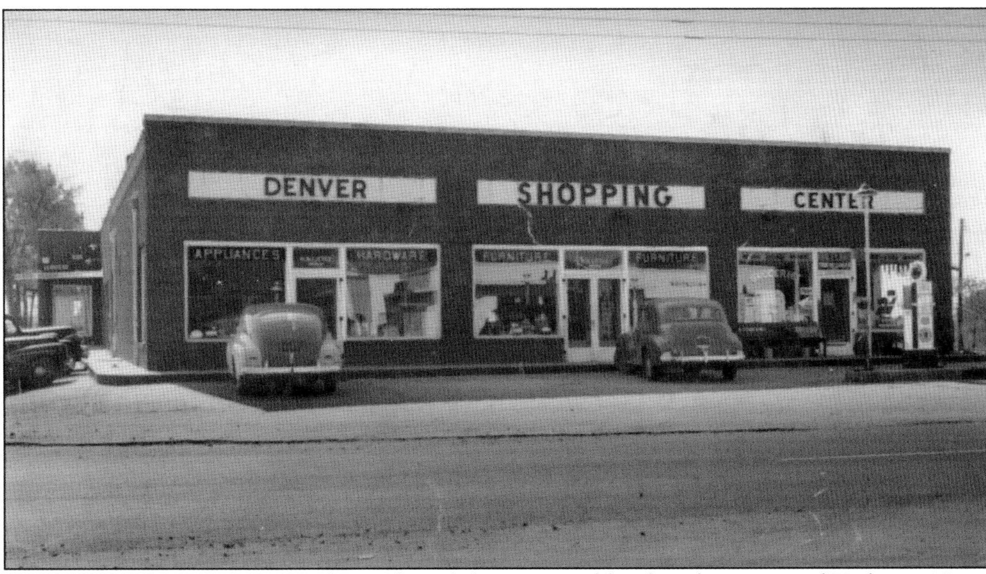

On January 16, 1939, H.N. Little purchased the store and land at the corner of Highway 16 and Forney Hill Road from Spencer Page Proctor for $1,150. Little and his wife, Callie, started the Denver Cash Store, a general mercantile store. In 1945, fire destroyed this building, and everything was lost. Little had to drive to Newton to get a fire truck to come. In 1946, the Littles built the Denver Shopping Center and sold hardware, furniture, and appliances. The name changed to Denver Furniture Center in 1989, and Marty Mull now operates it as Denver Furniture. (Courtesy of Shirley Mull.)

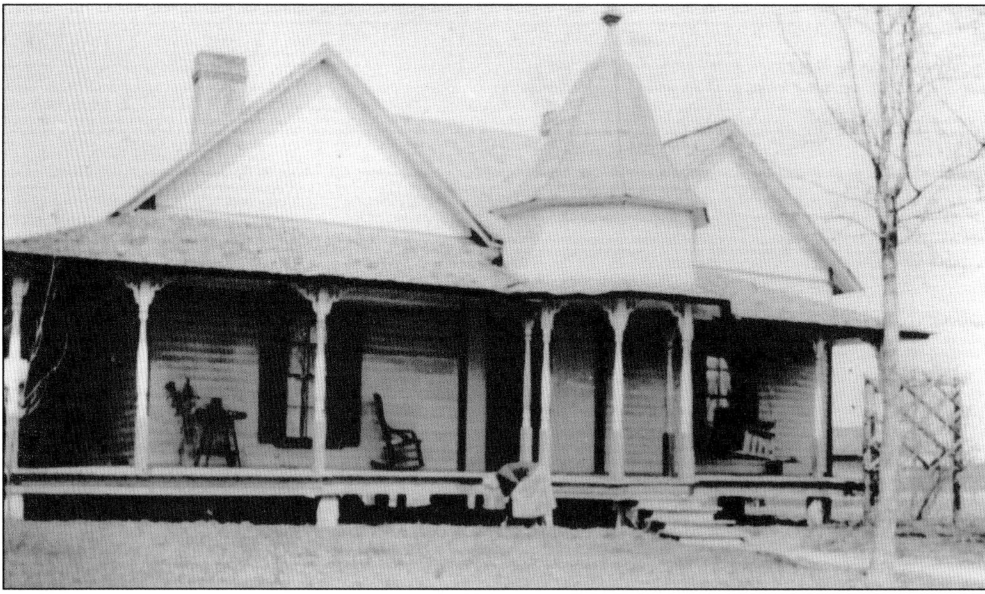

A cupola, a rare architectural element in Lincoln County, rises from the front of the Franklin T. Smith house on Campground Road in Denver. Eugenia B. Smith Paine bequeathed 27 acres of land on which this house stands to her brother Franklin Theodore Smith (1855–1932) in 1916, and he built this house on the property. The cupola, which the family called the "steeple," was removed during the 1960s. (Courtesy of Allen Broach.)

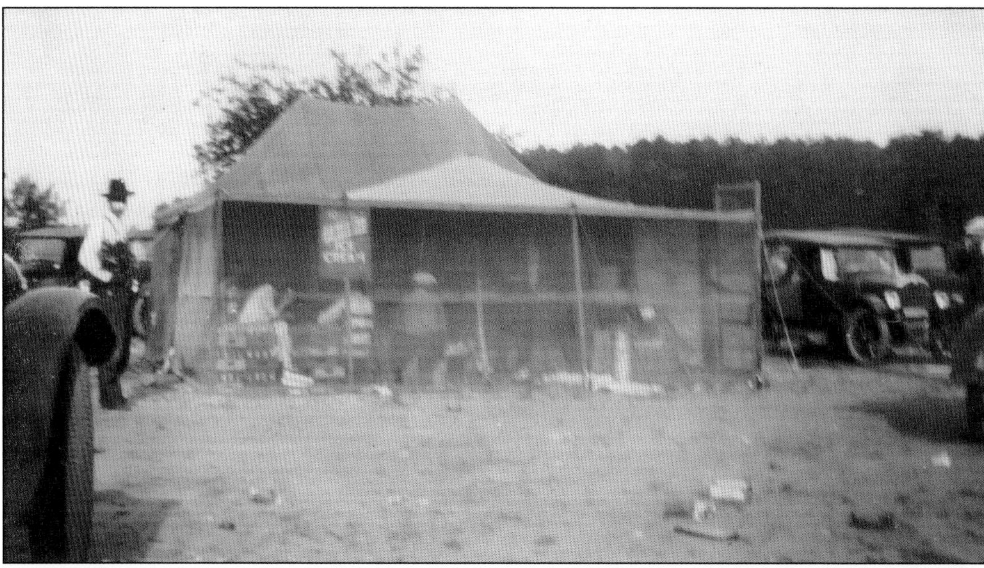

Pictured here are people waiting for Iron Station's faith healer Ellen Hilton Bynum to ease their ailments. Bynum's home was located at the site where the Timken Plant is located. Her faith healing started with a vision one morning on a trip to the spring house to get some milk. She was taken by a deep belief that she could alleviate suffering by transferring pain and disease to a nearby fruit tree. She sat inside a tent erected around her fruit tree, and as each patient approached her, they dropped money into the farm wife's large apron pocket. Newton restaurant operator Jake Huss set up a tent nearby where he served food and rented cots to the weary. (Courtesy of the Russell and Dot Cornwell family.)

Four

SOUL OF A SOCIETY
EDUCATION AND EDUCATORS

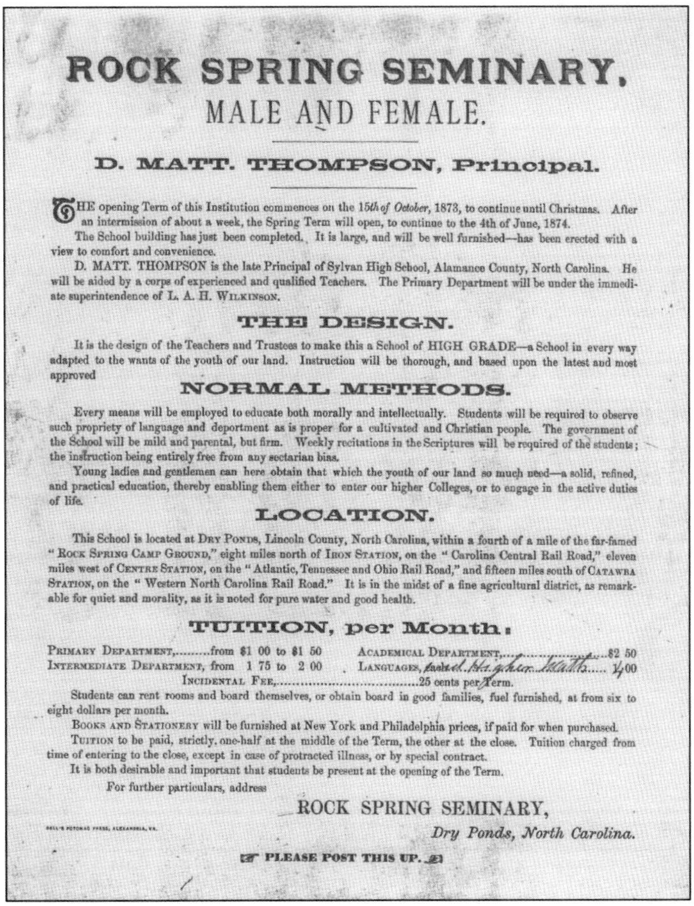

ROCK SPRING SEMINARY,

MALE AND FEMALE.

D. MATT. THOMPSON, Principal.

THE opening Term of this Institution commences on the *15th of October*, 1873, to continue until Christmas. After an intermission of about a week, the Spring Term will open, to continue to the 4th of June, 1874.

The School building has just been completed. It is large, and will be well furnished—has been erected with a view to comfort and convenience.

D. MATT. THOMPSON is the late Principal of Sylvan High School, Alamance County, North Carolina. He will be aided by a corps of experienced and qualified Teachers. The Primary Department will be under the immediate superintendence of L. A. H. WILKINSON.

THE DESIGN.

It is the design of the Teachers and Trustees to make this a School of HIGH GRADE—a School in every way adapted to the wants of the youth of our land. Instruction will be thorough, and based upon the latest and most approved

NORMAL METHODS.

Every means will be employed to educate both morally and intellectually. Students will be required to observe such propriety of language and deportment as is proper for a cultivated and Christian people. The government of the School will be mild and parental, but firm. Weekly recitations in the Scriptures will be required of the students; the instruction being entirely free from any sectarian bias.

Young ladies and gentlemen can here obtain that which the youth of our land so much need—a solid, refined, and practical education, thereby enabling them either to enter our higher Colleges, or to engage in the active duties of life.

LOCATION.

This School is located at DRY PONDS, Lincoln County, North Carolina, within a fourth of a mile of the far-famed "ROCK SPRING CAMP GROUND," eight miles north of IRON STATION, on the "Carolina Central Rail Road," eleven miles west of CENTRE STATION, on the "Atlantic, Tennessee and Ohio Rail Road," and fifteen miles south of CATAWBA STATION, on the "Western North Carolina Rail Road." It is in the midst of a fine agricultural district, as remarkable for quiet and morality, as it is noted for pure water and good health.

TUITION, per Month:

PRIMARY DEPARTMENT,.........from $1 00 to $1 50   ACADEMICAL DEPARTMENT,........................$2 50

INTERMEDIATE DEPARTMENT, from 1 75 to 2 00   LANGUAGES, and Higher Math..... 4 00

INCIDENTAL FEE,....................................25 cents per Term.

Students can rent rooms and board themselves, or obtain board in good families, fuel furnished, at from six to eight dollars per month.

BOOKS AND STATIONERY will be furnished at New York and Philadelphia prices, if paid for when purchased.

TUITION to be paid, strictly, one-half at the middle of the Term, the other at the close. Tuition charged from time of entering to the close, except in case of protracted illness, or by special contract.

It is both desirable and important that students be present at the opening of the Term.

For further particulars, address

ROCK SPRING SEMINARY,

Dry Ponds, North Carolina.

PLEASE POST THIS UP.

Eastern Lincoln County saw schools established as early as O'Reilly's School near Beatties Ford in 1826. In 1871, L.A.H. Wilkinson founded the Rock Spring Seminary in Denver. Wilkinson cut the logs to build the school, and before it opened, he hired a teacher to help with the instructions. Prof. D. Matt Thompson took over the school in 1873 and conducted it as a boarding school before moving to Lincolnton in 1884 to work with the Lincolnton City Schools. A number of professors succeeded Thompson at Rock Spring, including James F. Brewer, Charles L. Coon, Leon Cash, Sidney J. Whitener, and W.M. Brooks. Pictured is an 1873 advertisement for Rock Spring Seminary. (Courtesy of LCHA.)

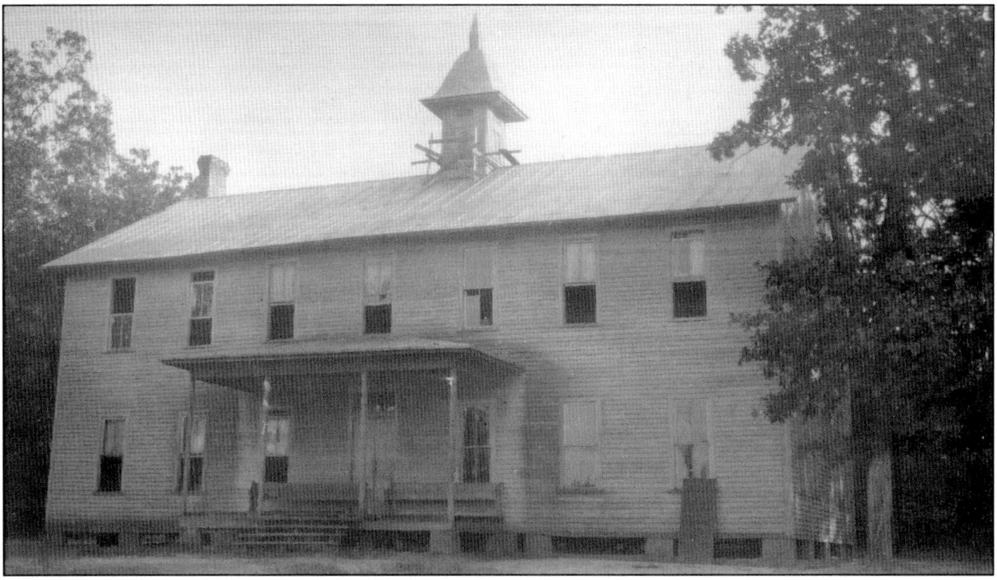

The first two free public high schools in Lincoln County opened at Denver and Crouse in 1907. In 1910, the new Denver High School was built, and under the supervision of Dr. Horace N. Abernethy, Charlotte Young, a native of Asheville and graduate of Carson-Newman College, became the first female principal hired in Denver. She taught here from 1910 to 1912. This building served the primary, intermediate, and high school levels until the early 1920s, when a $50,000 school bond was voted upon and approved for the construction of a modern brick schoolhouse that would consolidate the local one-room schoolhouses around Denver; it was Rock Springs High School. (Courtesy of LCHA.)

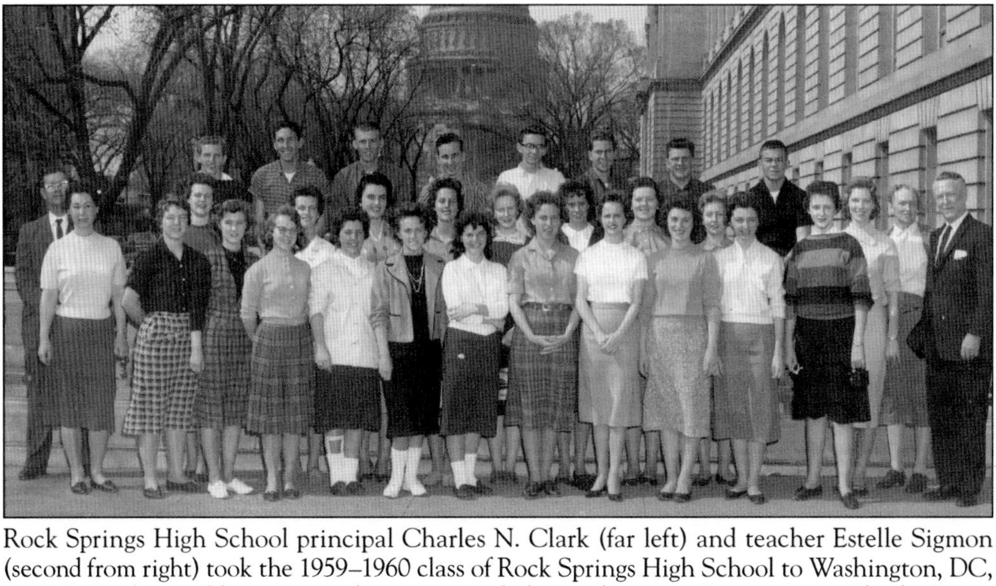

Rock Springs High School principal Charles N. Clark (far left) and teacher Estelle Sigmon (second from right) took the 1959–1960 class of Rock Springs High School to Washington, DC, in 1960. Students sold magazine subscriptions to help pay their way. Congressman Charles Raper Jonas (far right) took the time for a group photograph. He took the group on a tour of his office and the Capitol building, pictured here. While in Washington, students also toured the White House, the Washington Monument, the Lincoln Memorial, and the Smithsonian. (Courtesy of Kelli Gaskill Hogue.)

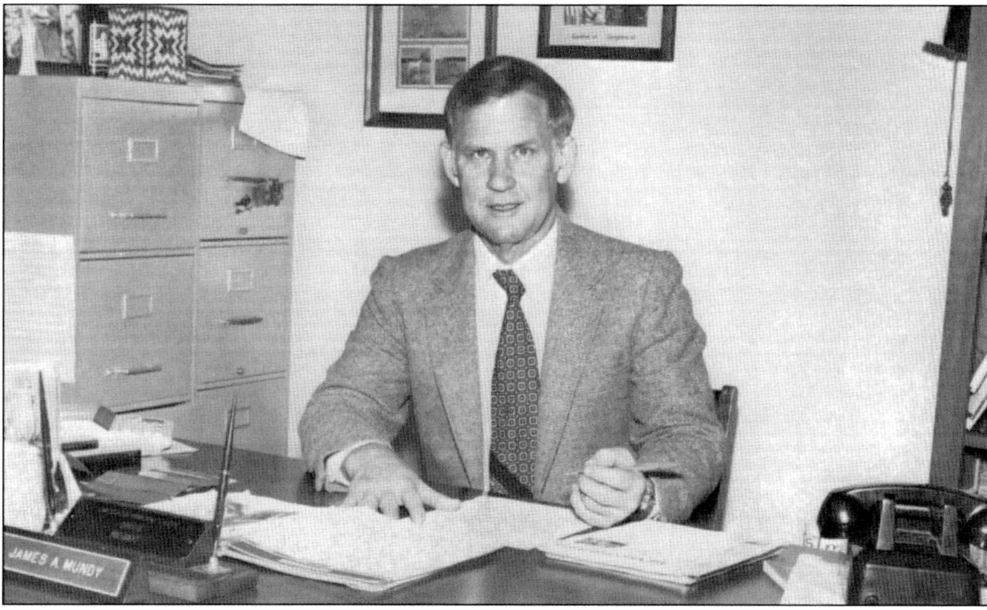

Principal James A. Mundy stops from the task at hand to pose for this early 1980s photograph in his office at Rock Springs Elementary School. Mundy was a 1955 graduate of Rock Springs High School and a stand-out athlete in several sports. He later became principal of the school. The school taught kindergarten through eighth grade during his first two years and an elementary school the remainder of his 20 years (1972–1992). He was inducted into the Lincoln County Sports Hall of Fame in 2011. (Courtesy of Rock Springs Elementary School.)

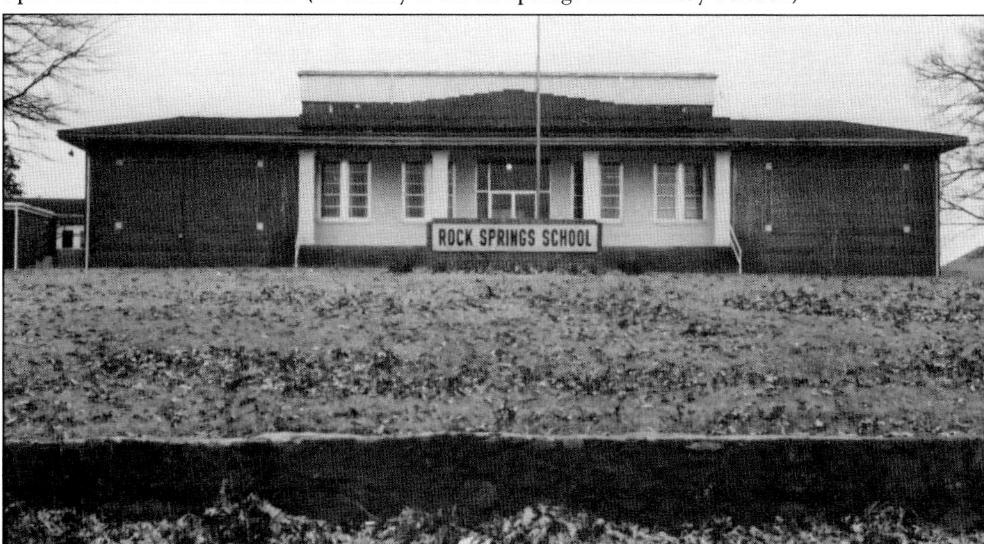

Built in the early 1920s as Rock Springs High School, this building looked much the same as it does in this 1970s photograph. The school stands above the original rock wall, which was built in 1926. When East Lincoln High School opened in the fall of 1967, Rock Springs High School was converted to teach kindergarten through eighth grade, and it remained an intermediate school until the fall of 1974, when East Lincoln Junior High opened. The school's mascot was the Warriors, and school colors were black and gold. This building was razed in 1996, and the current building has served the school since. (Courtesy of Rock Springs Elementary School.)

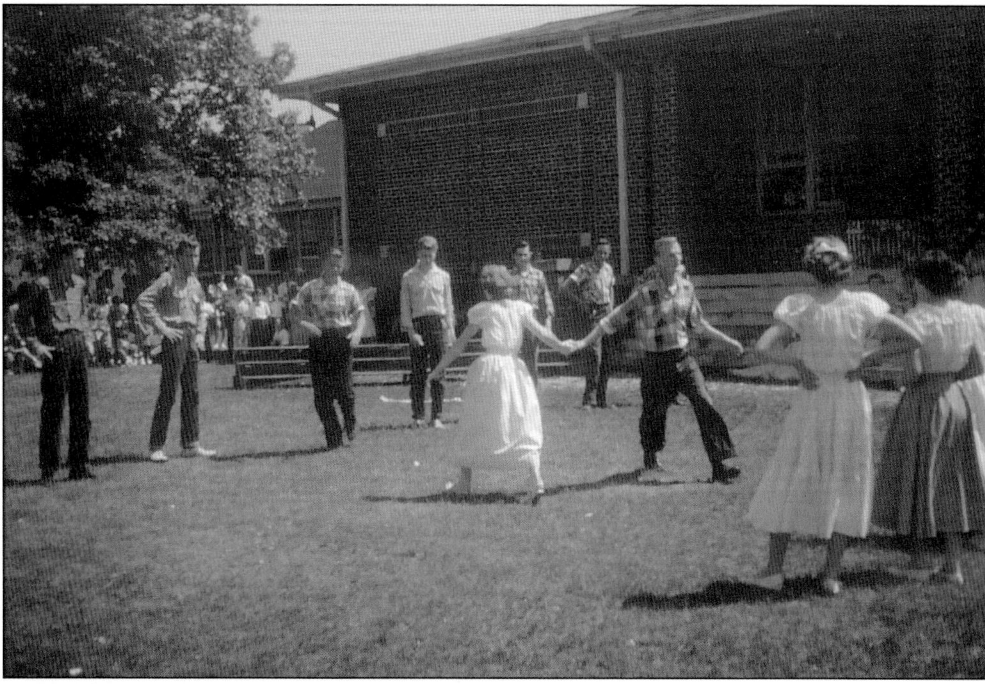

A select group of young men and women are the focal point of the May Day activities at Rock Springs High School for this 1950s photograph. Activities for May Day included the maypole, selection of the May Day queen, and square dancing. (Courtesy of LCHA.)

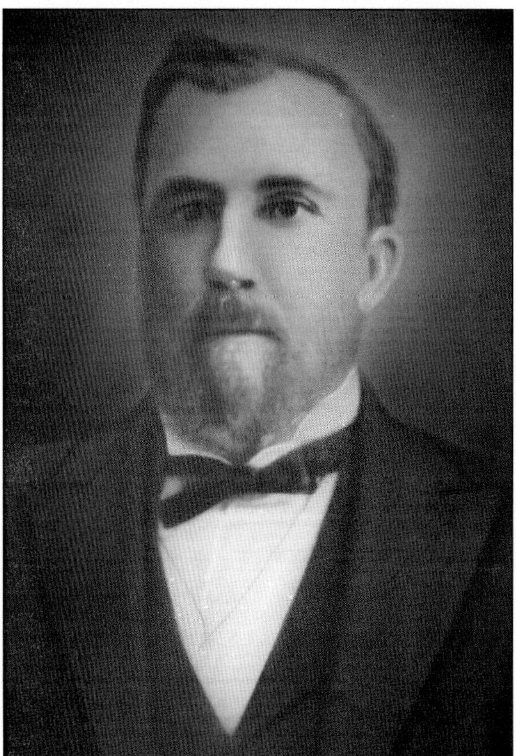

David Matthew Thompson (1844–1925), known as D. Matt Thompson, was born in Randolph County, North Carolina, and served in the 3rd and 19th North Carolina Regiments before coming to Lincoln County in 1872 to serve as the principal of Rock Spring Seminary in Denver. Under his leadership, from 1872 to 1884, he made the seminary one of the most noted and successful schools of the time in North Carolina. In 1884, he moved from Denver to Lincolnton to become the principal of Piedmont Seminary. He was principal of Piedmont Seminary until 1890 and, while in Lincolnton, served as the chairman of the board of education. He moved to Gainesville, Florida, in 1890 to serve as the superintendent of grade schools there. He is buried at Oakwood Cemetery in Statesville. (Courtesy of Rock Springs Elementary School.)

Locke Alexander Houston (L.A.H.) Wilkinson was appointed postmaster of Dry Pond in eastern Lincoln County on February 13, 1866, and is responsible for building Rock Spring Seminary in Denver in 1871. He married Nannie Ella Davenport (1854–1938), daughter of A.W. Davenport and Mary Cansler Davenport, of Gaston County, on February 17, 1876, and worked as a farmer and teacher in the Catawba Springs Township until moving out of the area after 1900. He was a traveling salesman in High Point in 1910, and in 1912, he is listed in the Charlotte City Directory as an agent for the Gate City Insurance Company. He died in 1915 and is buried in Forest Lawn Cemetery in Greensboro, North Carolina. (Courtesy of Rock Springs Elementary School.)

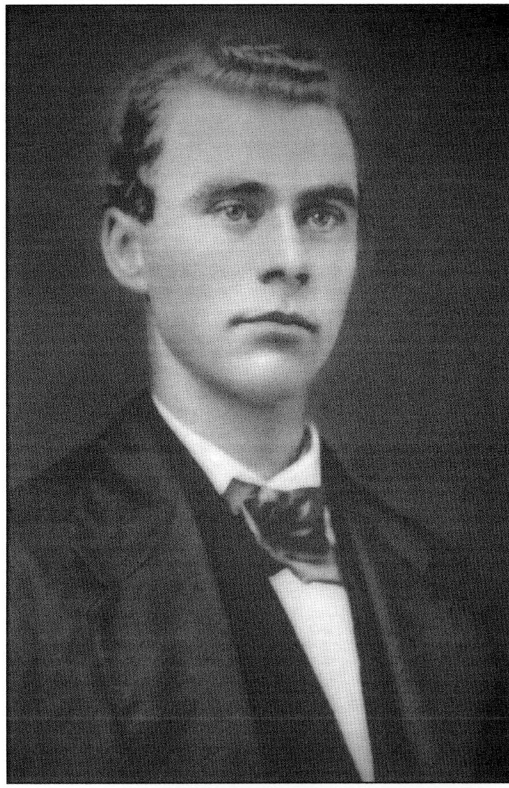

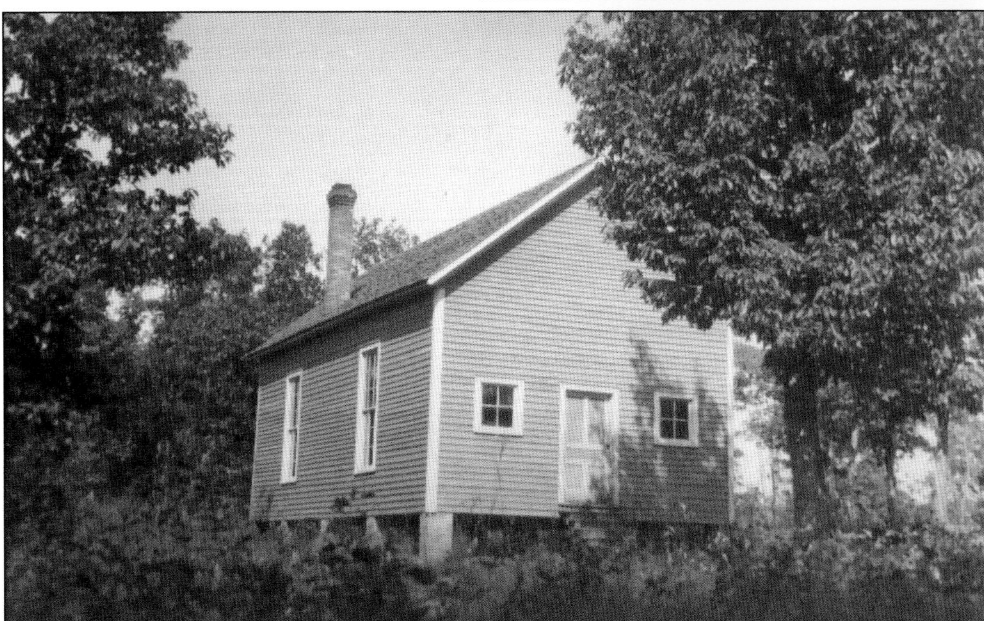

Graham School was a one-room schoolhouse located at the end of Graham Road in Triangle. The school served the area around Unity Church and Elmwood Plantation during the 1910s and 1920s until the new Triangle School was built in an effort to consolidate smaller schools throughout the eastern part of the county. (Courtesy of LCHA.)

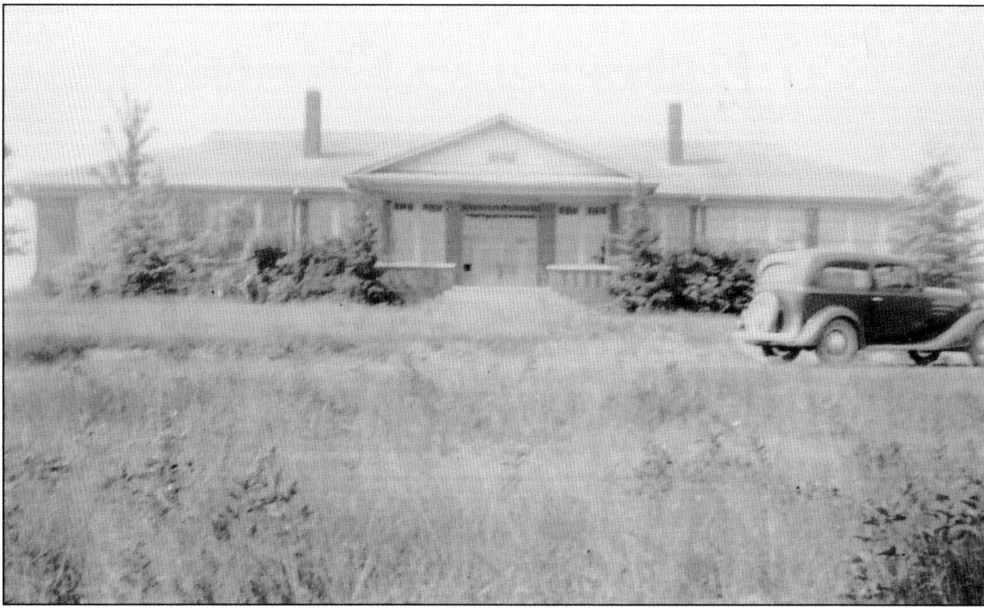

The modern brick building built as the Catawba Springs Consolidated School, later known as Machpelah School, in the Catawba Springs Township of eastern Lincoln County, was the focus of this photograph from the 1930s. This school holds many memories for students who attended here before the building burned in the spring of 1957. When the school burned, students went to the Triangle School. (Courtesy of LCHA.)

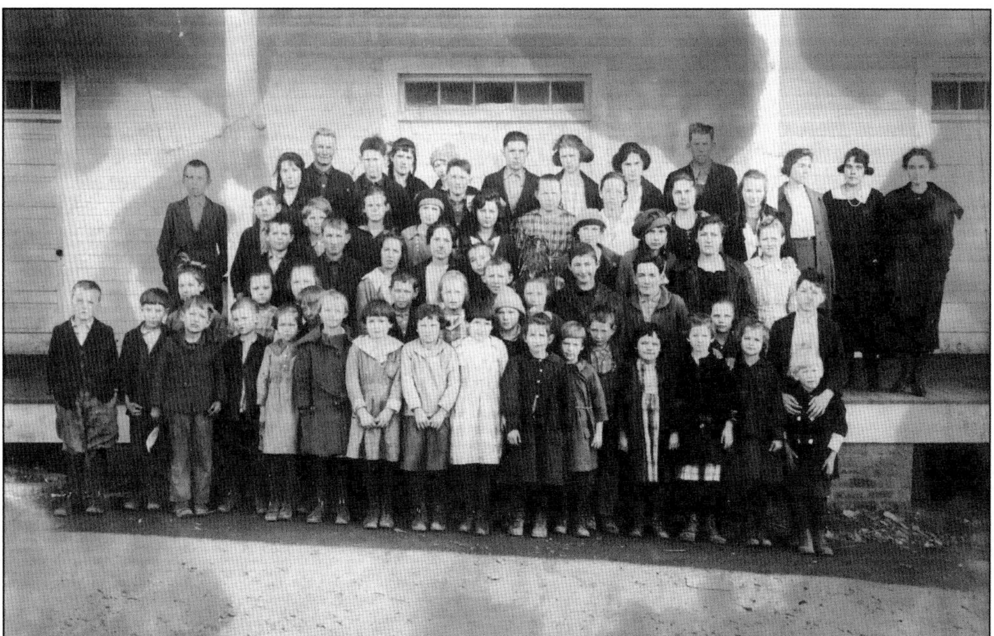

Young students of various grades stand in front of the Triangle School for this photograph from the late 1910s or early 1920s. In 1924, when the new Triangle School was built, these students and students from Graham's, McLean's, and the Lowesville District attended the new Triangle School. (Courtesy of Kelli Gaskill Hogue.)

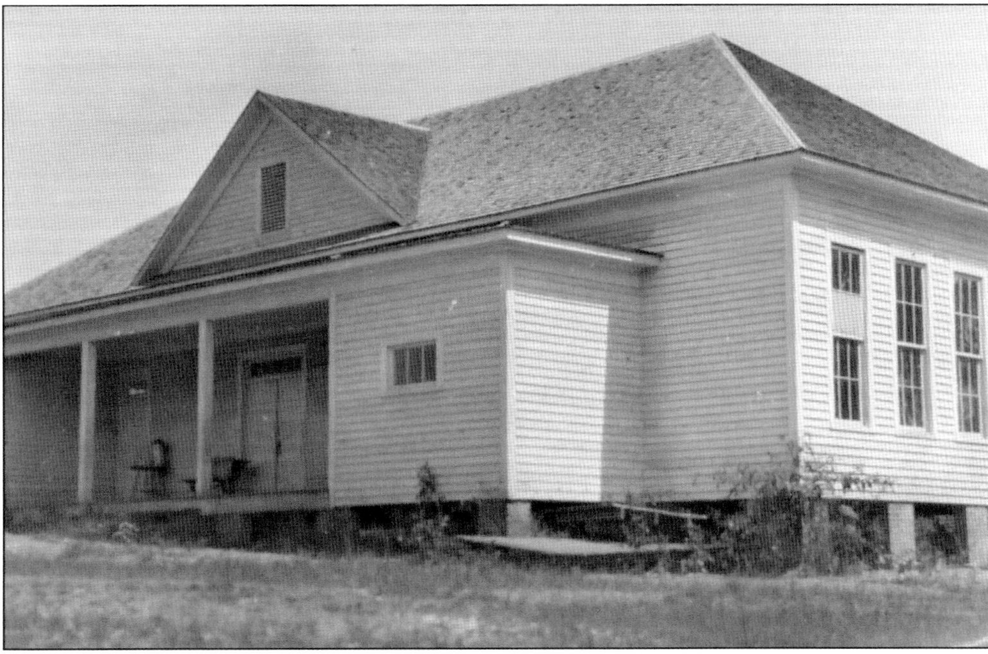

Triangle School was located in the field across the street from Big Bob Nixon's home on Triangle Circle from the 1910s into the early 1920s. This one-room, clapboard-sided structure fell victim to progress like many other small schools in the area when schools were consolidated in 1923. Apartments currently occupy this site. (Courtesy of Mary Abernathy.)

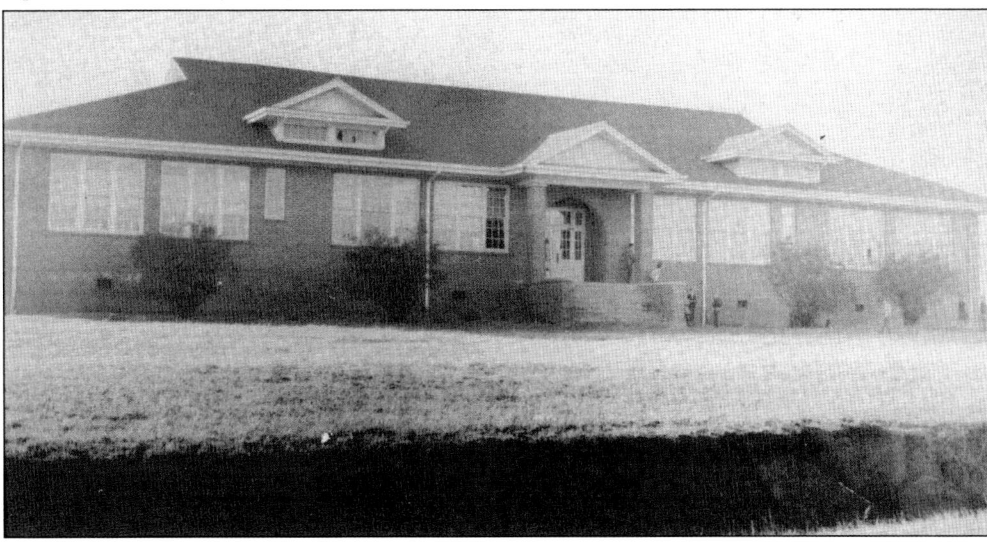

Early in the 1920s, schools in eastern Lincoln County underwent consolidation. A new brick structure with multiple classrooms and an auditorium was built on what is now Highway 16. In its early years, students went to Triangle through the eighth grade before going to Rock Springs High School. At one time, the school served the black community in southeastern Lincoln County. Throughout the 1970s and early 1980s, Triangle Elementary was kindergarten and first grade only and served as a feeder to Rock Springs Elementary in Denver. Triangle was closed when Catawba Springs Elementary School was opened in the 1980s. The old school is now Holy Spirit Catholic Church. (Courtesy of LCHA.)

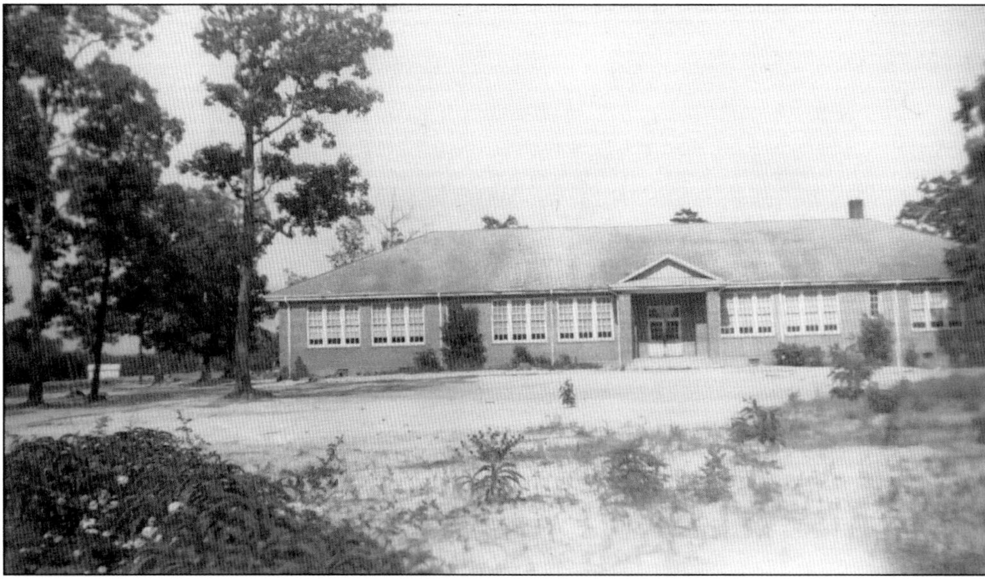

The construction of a large, modern brick school in Iron Station followed the many communities throughout Lincoln County who voted to consolidate small one- and two-teacher schools into larger facilities for educational advancement and community development. (Courtesy of LCHA.)

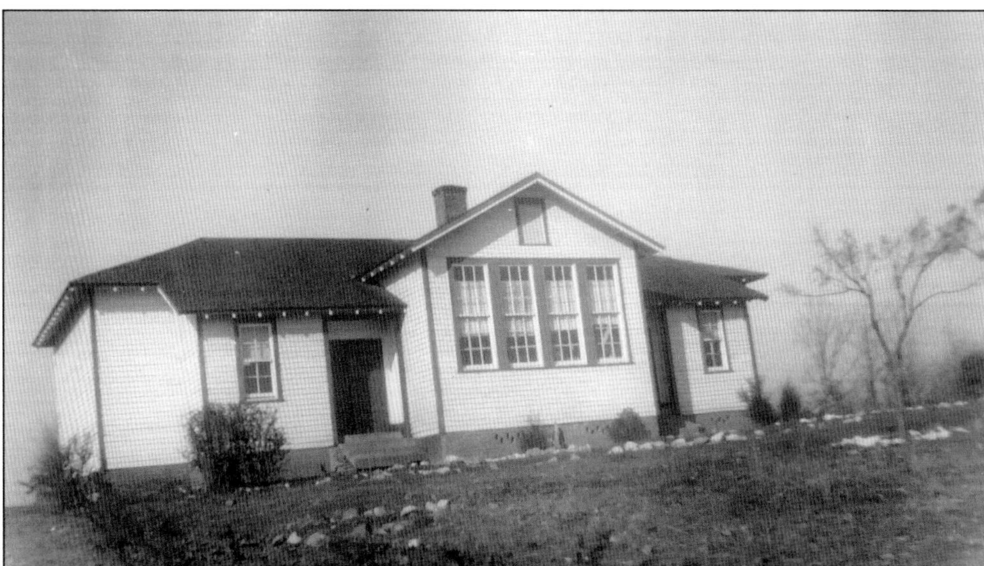

Built by 1924 to replace a smaller one-room school that was built on the site in 1902, the Mount Vernon Rosenwald School was originally a three-room, two-teacher rural schoolhouse for African American students. The two-teacher school design for Mount Vernon was from *Community School Plans*, Bulletin No. 3, issued by the Julius Rosenwald Fund in Nashville, Tennessee, in 1924. A matching grant from the Julius Rosenwald Fund helped fund the school's construction, which totaled $2,500, including $300 from local citizens, $1,500 from public funds, and a match of $700. The school held its last classes in the building in 1966, and it was later acquired by Mount Vernon Baptist Church. (Courtesy of LCHA.)

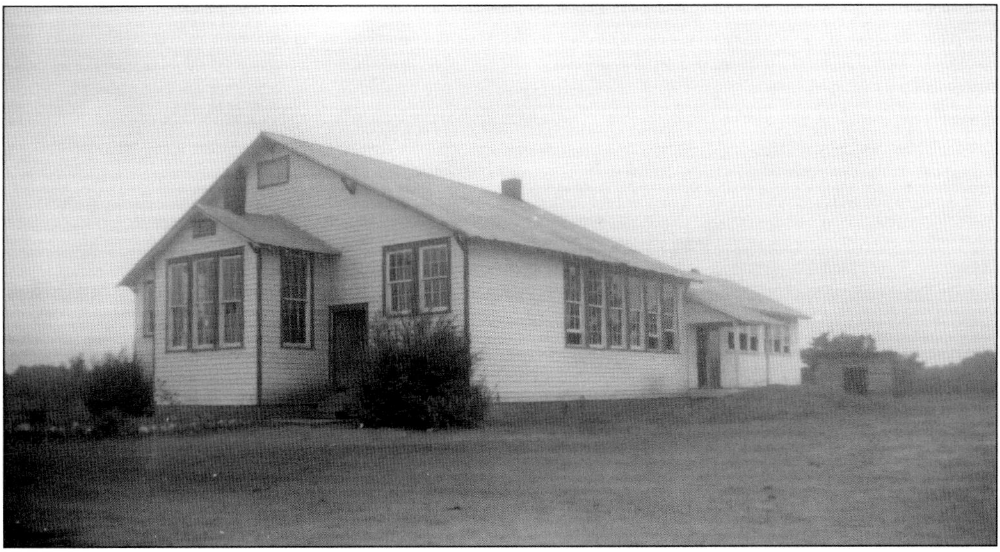

As one of five Rosenwald schools in Lincoln County, this frame front-gabled school building served the Tucker's Grove community in Iron Station. This school was a two-teacher type built between 1925 and 1926 at a total cost of $2,500. Contributions that supported the construction of the school building included $700 from the Julius Rosenwald Fund, $330 from the African American community, and $1,470 in public funds. (Courtesy of LCHA.)

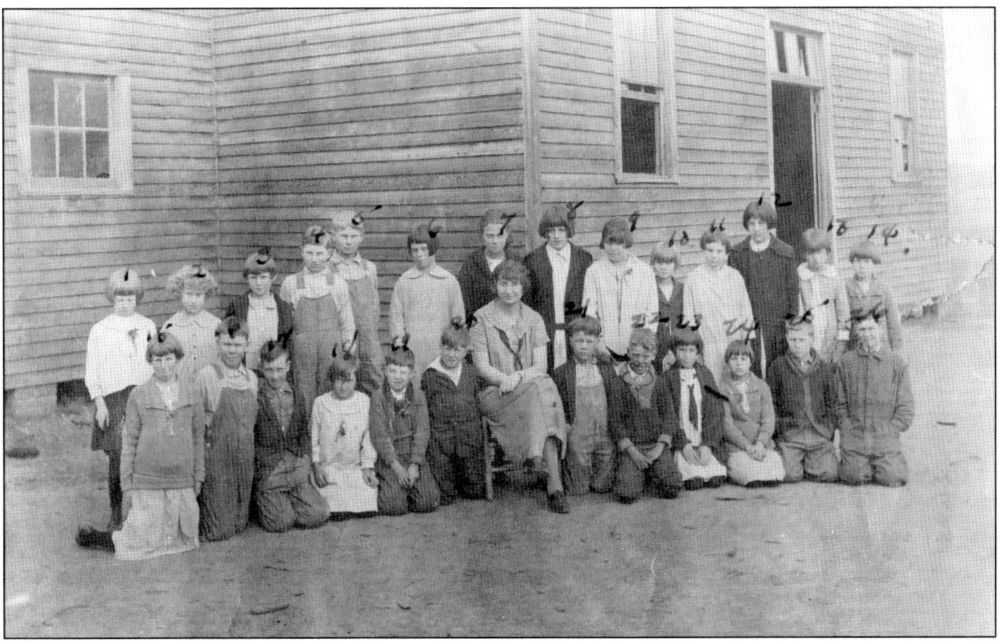

Third- and fourth-grade students at Lowesville School take a break from their work to have their class photograph taken in 1924. From left to right are (first row) Lucille Kelly, Yates Rogers, Lorrain Dellinger, Ruby Duckworth, Glenn Hager, Neal McIntosh, Roy Abernathy, Herron Grice, Elizabeth Robinson, Dorothy McConnell, Preston Henkle, and Irvin Duckworth; (second row) Marie Edwards, Louis Sifford, Addie Mae Kelly, James Hager, Paul Hager, Anna J. Abernathy, Margie Miller, Mary Helton, Virginia Rogers, Helen Duckworth, Mable Abernathy, Vida Helton, Edna Miller, and Ellen Jones. (Courtesy of LCHA.)

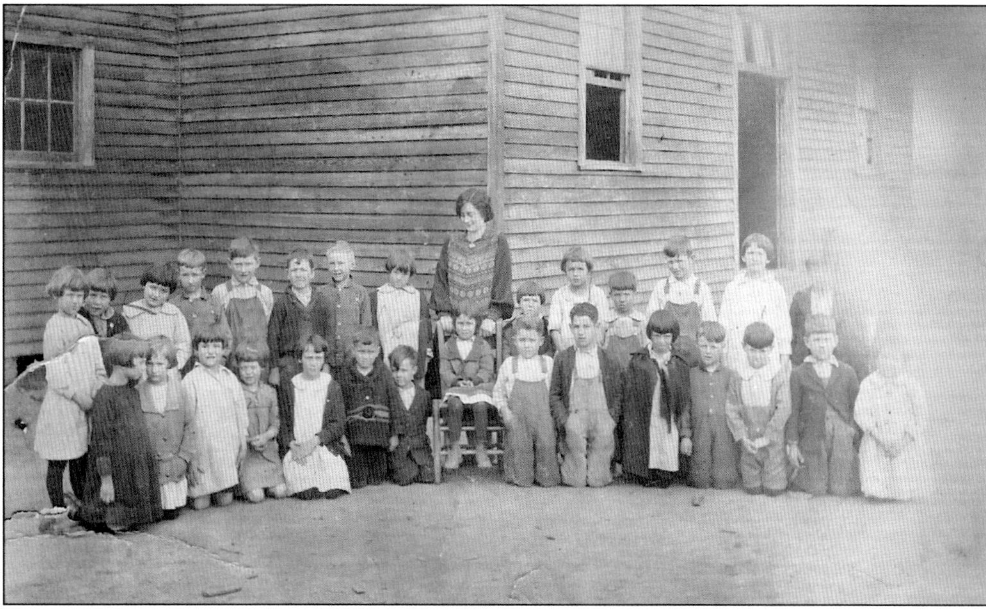

The Lowesville School, located near Hills Chapel Church, has its students assembled for a photograph during the 1920s. From left to right are (first row) Johnsie Lee Miller, Gladys Duckworth, ? Fortenberry, Helen McIntosh, Jessie Dellinger, unidentified, June Dellinger, ? Henkle, Roy Abernathy, Bennie Helton, Aldean Morrison, Grady Jones, Leonard Morrison, Oliver Duckworth, and Lottie B. Abernathy; (second row) Sylvia Nixon, Marie Rogers, Jannie Mae Hager, R.H. Dellinger, James Duckworth, Ernest Dellinger, ? Henkle, Sathel Little, teacher Nell Titman, Bernice Luckey, Velma Ree Duckworth, Roy Nixon, unidentified, Thelma Hager, Dorothy McConnell, and unidentified. (Courtesy of Mary Swift.)

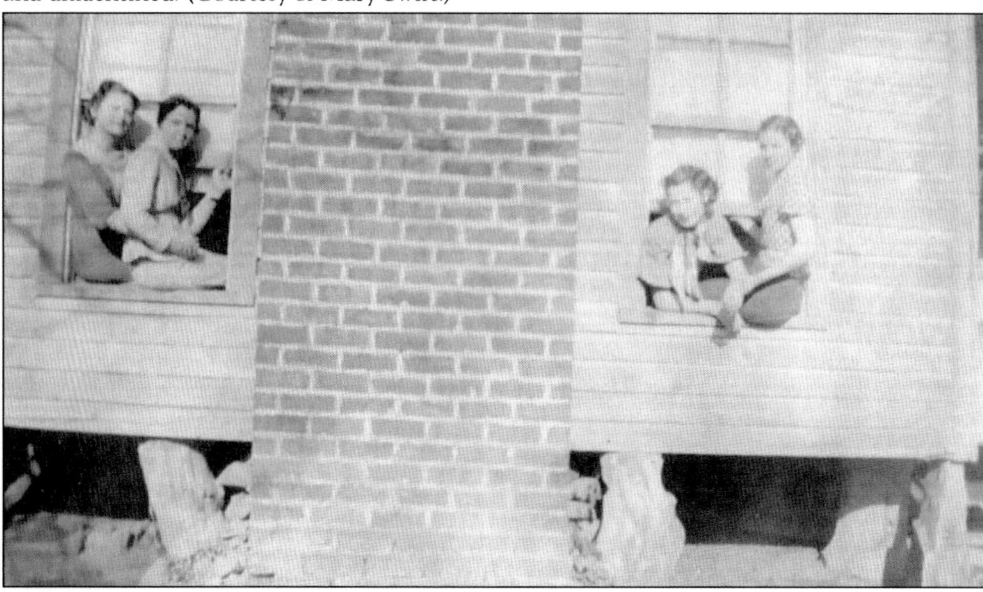

Stone piers support the frame Lowesville School building, while the brick chimney is flanked by some ladies who decided to raise those sashes and get some air during the late 1930s. From left to right are Edna Mae Miller, Vivian Jones Mundy, Johnsie Lee Miller, and Sylvia Nixon Camp. (Courtesy of Nancy Nixon Little.)

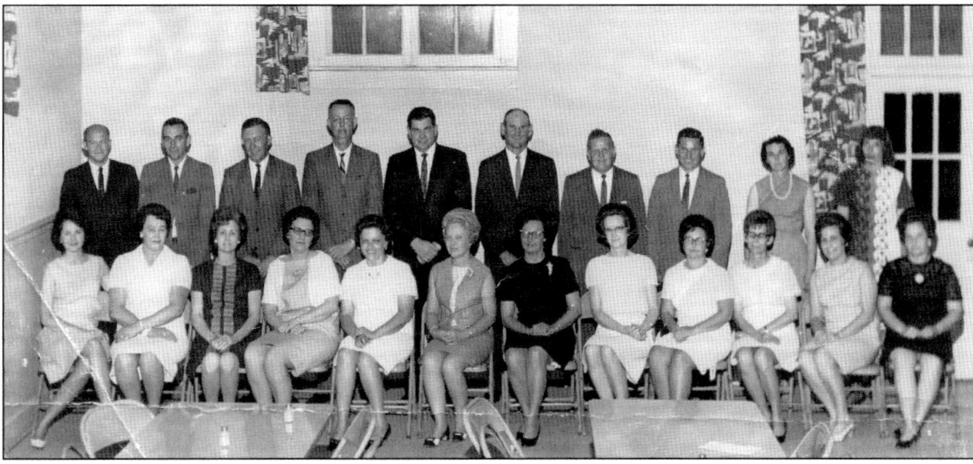

The men and women of the Rock Springs High School class of 1944 held this reunion in 1968. From left to right are (first row) Mabel Ruth Mundy, Blanche Henkel, Sue Betty Reel, Dorothy Armstrong, Allie Sue Heavner, Katharine Graham, Mary Fisher, Mary Lee Goodson, Sarah Sherrill Morris, Eva Sue Johnson, Nancy Senter, and Frances McIntosh Kiser; (second row) Curtis Brotherton, Blair Abernathy, Avery Black, Robert Howard, Ned McCall, Wiley Duckworth, Earl Setzer, Herman Sherrill, Mildred Hager, and Margaret Bynum. (Courtesy of Anne Eudy.)

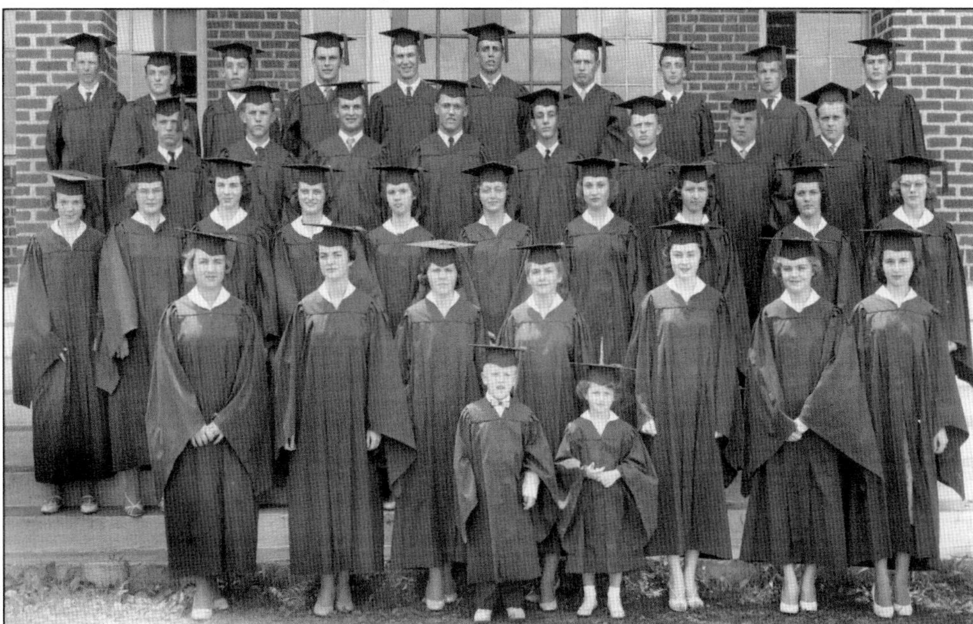

Students of Rock Springs High School's class of 1958 are, from left to right, (first row) mascots Mike Hoke and Marilyn Howard; (second row) Janice Chapman, Anna Beatty, Pinkie Barker, Emily Hager, Gloria Brotherton, Faye Drum, and July Lawing; (third row) Sarah Stillwell, Frances Duckworth, Doris Houk, Emily Loftin, Joyce Varner, Millie Dellinger, Brenda Schronce, Carol Jean Jetton, Jo Anne Nixon, and Shirley L. Richard; (fourth row) Reid McGinnis, Eugene Henley, Jerry Sigmon, Tony Cloninger, Donald Perkins, Tom Reel, David Ballard, and Tommy Ballard; (fifth row) Bobby Little, Calvin Blalock, Larry Reel, Kenneth Mundy, Jackie Thompson, Harold Ballard, Stamey Nixon, Clayton Ballard, Dariel Dellinger, and Roger Jones. Not pictured are Jeannette Graham Hager and Neal Reel. (Courtesy of Doris Houk Wilkinson.)

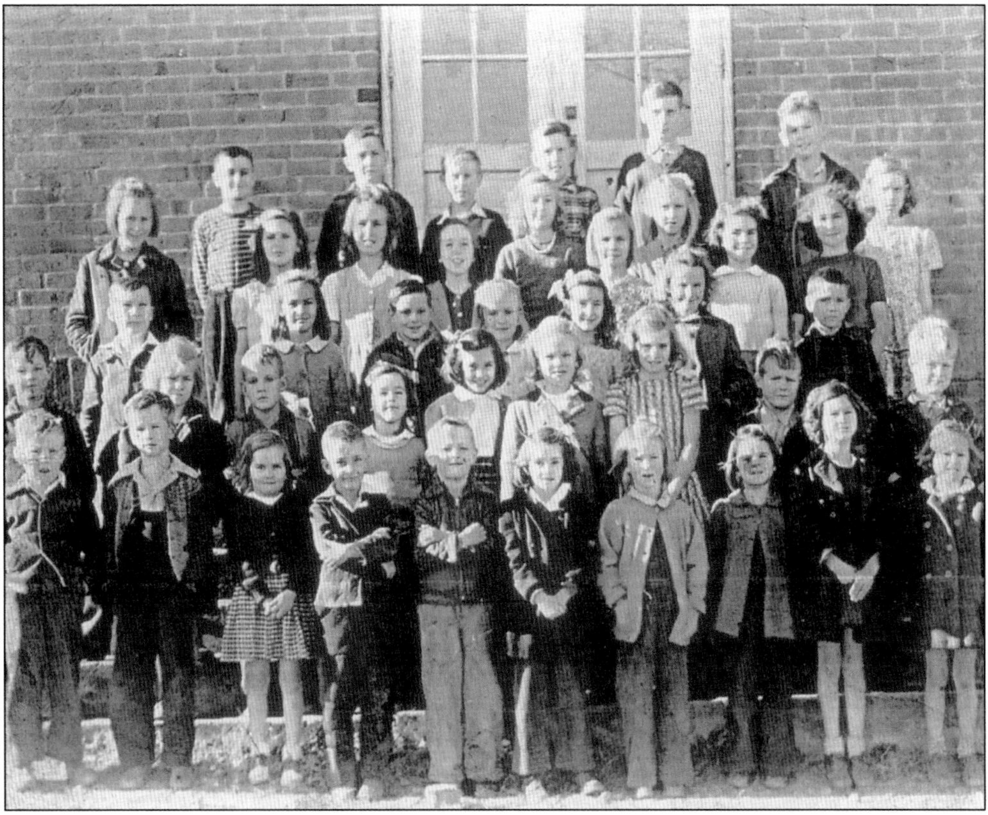

The students of Machpelah School in 1945 are, from left to right, (first row) Robert Christopher, Larry Dellinger, Linda Rudisill, Donald Perkins, Reid McGinnis, Linda Morrison, Evelyn Poole, Nancy Watts, Lucille Lynch, and Elsie Helton; (second row) Jimmy Poole, Judy Welch, unidentified, Barbara Poole, Sylvia Morrison, Jane Reep, Doris Ballard, Eddie Welch, and Tommy Welch; (third row) Walter Wilson, Joan Kennedy, unidentified, Verline Ballard, Jewell Perkins, Joyce Reel, and R.A. Watts; (fourth row) Audry Welch, Betty Ballard, Betty Poole, Joyce Sigmon, Shirley Perkins, Gertie O'Donahue, Dorothy Poole, Jackie Ledford, Betty Stroup, and Sue Avis Ballard; (fifth row) Billy Johnson, Bill Nantz, William Rumfelt, Benny Green, Frank Reel, and Kermit Sigmon. (Courtesy of Doris Houk Wilkinson.)

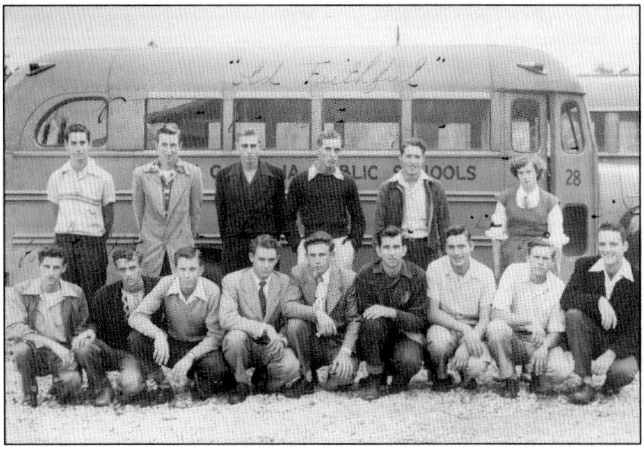

"Old Faithful" was the name of the bus in this 1951 photograph. The bus drivers are, from left to right, (first row) Paul Garrison, Joe Morrison, Joe King, Bill Lawing, Willie Little, Johnny Keever, William "Smilie" Mays, Leo Christopher, and Bill Nixon; (second row) Gray Jones, Clyde Sifford, Junior Gilleland, Melvin "Goat" Nixon, John Howie, and Barbara Jean Miller. (Courtesy of Bill and Lela Nixon.)

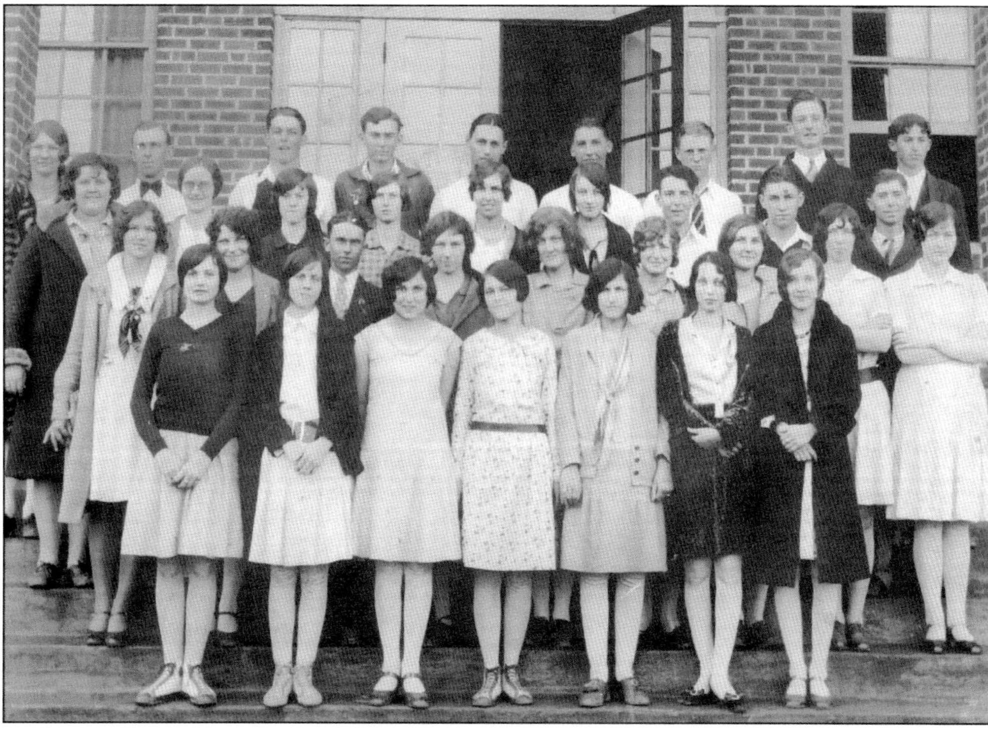

The Rock Springs High School class of 1930 is, from left to right, (first row) Ruby Long, Mildrew Edwards, Ethel Sigmon, Inez Cherry, Millie Cherry, Connie Ballard, and Janette Howard; (second row) Ruth Cherry, Jessie Bell Abernathy, Maurice Crouse, Ara Bell Nixon, Thelma Lazenby, Jessie Sifford, Leona Duckworth, Edith Nixon, and Louise King; (third row) Besse Mae Nixon, Dela Helderman, Willena Williamson, Vera Helderman, Julia Little, Excell Howard, Hugh Smith, Way Brotherton, and Austin Goodson; (fourth row) Lula Lee Cherry, Dennis Dellinger, Yates Wilkinson, Archie Keever, Billie Howard, Richard Little, Seth Lowe, Walter Canipe, and Ernest Nixon. (Courtesy of Nancy Nixon Little.)

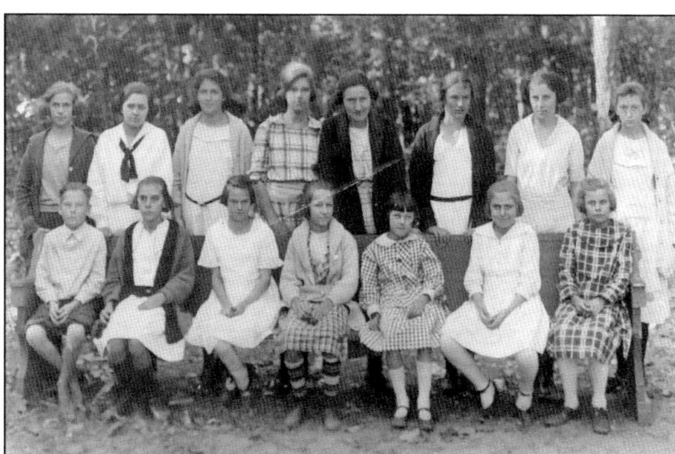

The Rock Springs School class of 1922 is, from left to right, (first row) Gene Bolick, Ethel Reed Bolick, Annie Derr Sigmon, Edith Nixon, Nixon, Betsy Shelton, and Ashley Gordon; (second row) Pinkie Howard, Faulabelle Hager Howard, Ann Little, Edna Earle Bolick, teacher Bessie Heavner, Leron Sigmon, Allie Mundy, and Nell Bollinger. (Courtesy of Shawn Howard.)

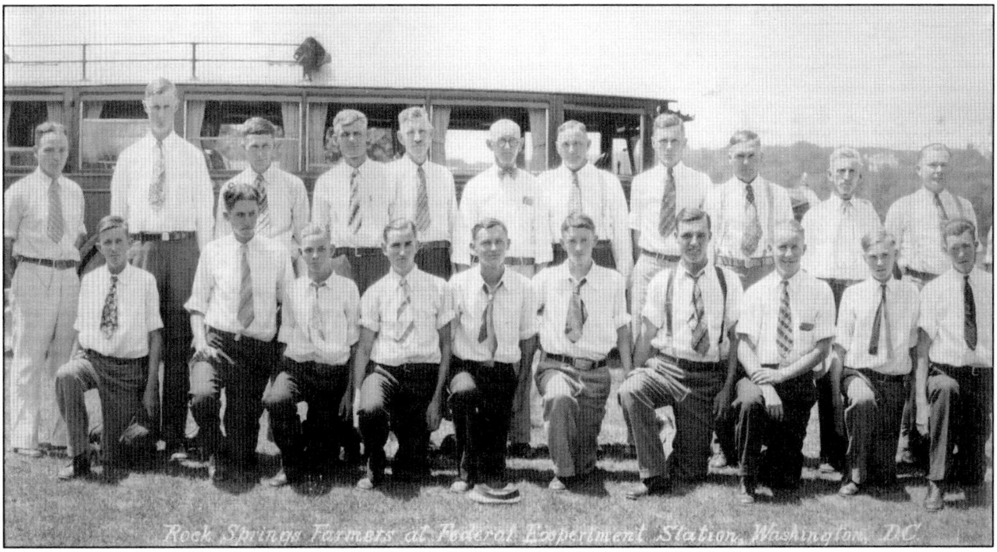

Twenty Lincoln County farmers, led by J. Alvin Wilson of the Rock Springs Vocational Agricultural Department, took a weeklong trip in July 1930 that culminated in two days and three nights in Washington, DC. There they visited the Experiment Station, Arlington National Cemetery, and federal buildings. Those who went on the tour included Joe King, E.S. Cherry, J.I. Cherry, Price Duckworth, F.P. Brotherton, Joe McCall, Coley Little, Donald Mundy, R.M. Goodson, M.M. Sherrill, J.A. Wilson, Perry Sigmon, Blair Sigmon, Yates Nixon, Joe Morrison, Junius Morrison, Paul Henkle, Ernest Nixon, Howie Keever, and another student whose name is only listed as Henkle. (Courtesy of Nancy Nixon Little.)

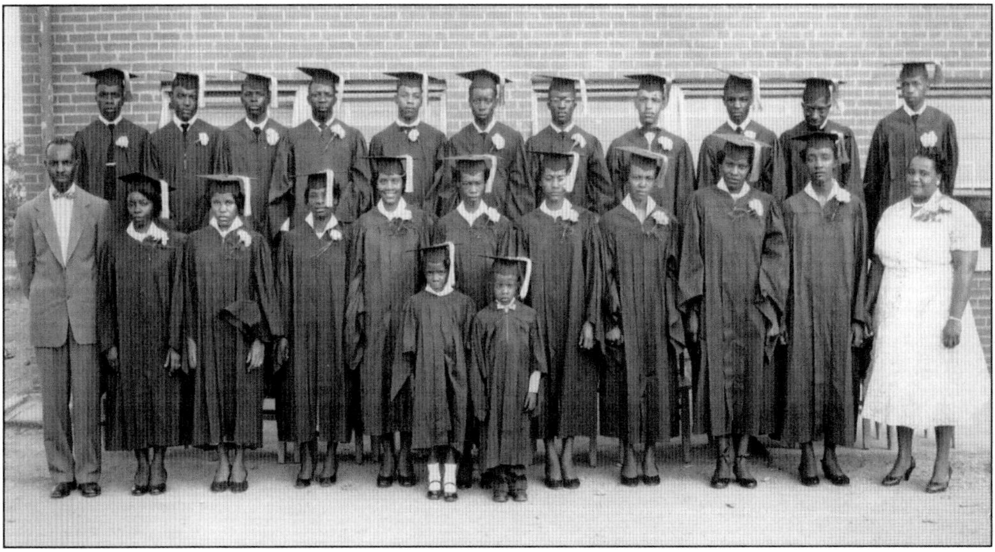

Newbold High School was a black high school in Lincolnton. From 1952 to 1968 under the "separate but equal" era, black students made the daily trip to Lincolnton from the farthest reaches of the county. Leroy Bost, fifth from the right in the back row, from Triangle, is just one of those students who would get up early in the morning, drive a bus, pick up the younger black students, drop them off at Tucker's Grove Elementary, and then make the trip to Lincolnton. He stands with the class of 1954 along with Principal G.E. Massey. Newbold is now an elementary school named in honor of its former principal G.E. Massey. (Courtesy of Leroy Bost.)

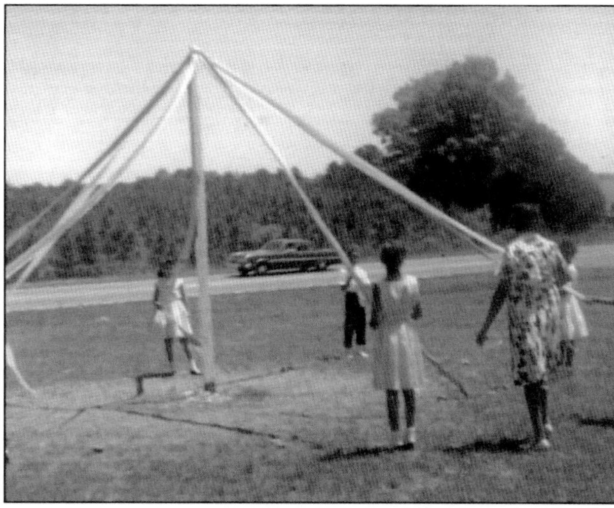

Kenneth Nixon Jr. and female members of his class take part in Rock Hill Elementary School's maypole activity during the 1960s in Triangle. Before schools were completely integrated in Lincoln County in the late 1960s, African American children attended Newbold, Mitchell, and Rock Hill Elementary. Lincoln County's Desegregation Plan of 1968, approved by the Department of Health, Education, and Welfare, closed these three schools during the 1969–1970 school year. (Courtesy of Thomas Nixon.)

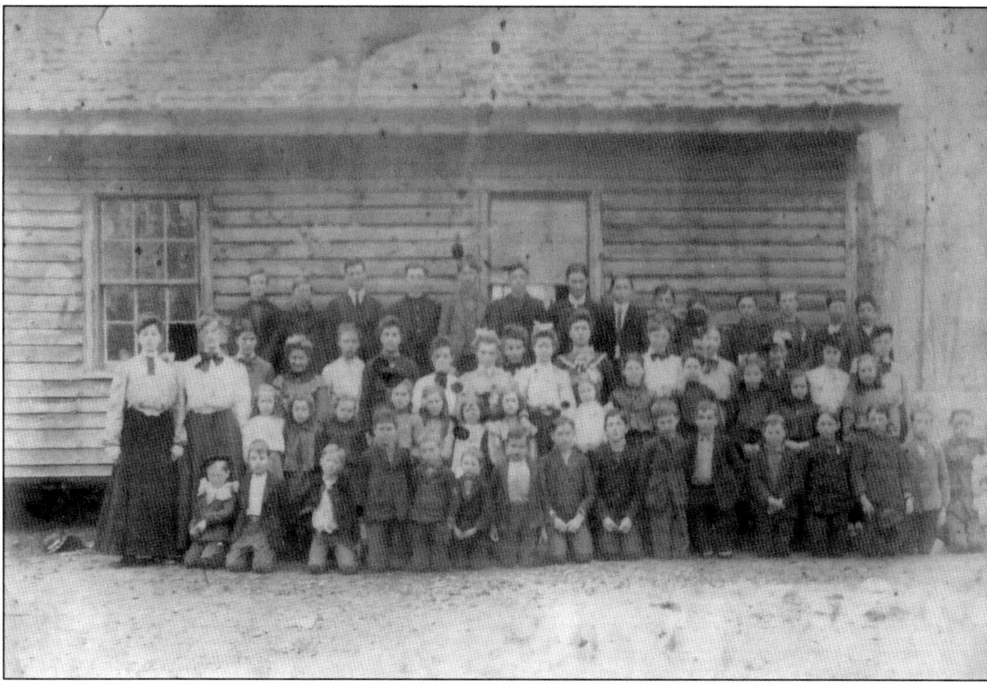

Students at the old Elbow School in Pumpkin Center around 1905 are, from left to right, (first row) Don Ewing, Lloyd Blalock, Lurie Ballard, Lat Poole, Alf Ballard, Horace Ballard, Hal Abernethy, Jack Moore, James Williams, Harlan Wilkinson, David Keever, Austin Reynolds, Willie Schronce, Fred Brotherton, Dan Keever, Luther Abernethy, and Ted Abernethy; (second row) teachers Leona and Maude Robinson, Edna Wilkinson, Luna Wilkinson, Ara Lowe, Lettie Poole, Carrie Keever, Agnes Reel, Ethel Reel, Alda Ewing, Ruth Reynolds, Lucy Dellinger, Zettie Moore, Connie Wilkinson, and Chloe Reel; (third row) Myrtice Ballard, Emma Ballard, Iva Ballard, Leckie Poole, Eunice Dellinger, Viola Reel, Sarah Douge Schronce, Anna Reel, Kate Poole, Ella Reynolds, Edna Keever, Elsie Ballard, Bess Dellinger, and Essie Wilkinson; (fourth row) Jesse Williams, David Reel, Otha Perkins, Walter Potts, Vance Wilkinson, Everett Wilkinson, Jim McCorkle, Ed Reel, Latt Potts, unidentified, Henry Dellinger, Raymond Ballard, Alf Smith, and Sully Perkins. (Courtesy of Emmitt and Sharon Poole.)

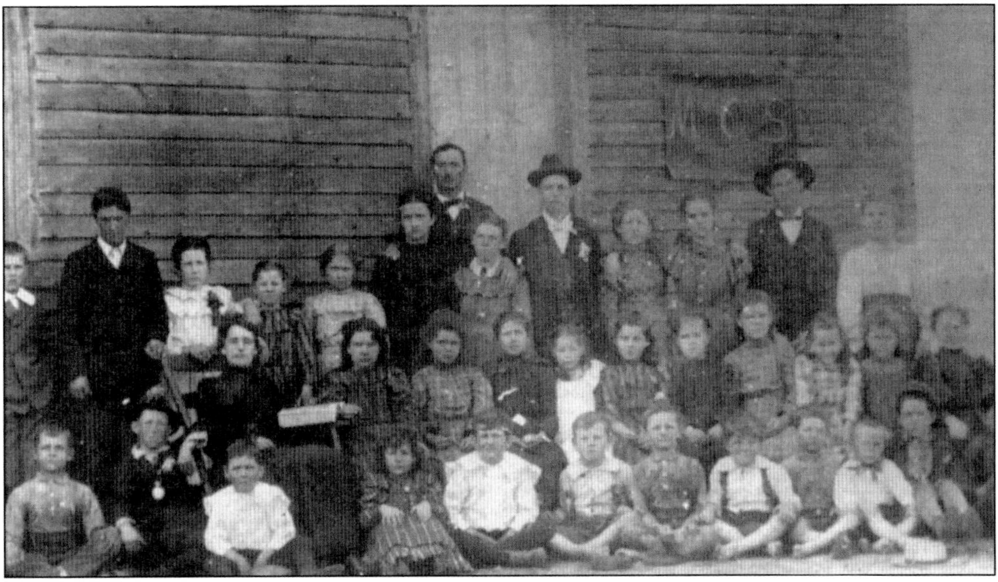

Labeled "M.C.S." on a primitive sign attached to the building's exterior, the McLean School, located at the corner of the old Cowan's Ford Road and Moore's Ferry Road, served children from various families in the area: Siffords, Nantzes, Moores, Hagers, Duckworths, McConnells, Joneses, McIntoshes, and Edwards. This photograph was taken around 1899–1900. (Courtesy of Frances Hampton.)

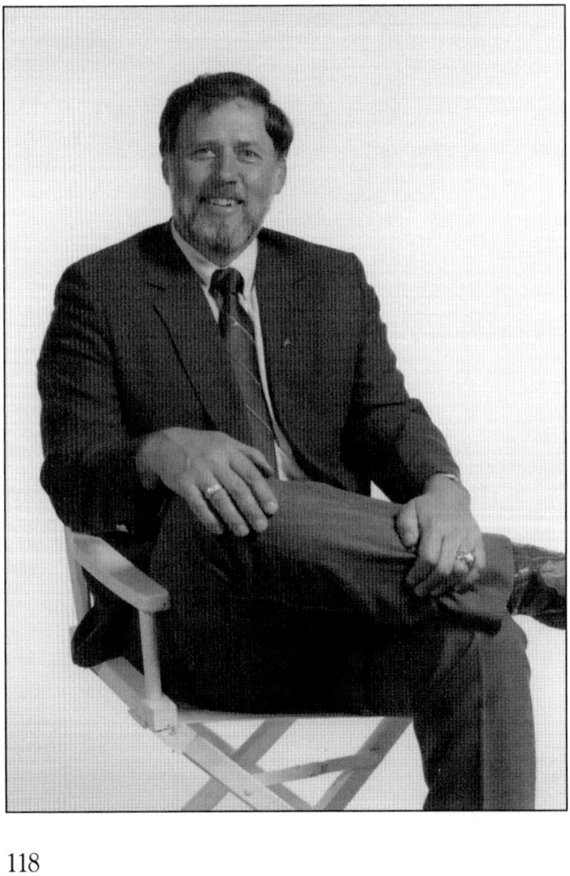

Principal Steve Cherry was a 1960 graduate of Rock Springs High School in Denver. After graduating from Western Carolina University, he taught and coached for several years at Quail Hollow Junior High in Charlotte. In 1967, East Lincoln High School opened, and he saw the opportunity to return to his native county. He accepted the position of assistant principal and all of the responsibilities that came along with it: athletic director, assistant football coach, head basketball coach, and golf coach. He received his first principal job at the new East Lincoln Junior High (1974–1983) and moved back to East Lincoln High as principal (1983–1993). After retirement from the school system, Cherry has spent the years coaching, farming, and raising horses at his farm, Cherry Acre Farm, on Unity Church Road in Triangle. (Courtesy of Steve Cherry.)

Five

Going the Distance

Memorable Teams and Athletes of Eastern Lincoln County

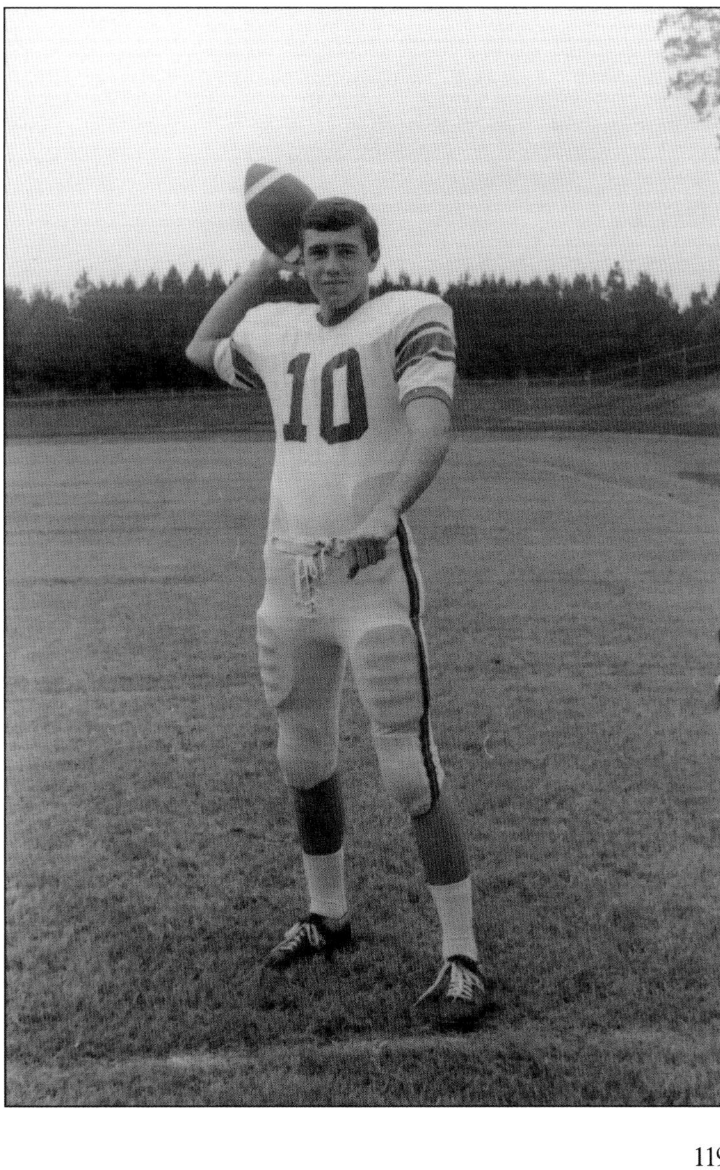

Tommy Lawing stands ready to make a pass for this photograph during his tenure at East Lincoln High School in Denver, where he was the first quarterback in 1967. He lettered in football, baseball, and basketball. He and his future wife, Annette Callaway, were part of the first fully integrated class at East Lincoln. Tommy graduated in 1969, and his son Todd carried on the family's football tradition at East Lincoln by playing quarterback. (Courtesy of LCHA.)

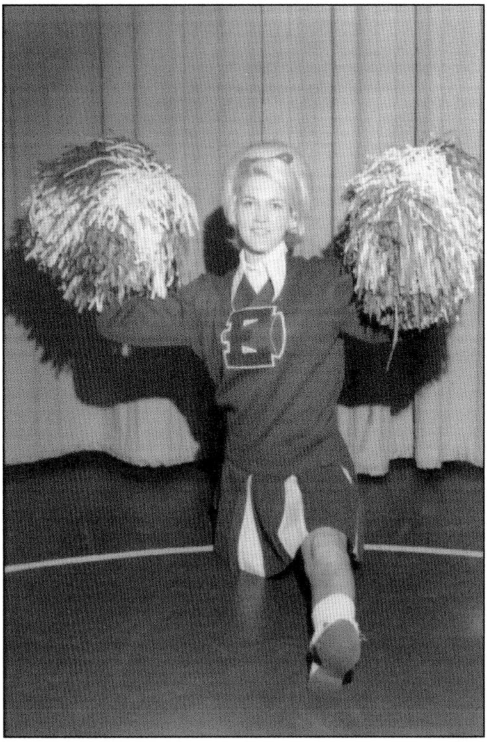

Annette Callaway proudly lifts her pom-poms as a cheerleader of East Lincoln High School's first cheerleading team. The squad held tryouts on the front lawn of Rock Springs School in Denver. Callaway lettered as a cheerleader from 1967 to 1970 and as a member of the basketball team during the 1968–1969 season. Callaway graduated in 1970 and married Tommy Lawing in 1972. All three of Tommy and Annette's sons, Michael, Todd, and Derek, became athletes at East Lincoln High School. (Courtesy of LCHA.)

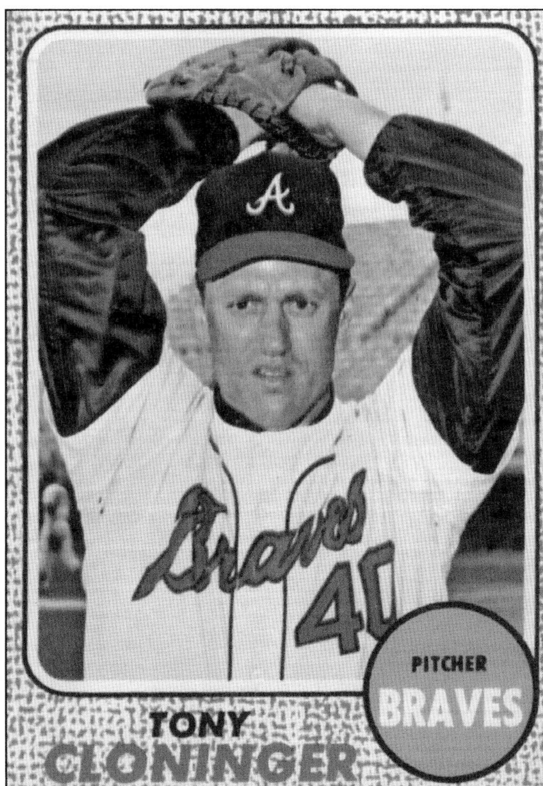

After Tony Cloninger from Iron Station missed out on a 1953 trip with the Cherryville American Legion team to Miami for the American Legion Series, he struck out 21 batters in an American Legion game against Charlotte. He signed a $100,000 contract with the Milwaukee Braves in 1958 and had a locker between Hank Aaron and Eddie Matthews. He was the Atlanta Braves' top winner in 1965, posting 24 victories. While playing for the Braves, Cloninger hit two grand slams in one game. He played for the Braves, Reds, and Cardinals from 1961 to 1972 and was the only pitcher in major-league history to hit two grand slams in one game. Cloninger retired as a player in 1972. From 1992 to 2001, Cloninger was the pitching coach for the New York Yankees, during which time the Yankees won five American League championships and four World Series. (Courtesy of LCHA.)

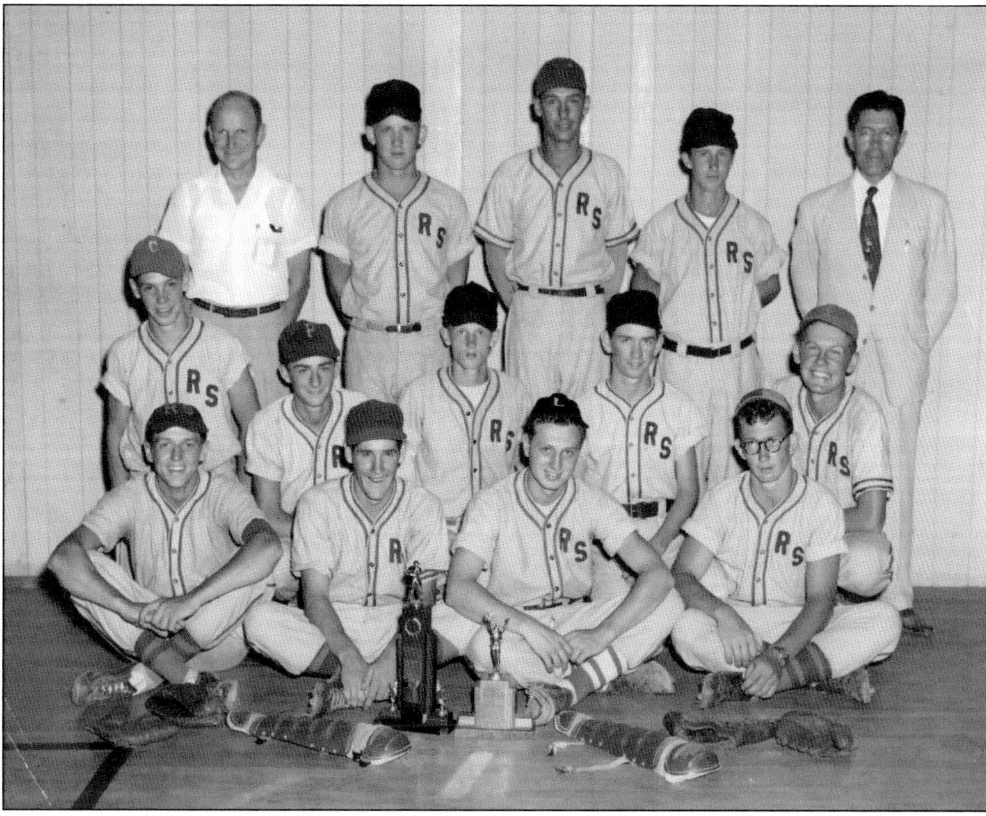

The 1953 Rock Springs High School baseball team won the Little 10 title, comprised of Gaston and Lincoln County teams, and the State Class A championship during its first conference year. Rock Springs defeated Eastern North Carolina state champs Hertford in a best-of-three series. Jim Mundy, who would later serve 20 years as principal of this school, is credited with hitting the winning run in the championship game. From left to right are (first row) Ray Cloninger, Grady Barker, Junior Barkley, and Tommy Little; (second row) C.E. McCorkle, Herbert Loftin, Richard Sherrill, Walter Mundy, and Kermit Sigmon; (third row) Lester Ballard, Jimmy Mundy, Donald Miller, Murrey Sherrill, and coach W.T. Long. (Courtesy of LCHA.)

The young men of the Triangle basketball team opt out of their uniforms for bibbed overalls in 1935. Joe Grice (kneeling) holds the team's basketball, which cements the date of the season for posterity. The team members are, from left to right, (first tow) Hugh Duckworth, Shellum Abernathy, Joe Grice, Harry Graham, and Tate Williamson; (second row) Stewart Helton and Carl McIntosh. (Courtesy of Ann Smith.)

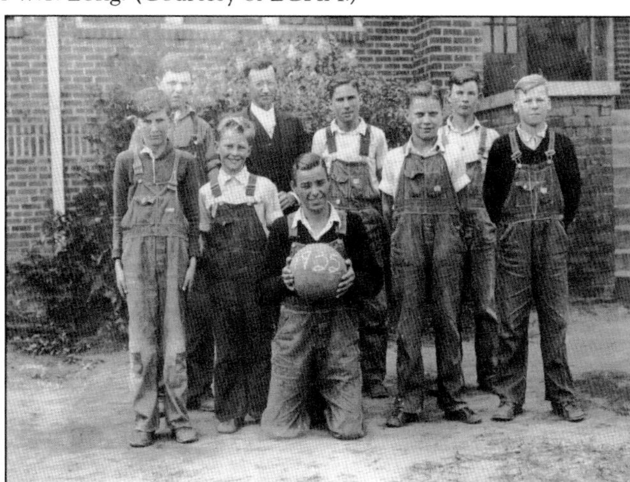

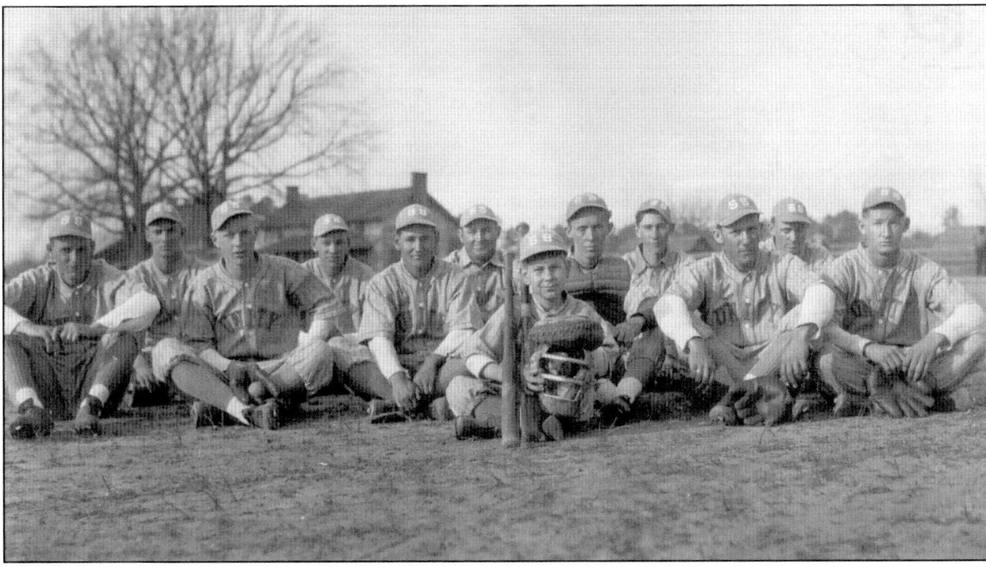

Regular games of baseball were played throughout the 1910s and 1920s in the fields around Denver. The Unity baseball team stops play to pose for this late 1920s photograph in Triangle in the field across from the home of Alfred Lee Cherry, seen in the background. Players are, from left to right, (first row) Roy Long, Harold Graham, Frank Cherry, Ted Smith Jr. (mascot), Wilson Graham, James Graham, and Bart Nixon; (second row) James Nixon, J.W. Nixon, Gene Cherry, unidentified, and Tom Cherry. (Courtesy of Ann Smith.)

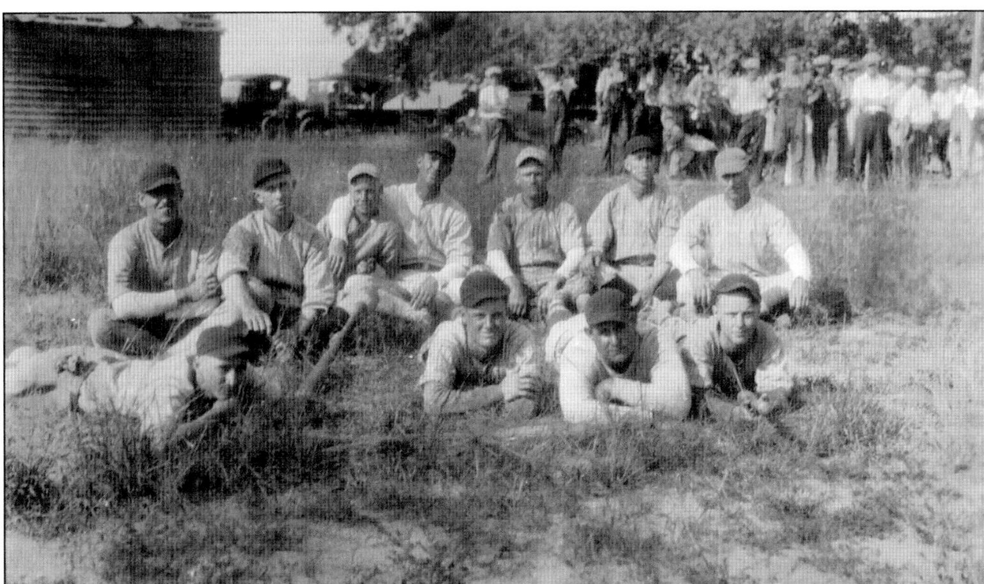

Camaraderie is evident as the men of the Unity baseball team lounge in an open field while a group of onlookers stands by as the photographer captures a special moment in time. (Courtesy of Ann Smith.)

In the early 20th century, before radio broadcasts brought major-league games into homes, young men organized baseball teams in many small towns, mill villages, and rural communities. In this c. 1918 photograph, the Triangle baseball team is clad in wool uniforms with high stockings and equipped with mitts and bats. From left to right are (first row) Dallas Barker and Marian Proctor; (second row) Harvey Cherry, Joe Cherry, Robert Nixon, and Rozzelle Proctor; (third row) Joe Graham, Ethridge Cherry, and Fred Long. (Courtesy of Kelli Hogue.)

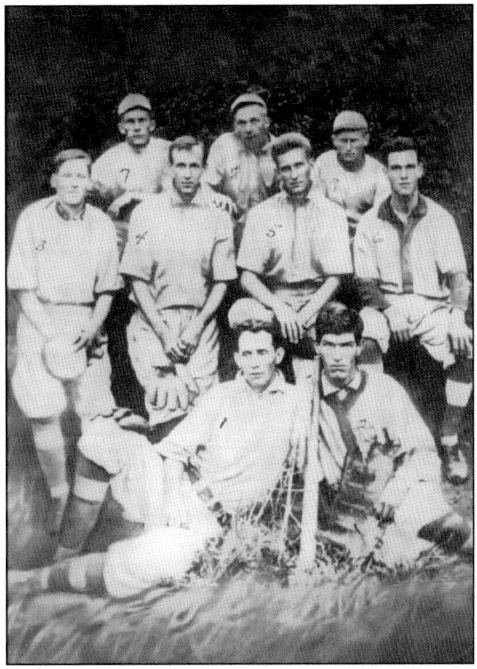

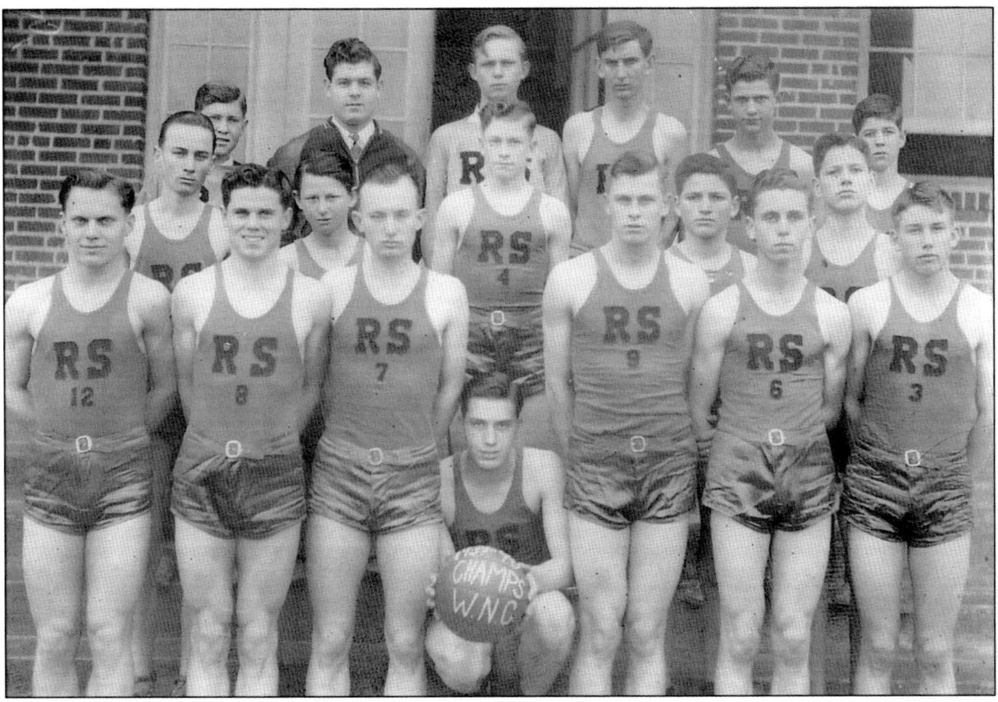

Fred McCall Jr. holds a basketball that tells the story of the Rock Springs High School's 1939–1940 season: "Champs, W.N.C." From left to right are (first row) Harry Graham, Rodney Sherrill, Grady Howard, Fred McCall Jr., Harven Crouse, Ab Lynch, and Olen Painter; (second row) Kenneth Jetton, Harold Howard, Horace Crouse, J.W. Sigmon, and L.G. McCall; (third row) Bill Ballard, Coach Joe Amendola, Howard Long, Hugh Duckworth, Aumon Sherrill, and Vaness Barker. (Courtesy of LCHA.)

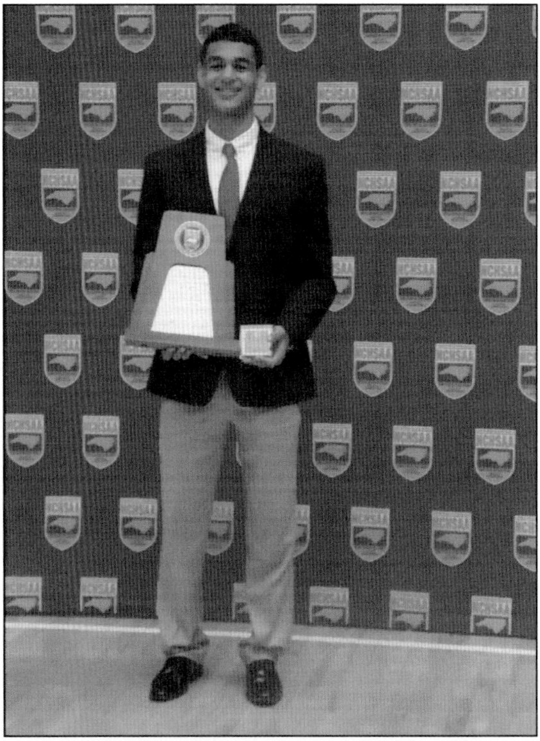

Chazz Surratt is a two-sport athlete at East Lincoln High School. He was part of the 2012 undefeated football state championship team, and, as quarterback, he led the Mustangs to an unbeaten season and a state football championship in 2014 and was was named MVP. In the fall of 2015, Surratt set state records for total responsible yards (16,593) and touchdown responsibilities (229). He was named the 2015–2016 North Carolina Gatorade Football Player of the Year and 2016 Parade All-America Football Player of the Year. In basketball, Surratt was the 2015 Southern District 7 Player of the Year and was a member of two state basketball championship appearances, in 2015 and 2016. In 2015, as a junior, Surratt was voted the North Carolina Male Athlete of the Year. (Courtesy of Brandi Surratt.)

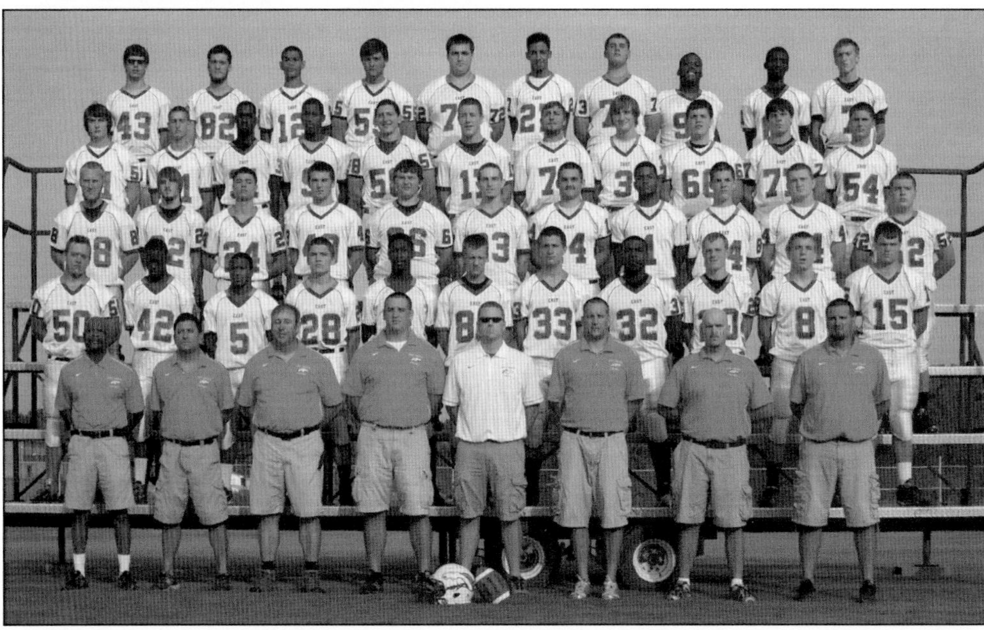

In 2012, the East Lincoln High School Mustangs reached a 16-0 record, winning the school's first North Carolina 2A championship in football. The Mustangs beat a very strong Tarboro High School Vikings team that had made five straight trips to the North Carolina 2A championship game and had won the three previous championships (2009–2011). The Mustangs beat the Vikings 24-20, and head coach Mike Byus celebrated his and the school's first of two state championships. (Courtesy of Mike Hensdill, the *Gaston Gazette*.)

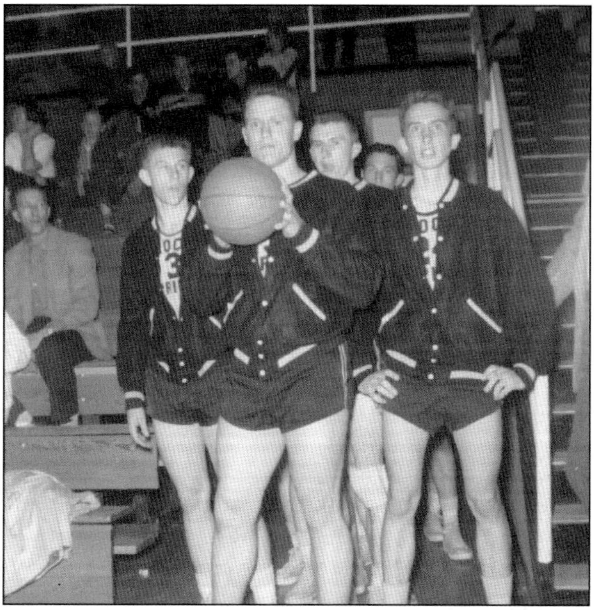

Standing strong in Converse All Stars while young boys look on with envy, the young men of Rock Springs High School's basketball team emerge from the back of Shuford Memorial Gym in Hickory, North Carolina, for this late 1950s photograph. Tony Cloninger leads the way with ball in hand while Gene Henley stands to his right and Jack Thompson and Steve Little stand to his left. (Courtesy of Jack Thompson.)

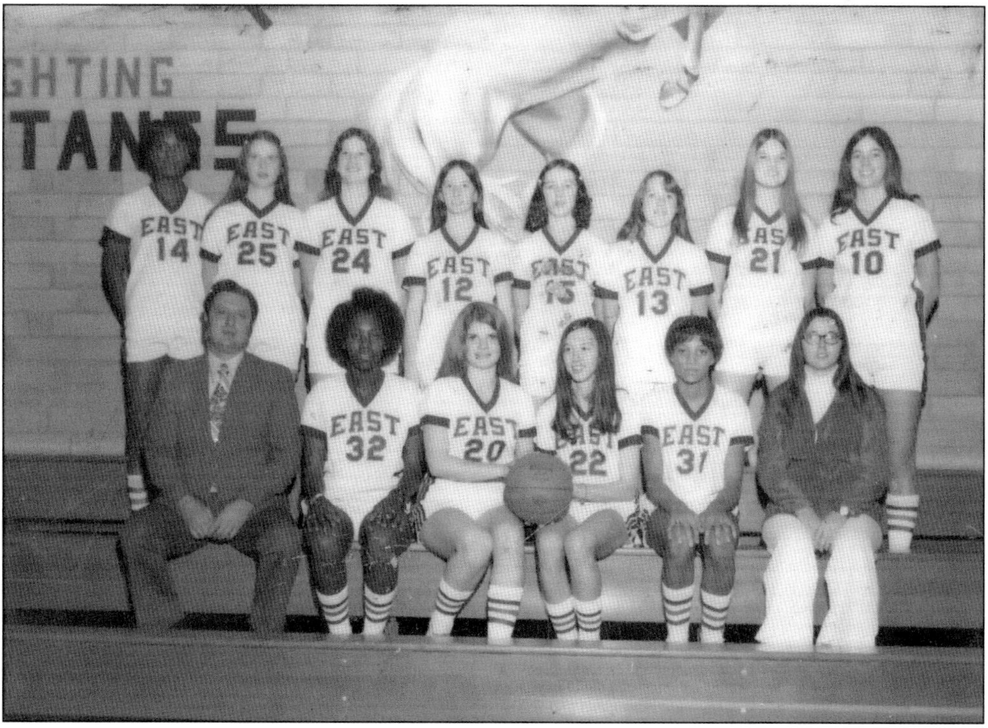

The East Lincoln girls' basketball team won the state championship in 1973 in High Point while winning four tournament titles along the way. Under coach Henry Barkley, pictured at left in the first row, the team won the state AA championship and boasted an impeccable 30-0 record. From left to right are (first row) Coach Barkley, Brenda Link, Donna Sigmon, Virginia Howie, Brenda Johnson, and manager Sheila Helton; (second row) Van Stewart, Cathy Peeler, Diane Helms, Pam Barker, Vickie Goodson, Sheila Barker, Sandy Sherrill, and Debbie Barker. (Courtesy of Henry Barkley.)

INDEX

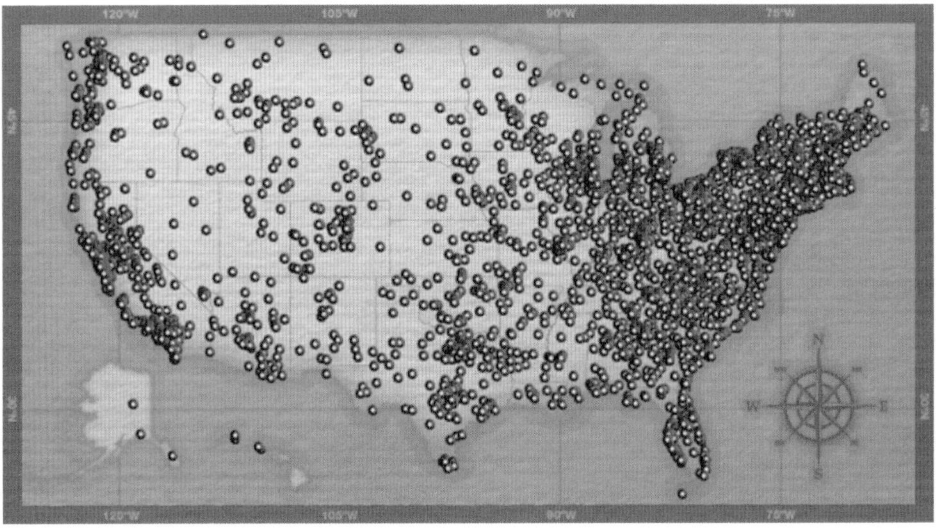